THE ULTIMATE BEGINNER SERIES®

ACOUSTIC GUITAR COMPLETE

Mark Hanson • Keith Wyatt

Alfred Publishing Co., Inc.
16320 Roscoe Blvd., Suite 100
P.O. Box 10003
Van Nuys, CA 91410-0003
alfred.com

Book and DVD (with case)
ISBN-10: 0-7390-5618-2
ISBN-13: 978-0-7390-5618-9

Book and DVD (without case)
ISBN-10: 0-7390-5619-0
ISBN-13: 978-0-7390-5619-6

Cover photographs:
Martin Dreadnought courtesy of Martin Guitars
Blue energy © istockphoto.com/Raycat

CONTENTS

Introduction 4

BASIC GUITAR

The Basics 6
- Guitar Types 7
- Parts of the Guitar 8
- Tuning Methods 10
- Changing Strings 12
- Reading Rhythm Notation 13
- Reading Music Notation 14
- Reading Tablature and Fretboard Diagrams 15

Open Position Chords 16
- The Blues Progression 20
- Down-Up Strumming 22
- Bass/Chord Strum Patterns 23
- The Alternating Bass/Strum Pattern 26
- Minor Chords 30
- Dominant Chords 31

Fingerpicking 33

Hammer-Ons and Pull-Offs with Chords 37
- The Capo 40

Barre Chords 41
- The "E" Type Barre Chord 42
- The "A" Type Barre Chord 43

BLUES GUITAR

Review: Open Position Chords 45
- E Blues 48
- A Blues 49
- C Blues 51

Blues Progressions 52
Rhythm 55
Bass Lines 59
Blues in A 67
Solo Acoustic Blues Guitar 71
Blues Licks 72
Blues Chord Soloing 77
The Blues Scale 82
Fingerstyle Blues 87
Putting It All Together 93

FINGERSTYLE GUITAR

Arpeggios 100
Right-Hand Position 103
Canyon Canon 104
Fingerpicking in ¾ Time 108
Windows 111
The Travis Picking Pattern (Alternating Bass) 114
Wheels 116
Other Alternating Bass Patterns 119
Four Per Bar 122
Other Accompaniment Patterns Using the Travis Style 125
Key to the Kingdom 129
Taylor's Ferry 132
Brahms' Lullaby 137

CONTENTS

INTRODUCTION

The acoustic guitar is one of the most versatile and enjoyable instruments you can play. With this book and DVD, you will learn all the basics you need to start playing and build a solid foundation that will enable you to play blues and fingerstyle music.

The Basics section will get you started by teaching you about the guitar, how to tune, how to read music and TAB, how to play chords, picking techniques, and much more.

The Blues section teaches you to play traditional, roots-oriented blues. You'll start off learning the basics: chord shapes, progressions, chord embellishments, strum patterns, bass lines, the shuffle groove, and turnarounds. You'll then focus on solo-style blues guitar: scales, melodic patterns, licks, and fingerpicking.

The Fingerstyle section will provide you with a wealth of information designed to move you well along the road to becoming a fine fingerstyle guitarist. Topics include arpeggio patterns, Travis picking, and alternating bass. You will play performance-quality pieces that use all the techniques you have learned.

Also included are play-along tracks featuring legendary recording artists that will enable you to instantly apply the new rhythms, techniques, and licks to your playing.

Let's dig in and get started playing acoustic guitar.

The included DVD contains MP3 audio files of every example in the book. Use the MP3s to ensure you're capturing the feel of the examples and interpreting the rhythms correctly.

To access the MP3s on the DVD, place the DVD in your computer's DVD-ROM drive. In Windows, double-click on My Computer, then right-click on the DVD drive icon. Select Explore, then double-click on the DVD-ROM Materials folder. For Mac, double-click on the DVD icon on your desktop, then double-click on the DVD-ROM Materials folder.

BASIC GUITAR

The Basics

The Three Basic Guitar Types

Nylon String Acoustic (Classic Guitar)

The nylon string acoustic guitar has a nice mellow tone and has several advantages for beginners. The strings are much easier to press to the fretboard so they don't cut into your fingers the way steel strings do. Also, the neck is wider than on a typical steel string guitar which makes fingering chords a little easier. The classic guitar is perfectly suited to intimate, unaccompanied guitar performances.

The Electric Guitar

The electric guitar has come to dominate popular music. It is an extremely versatile instrument capable of producing everything from mellow jazz tones and biting funk riffs to the screaming, over-the-top, dizzying pyro-technics of rock's reigning guitar virtuosos.

The Steel String Acoustic

The steel string acoustic guitar is perhaps the most versatile and common guitar type. Although it is a little bit harder to play than the nylon string guitar, the steel string acoustic has a loud, bright, ringing tone that clearly projects to the listener. The steel-string acoustic is the backbone of most country and bluegrass bands. It's perfect for backing a singer and, in the hands of today's new acoustic performers, its stylistic palette encompasses everything from New Age and Country Blues, to hot Bluegrass flatpicking, jazz fusion and "unplugged" rock.

Parts of the Guitar

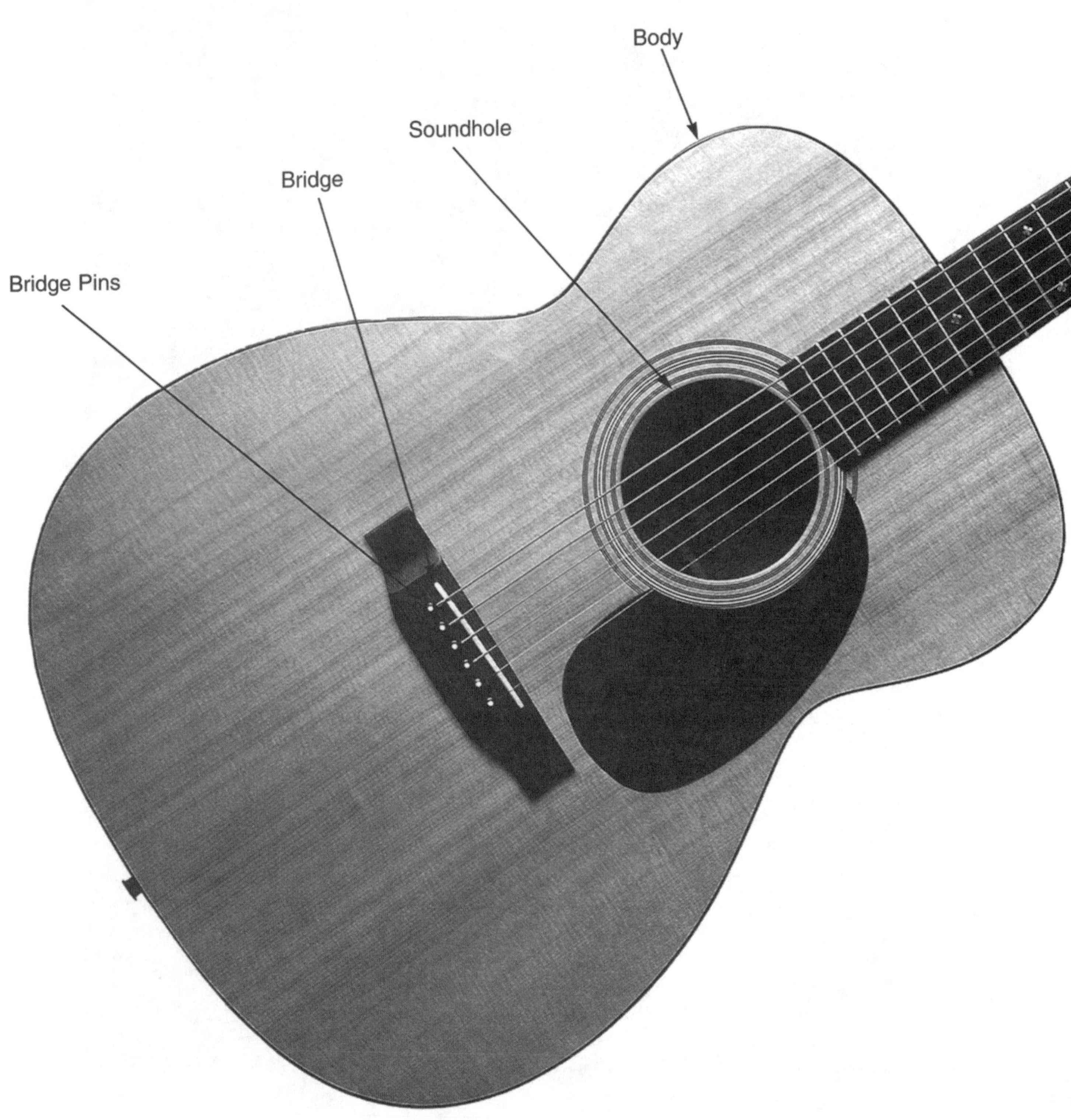

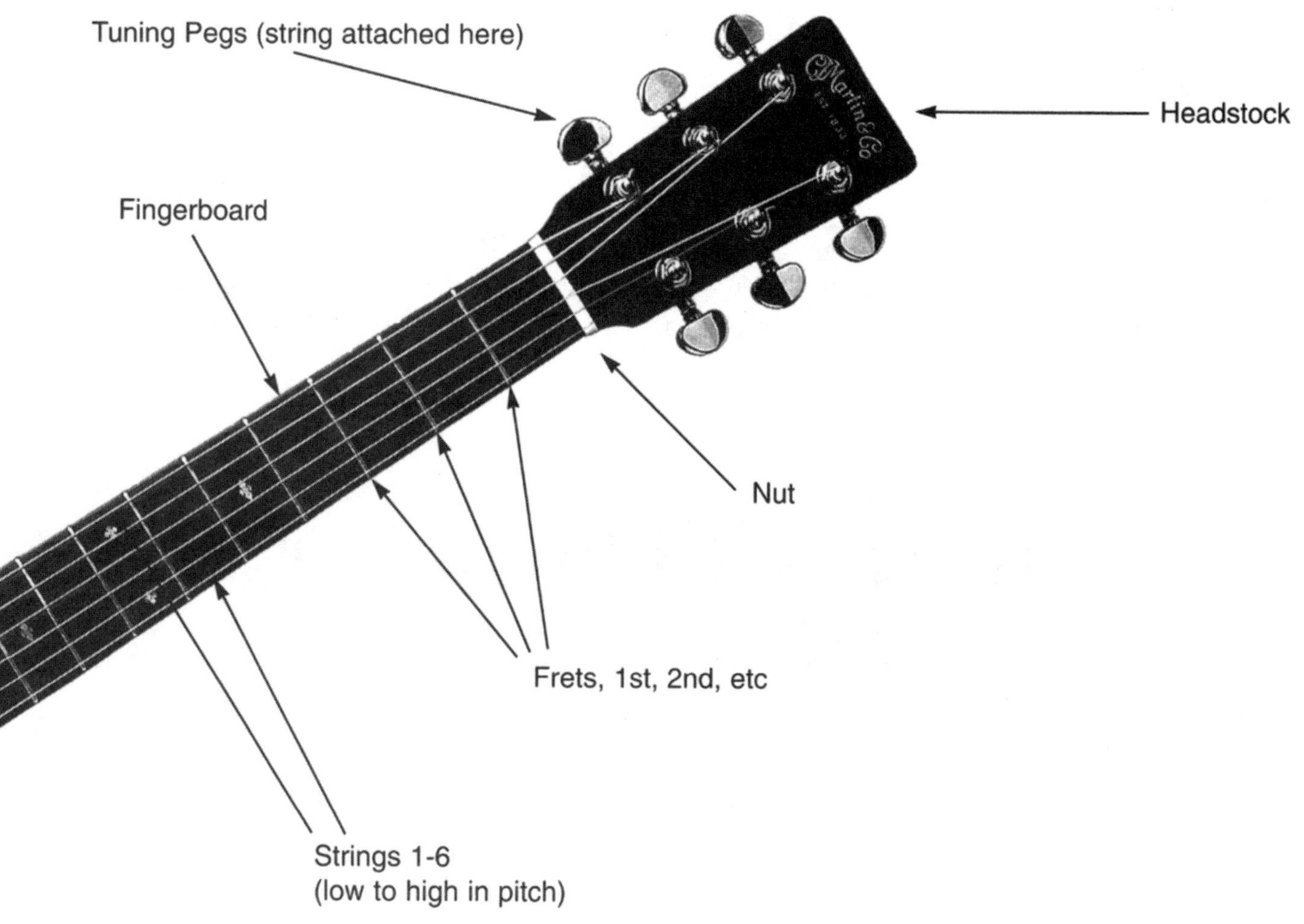

Strings: Strings are available in three basic gauges, light, medium and heavy. I suggest you begin with light or medium gauge strings.

Picks: Picks come in many shapes, sizes and thicknesses. For acoustic guitar, I recommend light to medium thickness. For electric, the thicker picks seem to work best. Experiment to find the size and shape you are most comfortable with.

Tuning Methods

Tuning to a Keyboard:

The six strings of a guitar can be tuned to a keyboard by matching the sound of each open guitar string to the keyboard notes as indicated in the diagram.

Note: You will hear the intonation better, and your guitar will stay in better tune, if you loosen the strings and tune them **up** to pitch rather than bringing them from above the pitch and tuning down.

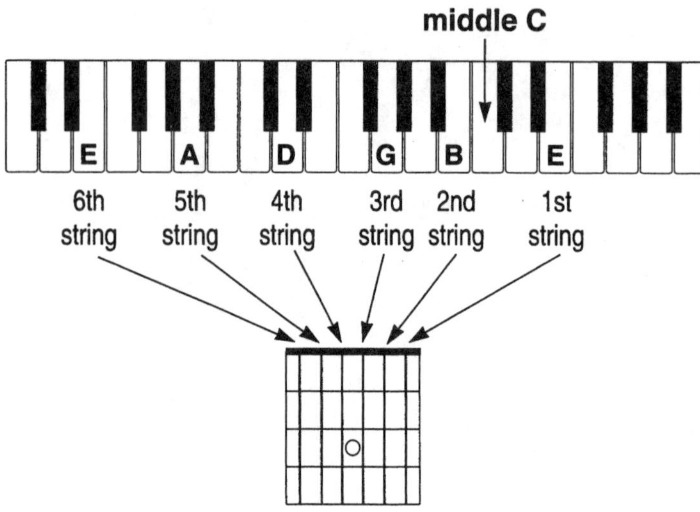

Electronic Tuners:

Many brands of small, battery operated tuners are available. These are excellent for keeping your guitar in perfect tune and for developing your ear to hear intonation very accurately. Simply follow the instructions supplied with the electronic tuner.

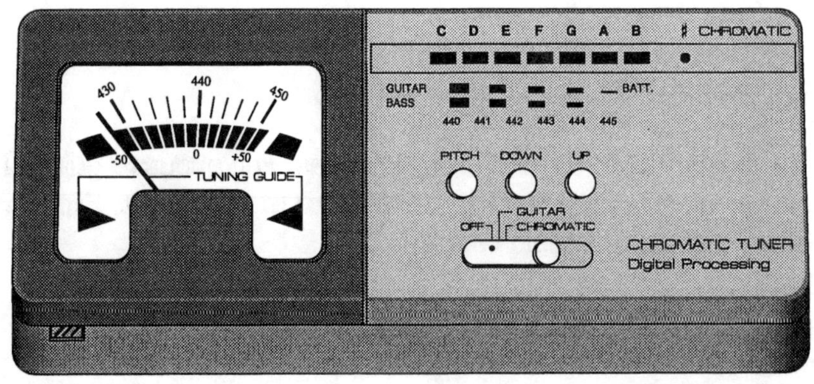

Tuning the Guitar to Itself – The "Fifth Fret" Method:

1) Either assume your 6th string "E" is in tune or tune it to a piano or some other fixed pitch instrument.

2) Depress the 6th string at the 5th fret. Play it and you will hear the note "A," which is the same as the 5th string played open. Turn the 5th string tuning key until the pitch of the open 5th string (A) matches that of the 6th string/5th fret (also A).

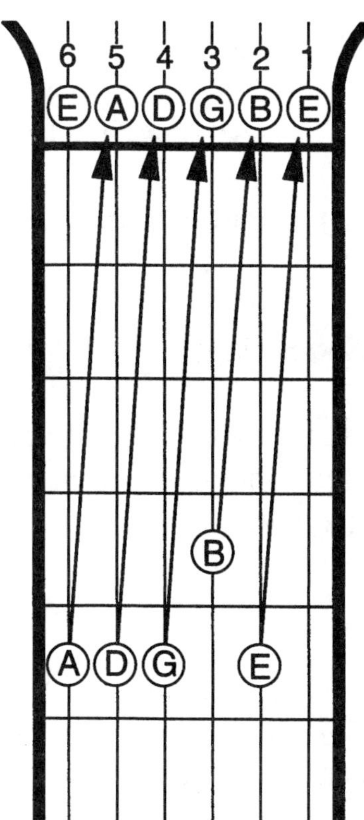

3) Depress the 5th string at the 5th fret. Play it and you will hear the note "D," which is the same as the 4th string played open. Turn the 4th string tuning key until the pitch of the open 4th string (D) matches that of the 5th string/5th fret (also D).

4) Depress the 4th string at the 5th fret. Play it and you will hear the note "G," which is the same as the 3rd string played open. Turn the 3rd string tuning key until the pitch of the open 3rd string (G) matches that of the 4th string/5th fret (also G).

5) Depress the 3rd string at the 4th fret (not the 5th fret as in the other strings). Play it and you will hear the note "B," which is the same as the 2nd string played open. Turn the 2nd string tuning key until the pitch of the open 2nd string (B) matches that of the 3rd string/4th fret (also B).

6) Depress the 2nd string at the 5th fret. Play it and you will hear the note "E," which is the same as the 1st string played open. Turn the 1st string tuning key until the pitch of the open 1st string (E) matches that of the 2nd string/5th fret (also E).

Changing Strings

Eventually, whether because a string has broken on its own, or because through repeated use it is no longer "tunable," you will have to change your strings. Be prepared! Always keep in your guitar case:

1) A set of extra strings
2) A pair of wire cutters
3) A string winder

All available at your local music store.

Changing Strings:

1) First, remove the bridge pin to release the ball end from the bridge. Unwrap the other end of the string from around the tuning peg.

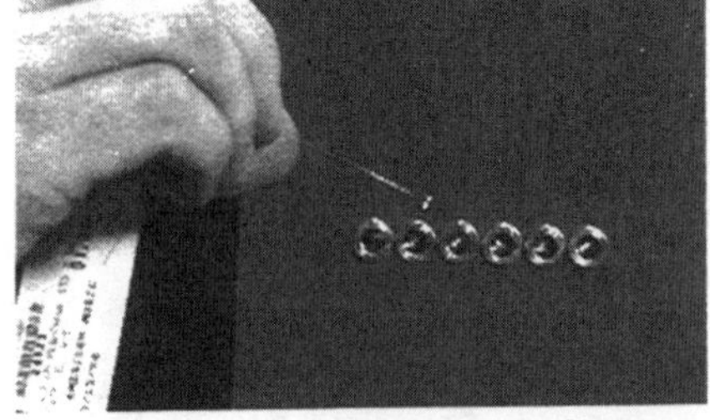

2) Insert the ball end of the new string into the hole in the bridge and replace the bridge pin.

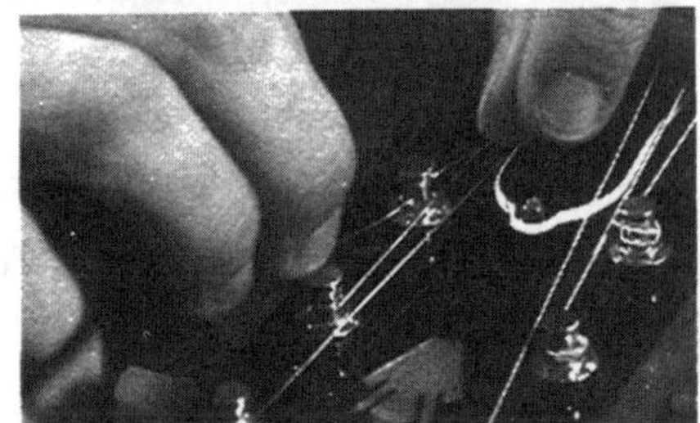

3) Once the string has been inserted into the bridge, feed the other end through the hole in the tuning peg, make sure to leave some slack in the string.

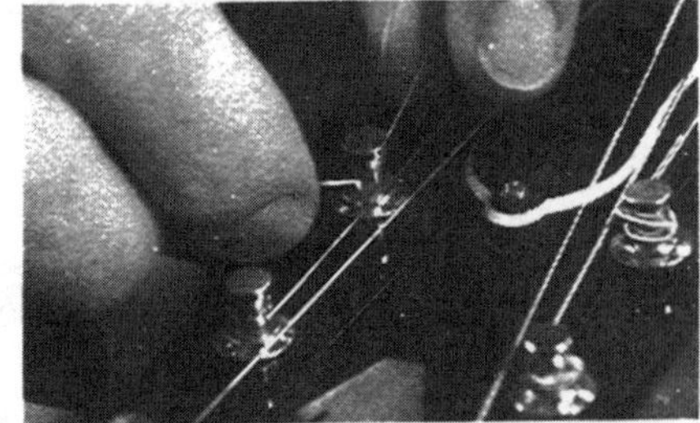

4) Bend the end slightly, and with your string winder, begin to tighten the string.

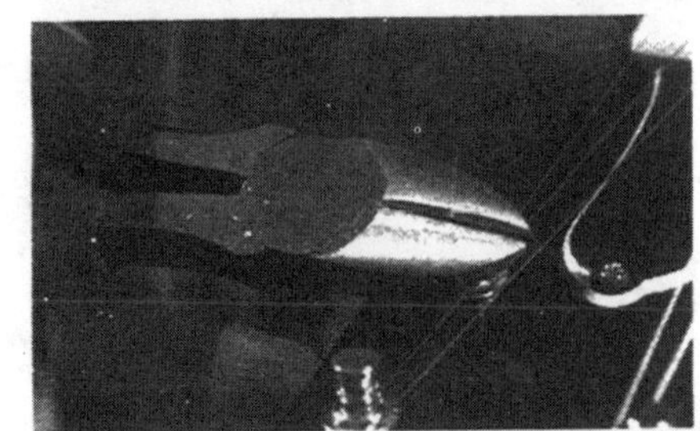

5) Trim the excess string off with your wire cutters.

Reading Rhythm Notation

At the beginning of every song is a time signature. 4/4 is the most common time signature:

4 FOUR COUNTS TO A MEASURE
4 A QUARTER NOTE RECEIVES ONE COUNT

The top number tells you how many counts per measure.
The bottom number tells you which kind of note receives one count.

The time value of a note is determined by three things:

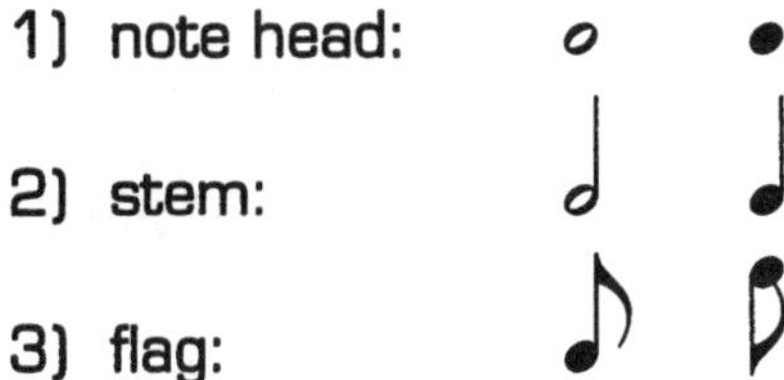

This is a whole note. The note head is open and has no stem. In 4/4 time a whole note receives 4 counts.

This is a half note. It has an open note head and a stem. A half note receives 2 counts.

This is a quarter note. It has a solid note head and a stem. A quarter note receives 1 count.

This is an eighth note. It has a solid note head and a stem with a flag attached. An eighth note receives 1/2 count.

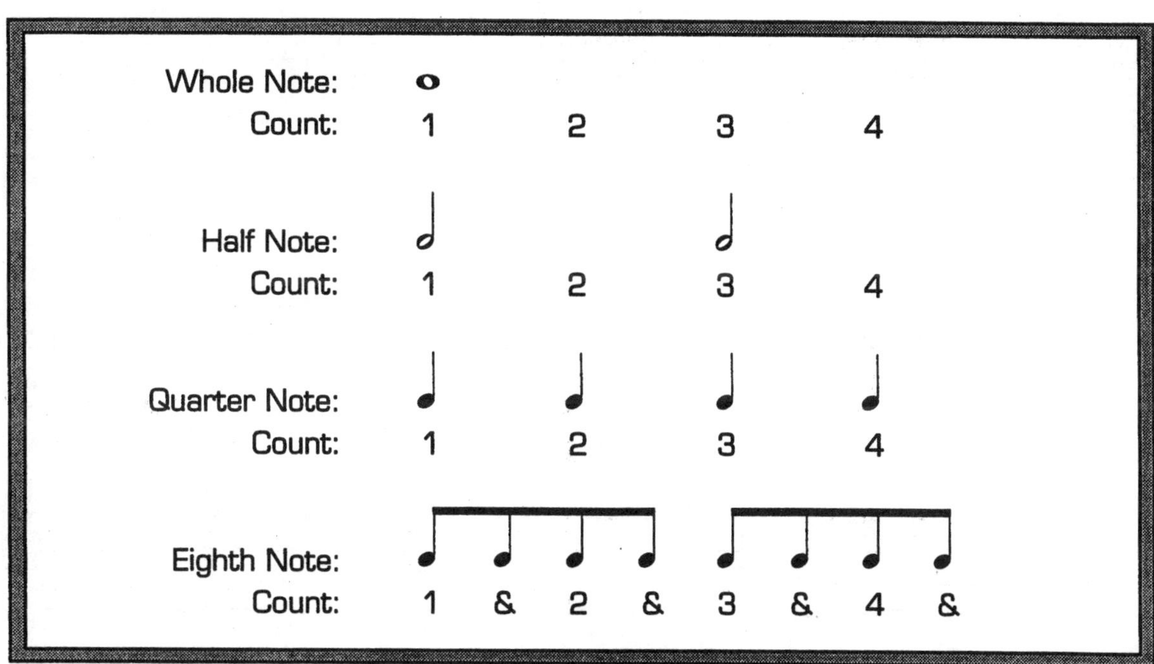

Reading Music Notation

Music is written on a **staff**. The staff consists of five lines and four spaces between the lines:

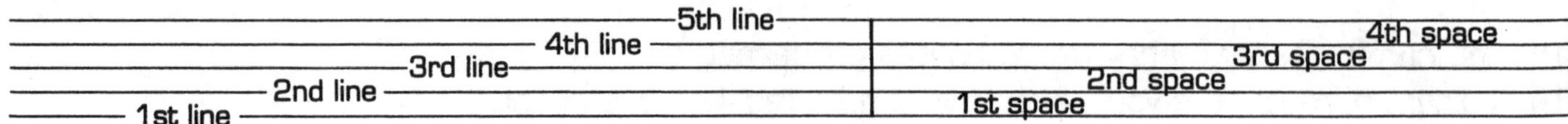

The names of the notes are the same as the first seven letters of the alphabet: A B C D E F G.

The notes are written in alphabetical order. The first (lowest) line is "E":

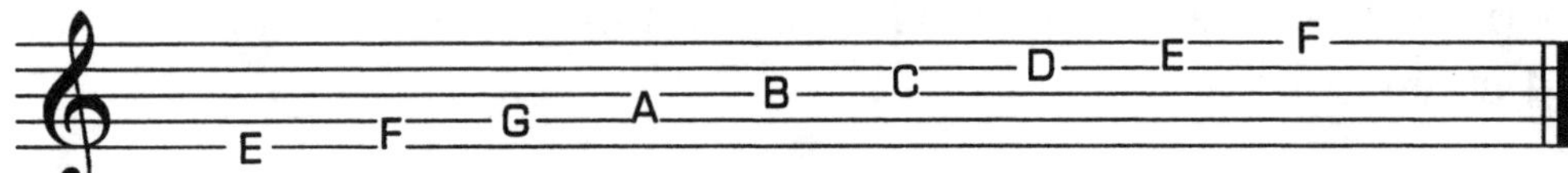

Notes can extend above and below the staff. When they do, **ledger lines** are added. Here is the approximate range of the guitar from the lowest note, open 6th string "E," to a "B" on the 1st string at the 17th fret.

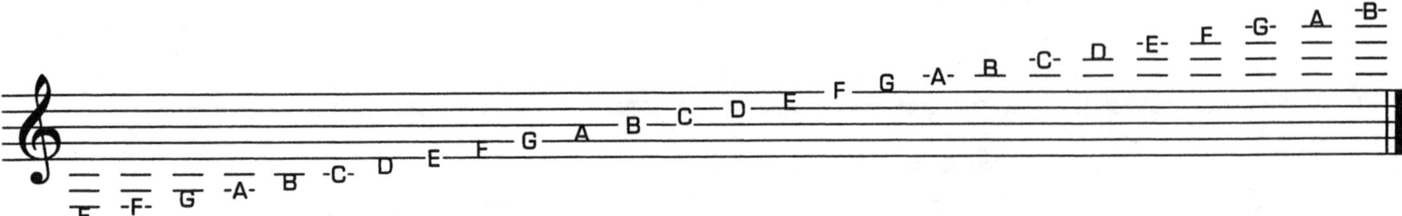

The staff is divided into **measures** by **bar lines**. A heavy double bar line marks the end of the music.

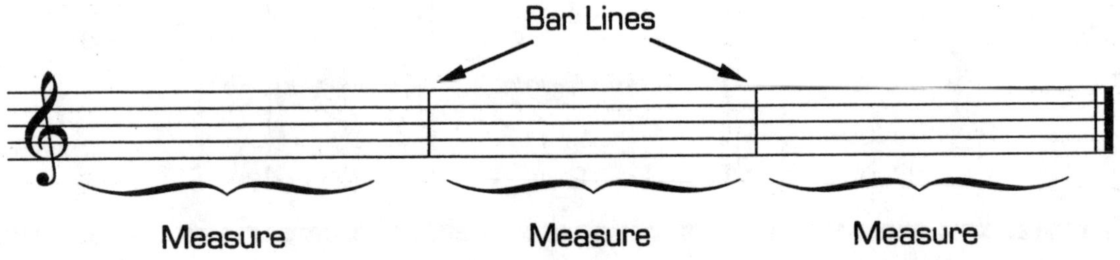

Reading Tablature and Fretboard Diagrams

Tablature illustrates the location of notes on the neck of the guitar. This illustration compares the six strings of a guitar to the six lines of tablature.

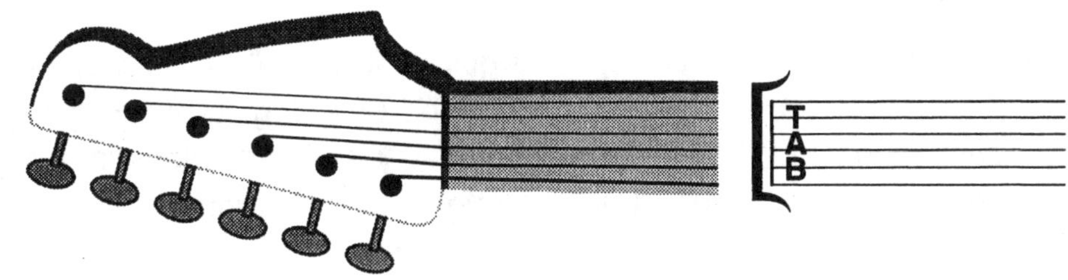

Notes are indicated by placing fret numbers on the strings. An "O" indicates an open string.

This tablature indicates to play the open, 1st and 3rd frets on the 1st string.

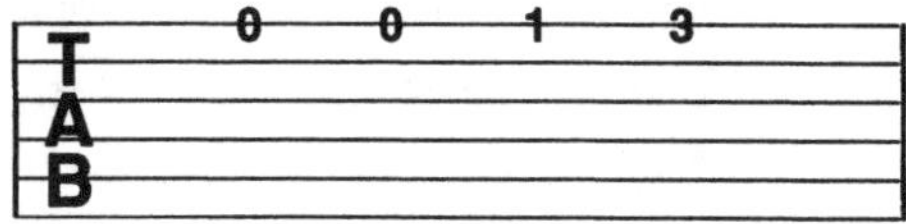

Tablature is usually used in conjunction with standard music notation. The rhythms and note names are indicated by the standard notation and the location of those notes on the guitar neck is indicated by the tablature.

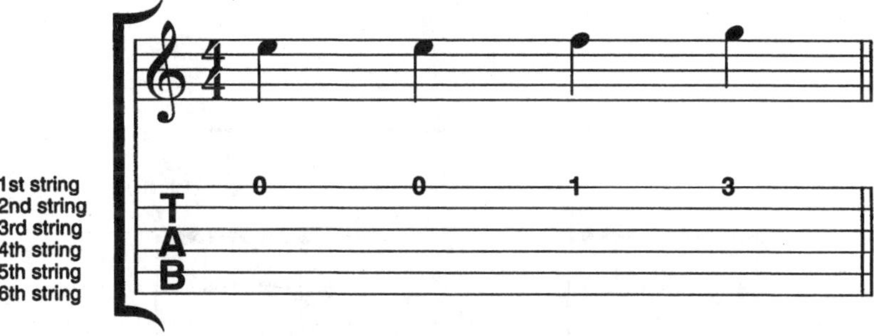

Chords are often indicated in **chord block diagrams**. The vertical lines represent the strings and the horizontal line represent the frets. Scales are often indicated with guitar **fretboard diagrams**. Here the strings are horizontal and the frets are vertical.

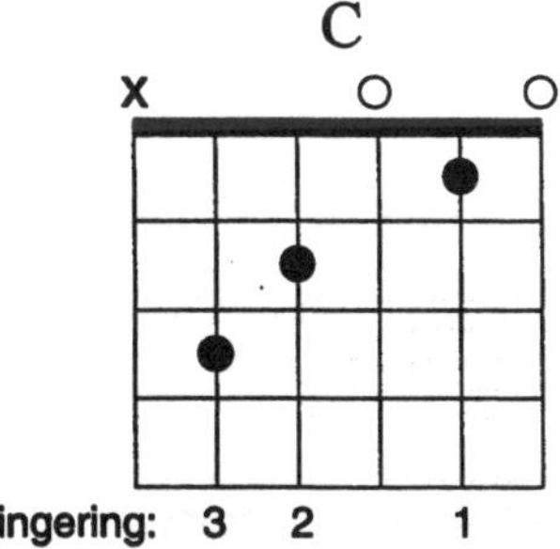

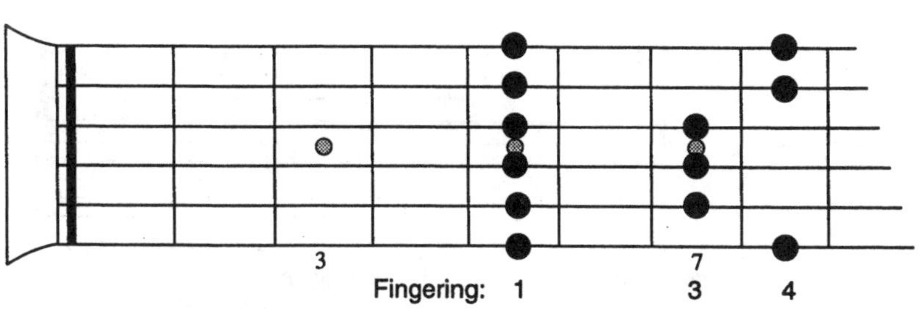

Open Position Chords

The Six Basic Open Position Chords

These are the most fundamental chords to all styles of guitar playing. "Open" position chords contain open strings which ring out loud and clear. The sound of a ringing open chord is probably the most identifiable guitar sound there is. Whether you play acoustic or electric guitar, these six chords will be some of the main chords you will use throughout your lifetime.

The E Major Chord

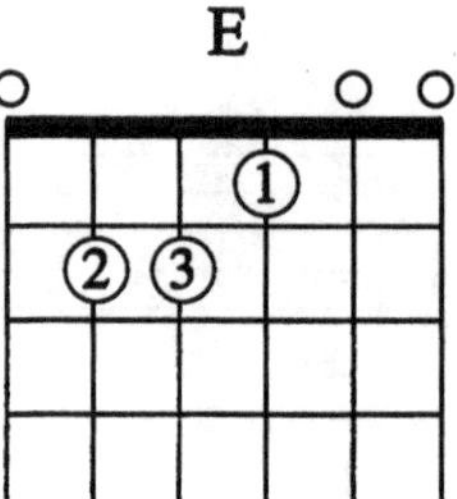

The dots indicate which notes to play with your finger, the open circles indicate open strings and "x" indicates a string that should not be played. The numbers under the chord frame indicate which left-hand finger to use. Play the E chord. Make sure you get a clear sound without any buzzing or muffled notes. Your fingertips should be placed just behind the fret—not on top of it or too far behind it. Also, the fingertips should be perpendicular to the fingerboard; if they lean at an angle they will interfere with the other strings and prevent them from ringing.

The A Major Chord

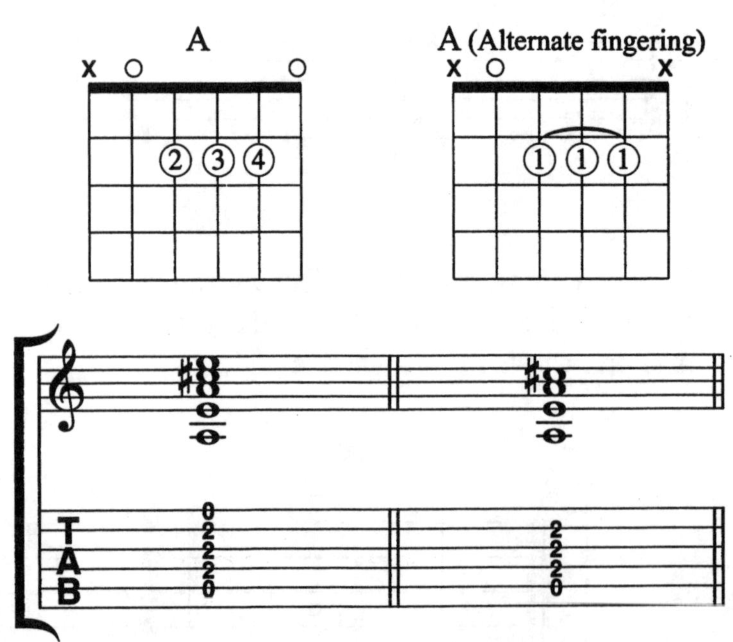

Notice that in the alternate fingering there is no 1st string E. This is OK, it's still an A chord.

The D Major Chord

The D chord uses just the top four strings. Play the chord making sure you can get a good clear, ringing tone.

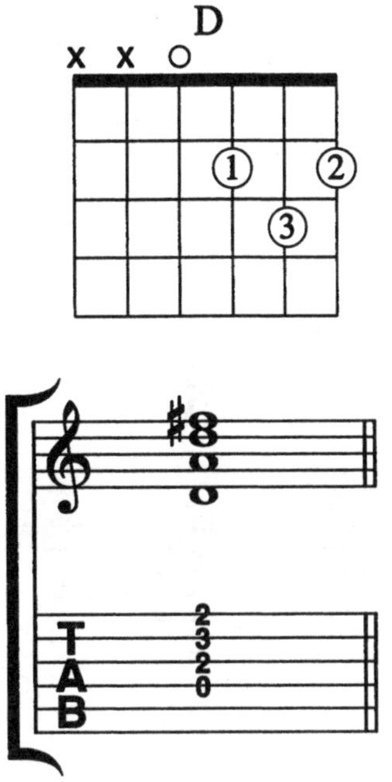

Strumming:

Relax your left-hand and strum with a constant down-up motion from your wrist. Strike the strings evenly with both the down-strum and, as your hand returns to playing position, with the up-strum.

Example 1: First Strumming Pattern

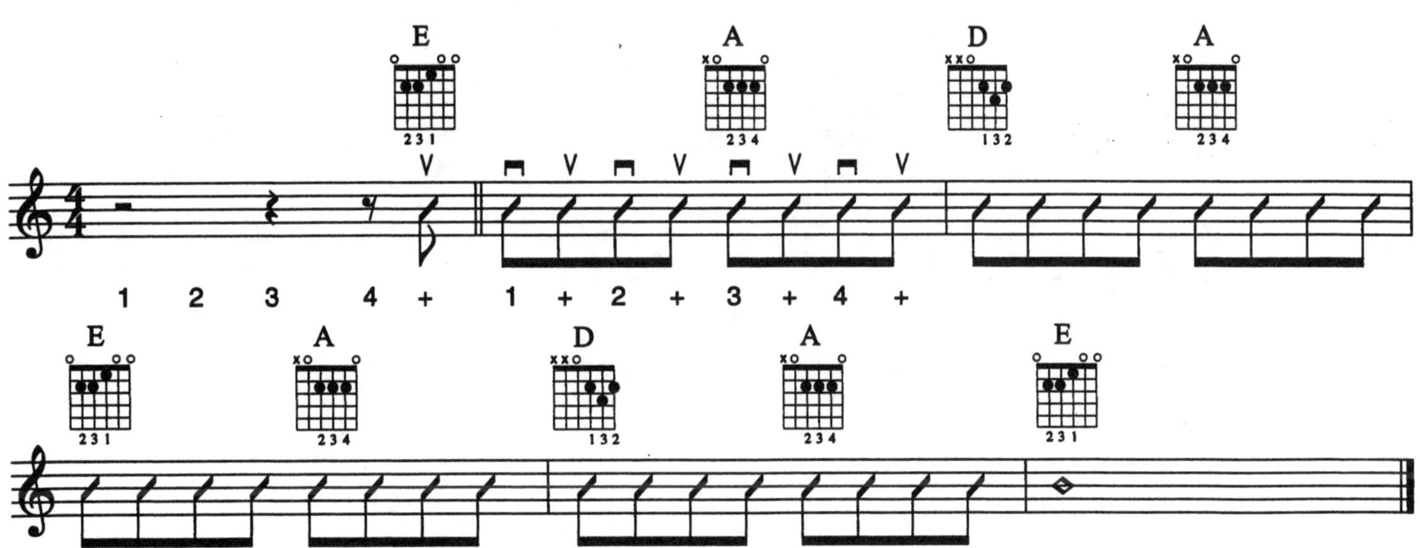

Note: Down-strums are indicated with this symbol: ⊓. Up-strums are indicated with this symbol: V.

G Major

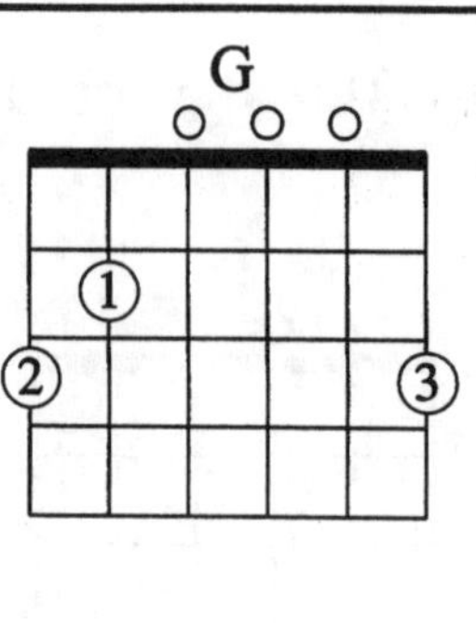

Tip: In order to play this chord cleanly, it is essential that you play on your fingertips, holding your fingers perpendicular to the neck. Keeping your left-hand thumb down in the center of the neck will help keep your fingers in the best position to avoid interfering with the other strings.

Example 2

Now try combining the G chord with the D chord. Notice both chords use the same three fingers:

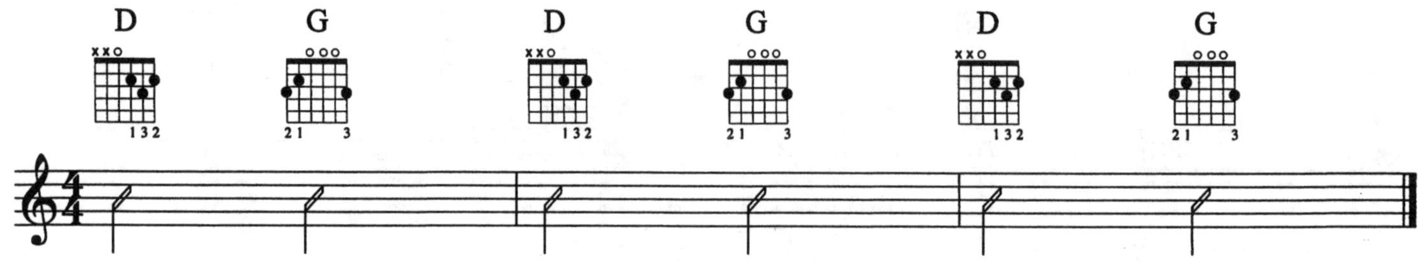

C Major

Remember: Hold your fingers perpendicular to the neck making sure they touch only the strings they are playing and do not interfere with the other strings.

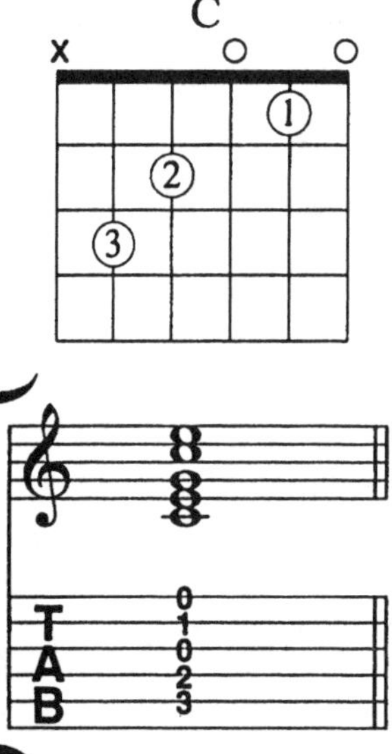

Example 3

Practice moving back and forth between the C and G chords.

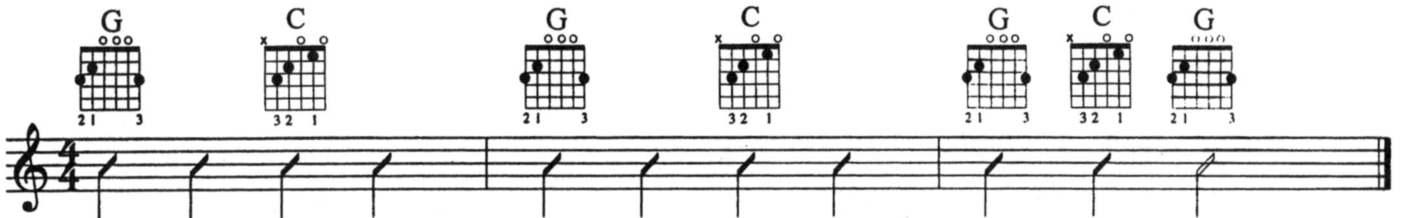

B7 Chord

The G, D, C and E chords each contain three different notes. The B7 is a four-note chord (B, D♯, F♯, A).

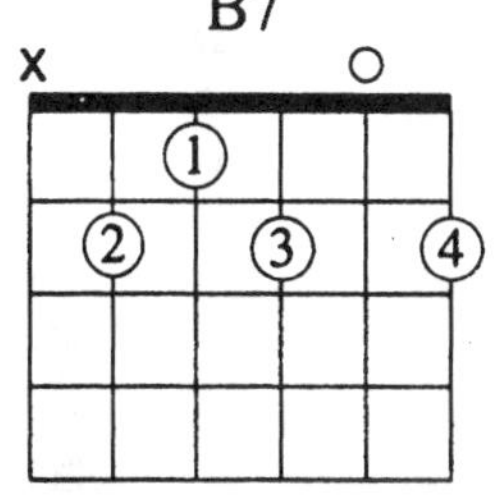

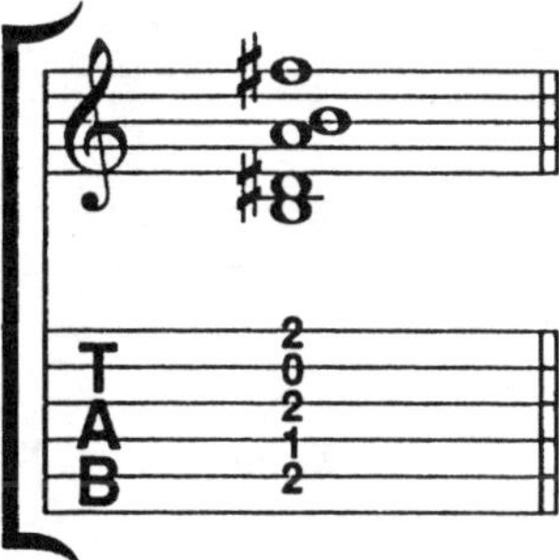

Example 4

Now try this next example which switches between the E and B7 chords.

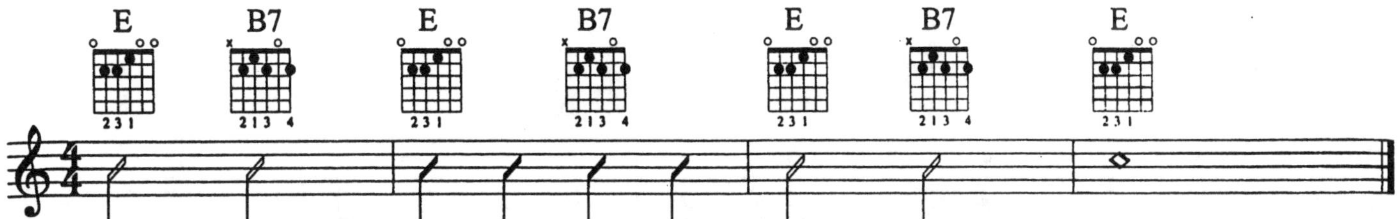

The Blues Progression (in four keys)

The blues progression is the most common chord progression. The typical blues progression is 12 measures long and uses the 1st, 4th and 5th chords of the key. To find the 1st, 4th and 5th chords (usually indicated with Roman numerals: I, IV and V) simply count up through the alphabet from the key note.

For Example:

Blues in the key of "A":	A	B	C	D	E	F	G	A
	I			IV	V			
Blues in the key of "G":	G	A	B	C	D	E	F	G
	I			IV	V			
Blues in the key of "E":	E	F	G	A	B	C	D	E
	I			IV	V			
Blues in the key of "D":	D	E	F	G	A	B	C	D
	I			IV	V			

Example 5: Strum Pattern A

The next progression can be played with a variety of "strum" patterns. First try this simple "quarter-note" (one strum per beat) pattern. It can be played with either your pick, for a clear, bright sound; or your thumb, which gives it a darker, warmer sound. Listen to the recording to hear the difference.

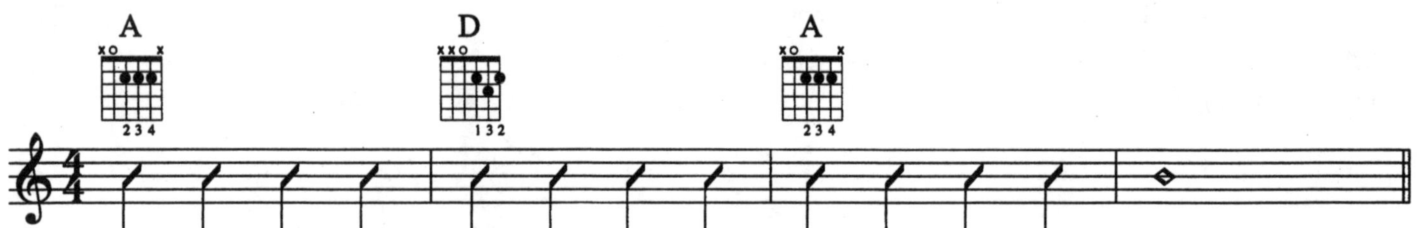

Example 6: Strum Pattern B

This next pattern uses both down- and up-strokes of the pick. Your right hand should maintain a constant down-up motion, but you'll hit the strings on both the down-stroke, and on some of the up-strokes.

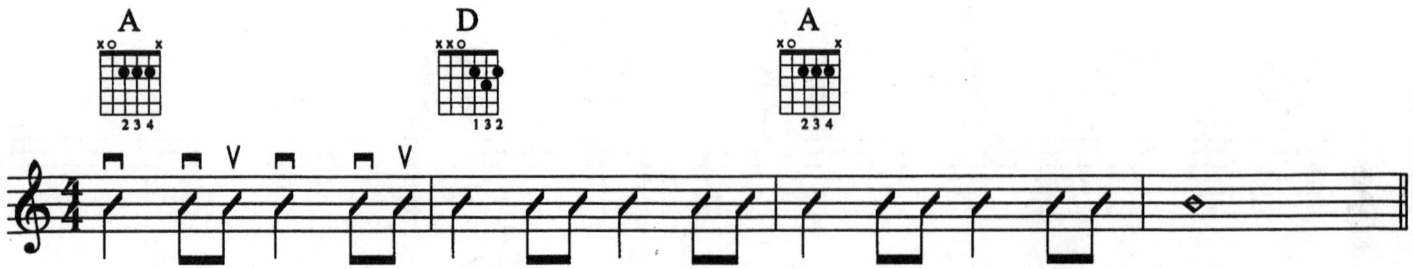

Example 7

This strumming example takes the blues progression through four keys: A, G, E, and D. It uses just the six chords you've learned so far: A, D, E, G, C and B7. Play along with the recording using the two rhythms you've just learned. When you're comfortable with the chord changes, try making up some rhythms of your own.

Blues in Four Keys

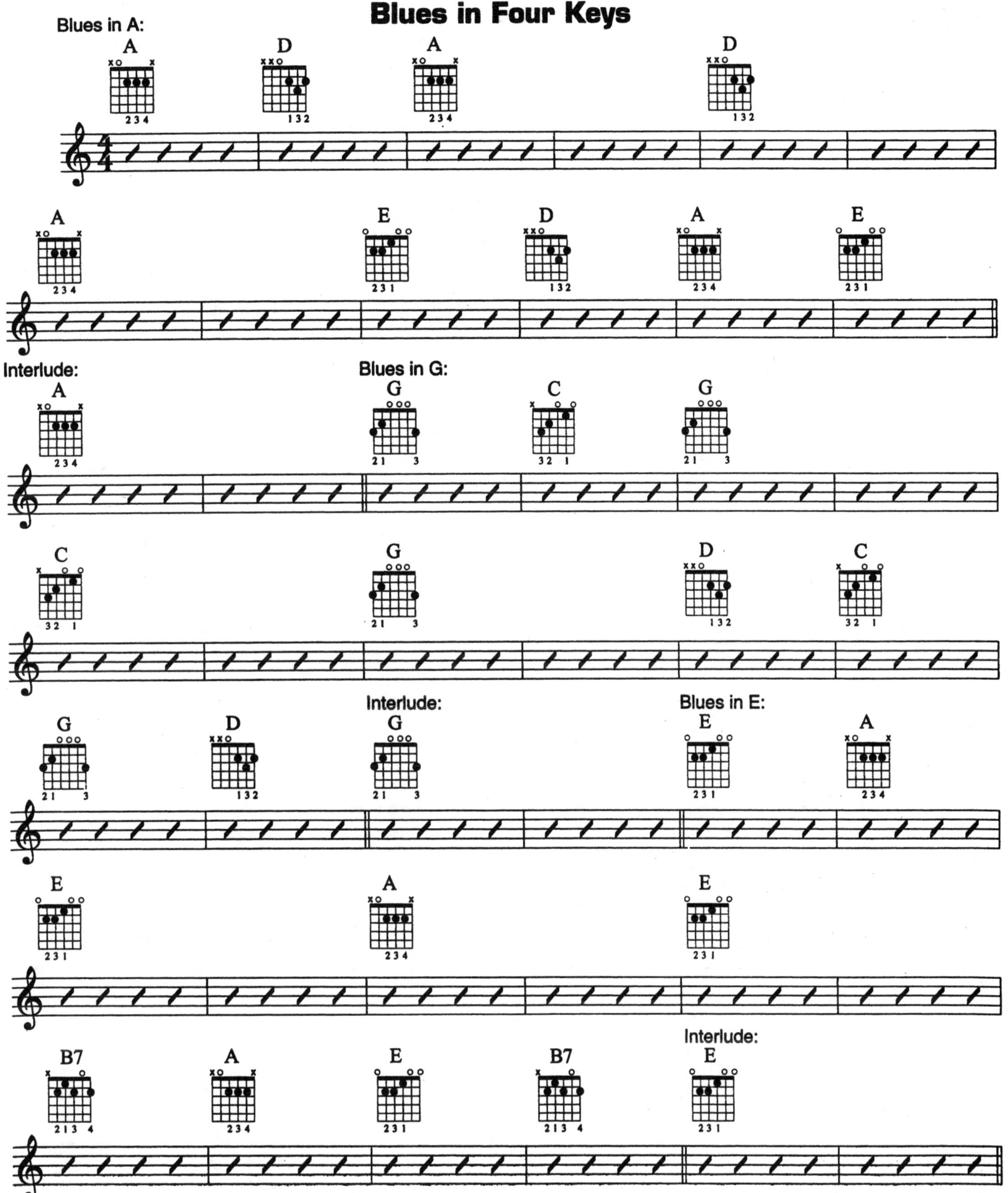

Blues in D:

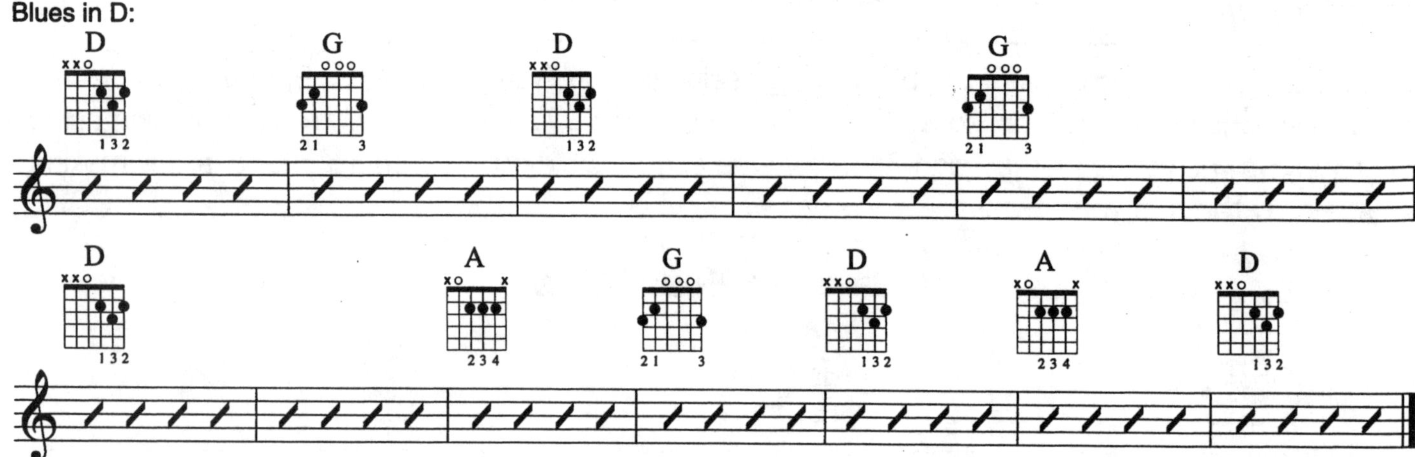

Down-Up Strumming

As you've already seen in Example 6, picking (or strumming) consists of two elements: the down-stroke and the up-stroke. Again, your right hand should maintain a constant down-up motion, striking the strings on not only the down-stroke, but also on some of the up-strokes.

Example 8

Here is a typical alternating strum pattern played over an E chord.

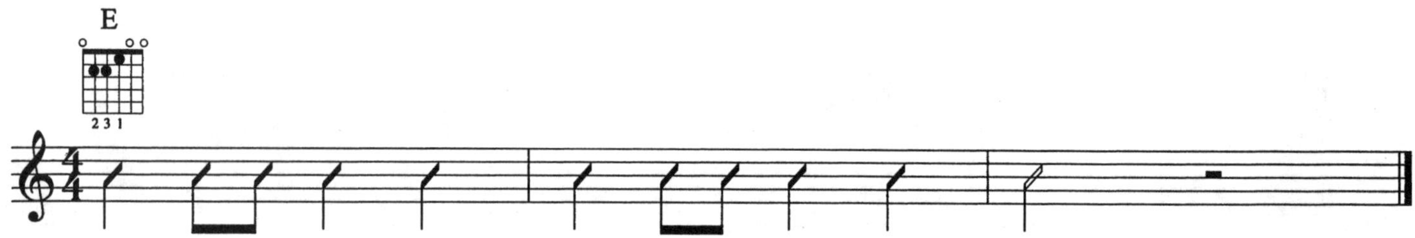

Example 9

Now let's apply the strum pattern from the previous example to the chord progression: E - D - A - E.

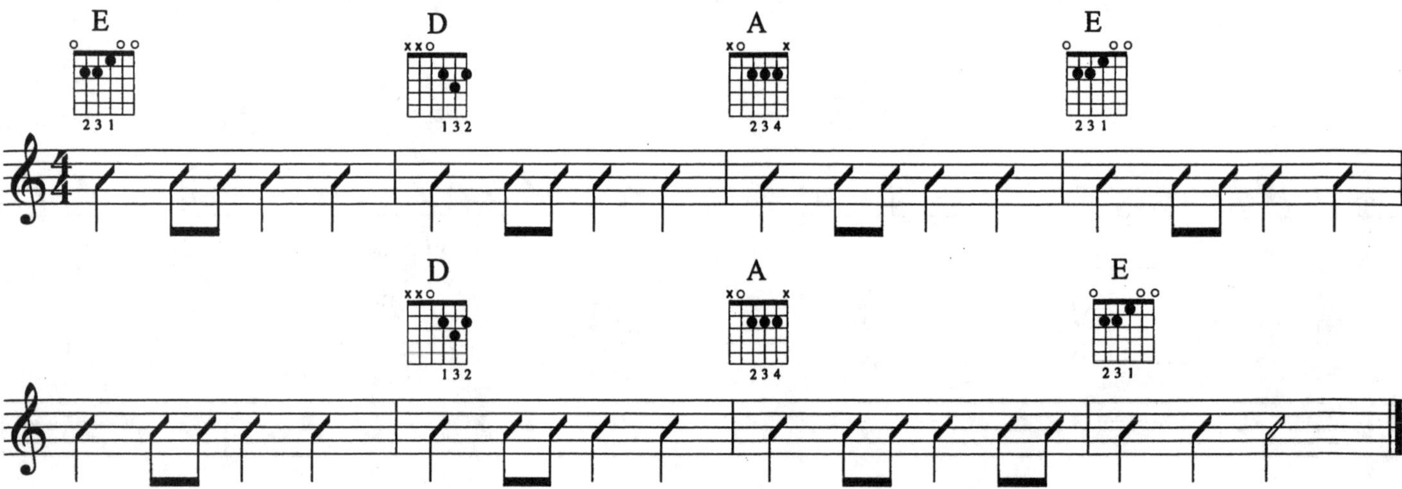

Bass/Chord Strum Patterns

One of the most common acoustic guitar strumming techniques is the bass/chord strumming pattern. First play the bass note (the root) of the chord, then strum the rest of the chord.

Example 10

Here is an example using an E chord. Play the lowest note (E on the 6th string) and then strum the higher strings. Use all down strokes.

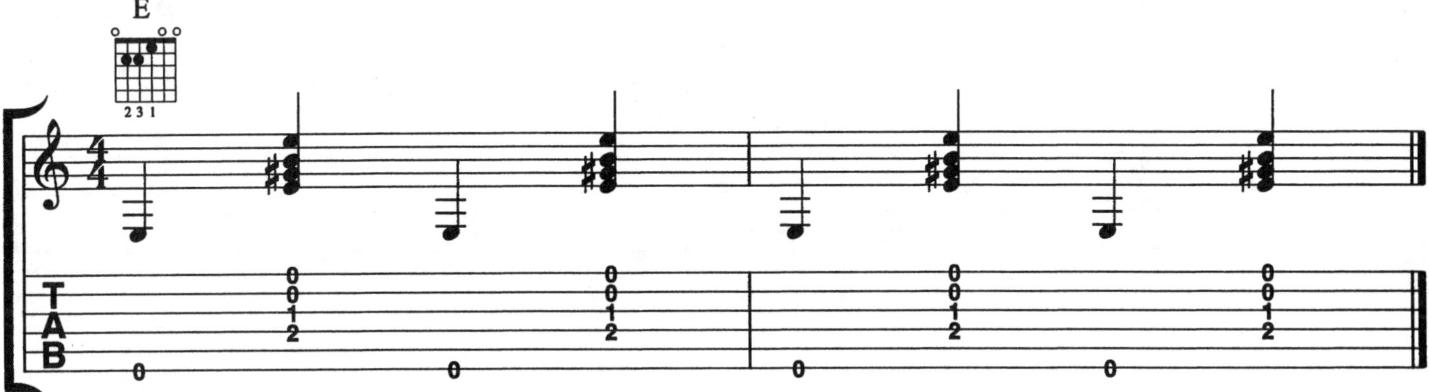

Example 11

Here is an example using an A chord. Play the lowest note (A on the 5th string) and then strum the higher strings. It's okay to look down at your picking hand if that helps.

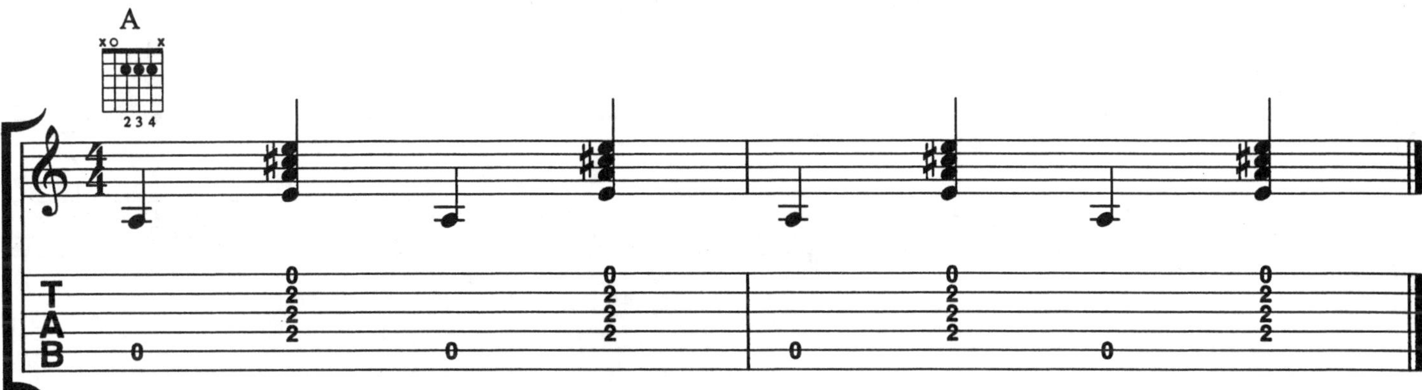

Example 12

Here is an example using a D chord. Play the lowest note (D on the 4th string) and then strum the higher strings.

Example 13

Now try the bass/strum technique with the G chord. Again, play the lowest note (G on the 6th string) and then strum the higher strings.

Example 14

Now try the bass/strum technique on the C chord. The root is the 5th string "C."

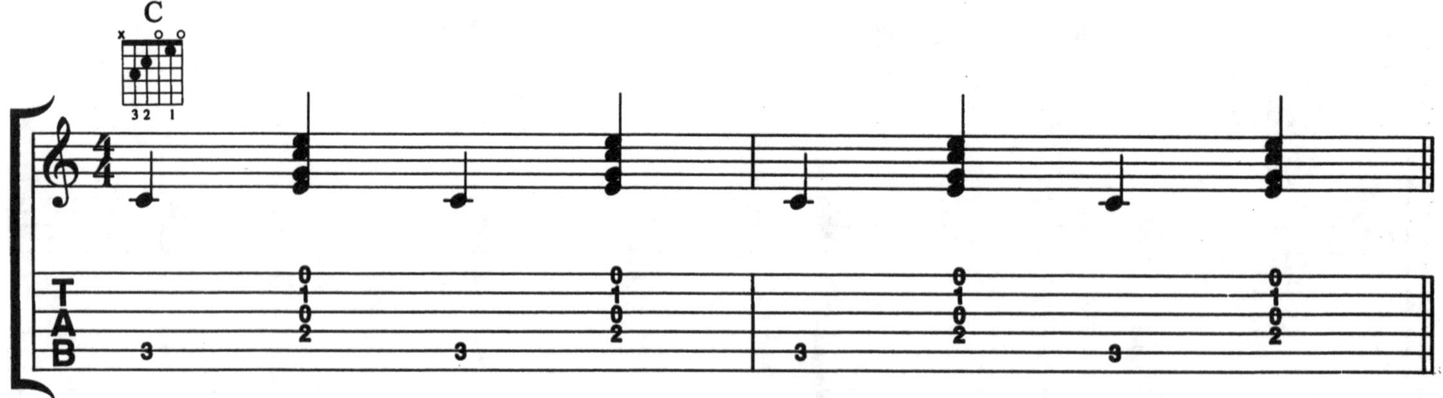

Example 15

Finally, let's try the bass/strum technique on the B7 chord. The root is the 5th string "B."

Example 16

Now put the bass/strum pattern in the context of a song using the chords G, C and D. Practice the example until you can shift smoothly from one chord to the next without stopping or breaking up the rhythm.

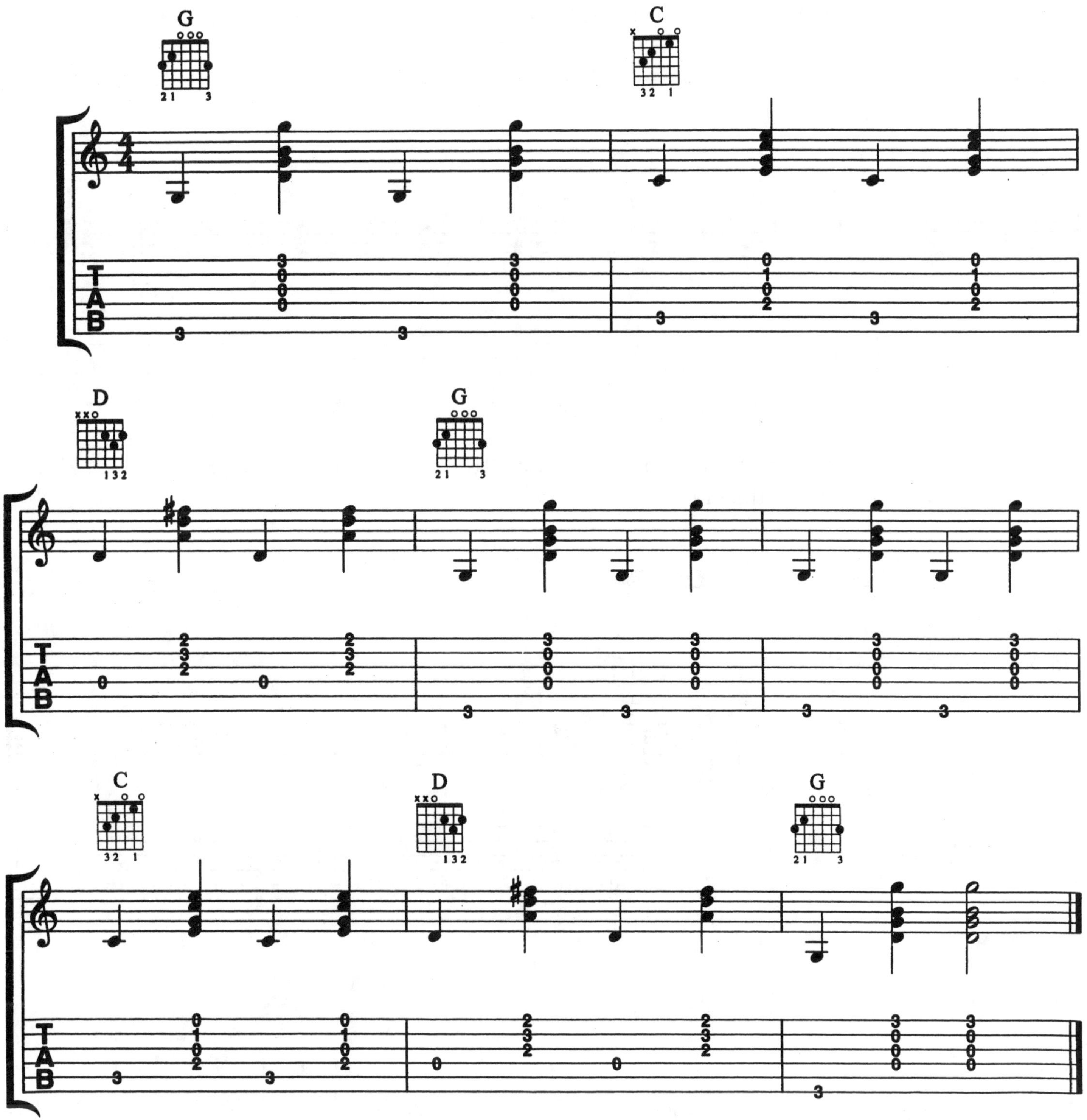

The Alternating Bass/Strum Pattern

The most common variation on the bass/strum pattern is to alternate between two different bass notes.

Example 17

The simplest alternating bass pattern is to first play the lowest note, strum, then play the next highest bass note, then strum again. So for an E chord the pattern would be: 6th string E–strum–5th string B–strum. Again, use all down-strokes.

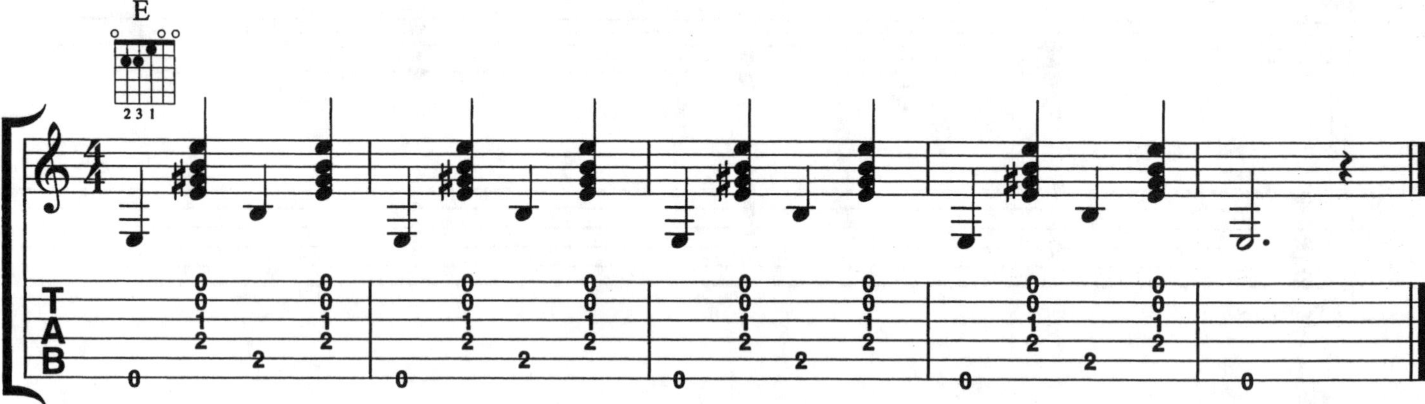

Note: Usually when playing alternating bass/chord patterns it sounds best to "skip" or "miss" the bass notes when you strum the chord.

Example 18

Now try the pattern over the A chord. Example 18A shows the previous pattern applied to the A chord. First play the 5th string A, strum, then play the 4th string E, then strum again.

Ex. 18A

Ex. 18B

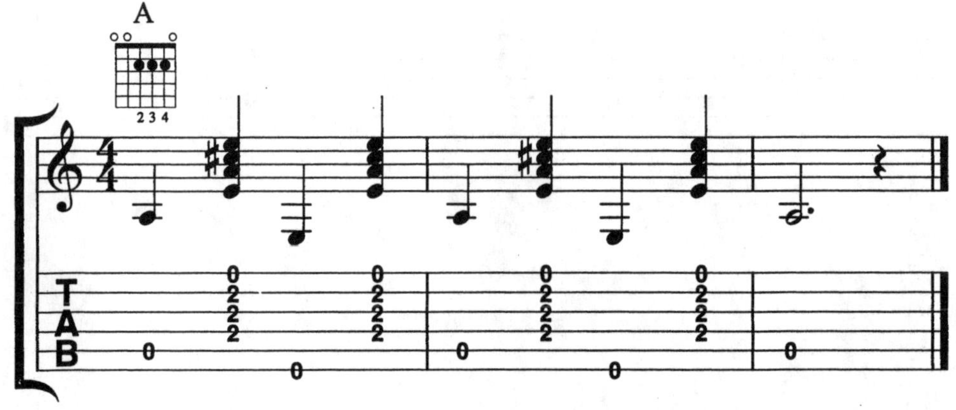

Example 18B shows a variation on the pattern: First play the 5th string A, strum, now instead of playing the 4th string E play the low 6th string E, then strum again. Again, use all down-strokes.

Example 19

Ex. 19A

Now try the pattern over the D chord. Example 19A shows the basic pattern applied to the D chord. First play the 4th string D, strum, then play the 3rd string A, then strum again.

Ex. 19B

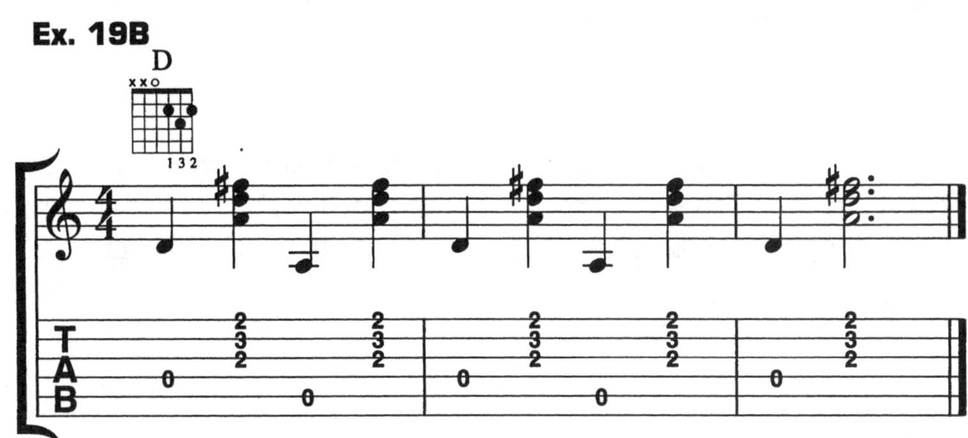

Since the 3rd string A is a little too high to provide a good bass, try using the 5th string as the alternate bass note instead: First play the 4th string D, strum, now instead of playing the 3rd string A play the low 5th string A, then strum again.

Example 20

Ex. 20A

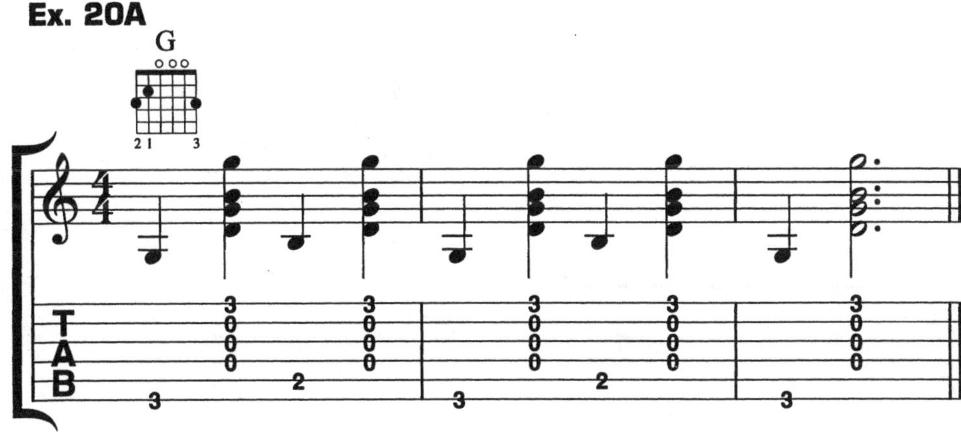

Now try the pattern over the G chord. Example 20A alternates between the 6th string G and the 5th string B.

Ex. 20B

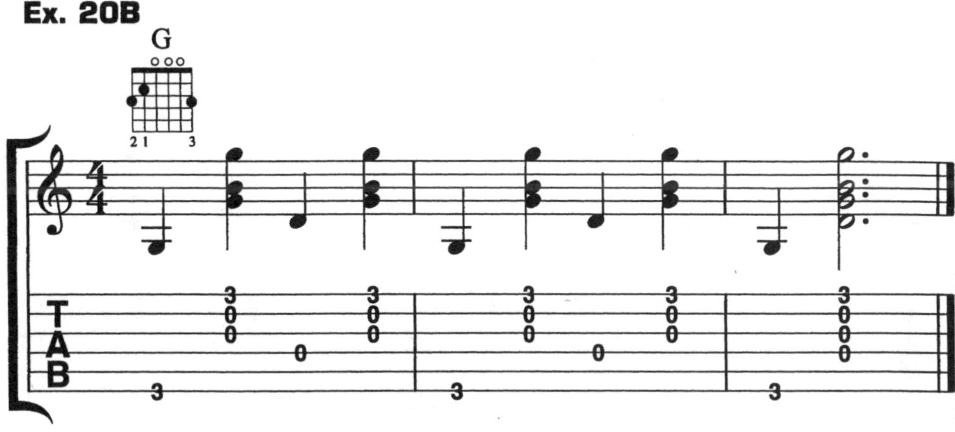

Example 20B alternates between the 6th string G and the 4th string D. (Again, notice how we "skip" the bass note "D" on the strum.)

Example 21

For the C chord alternate between the 5th string C and the 4th string E.

Ex. 21A

Example 21B shows a nice variation on the alternating bass pattern. Play the 5th string C, strum, then shift your 3rd finger from the C to the 6th string G, then strum again. Notice that we only strum the top four strings. This pattern will take a little practice but soon you'll have it down.

Ex. 21B

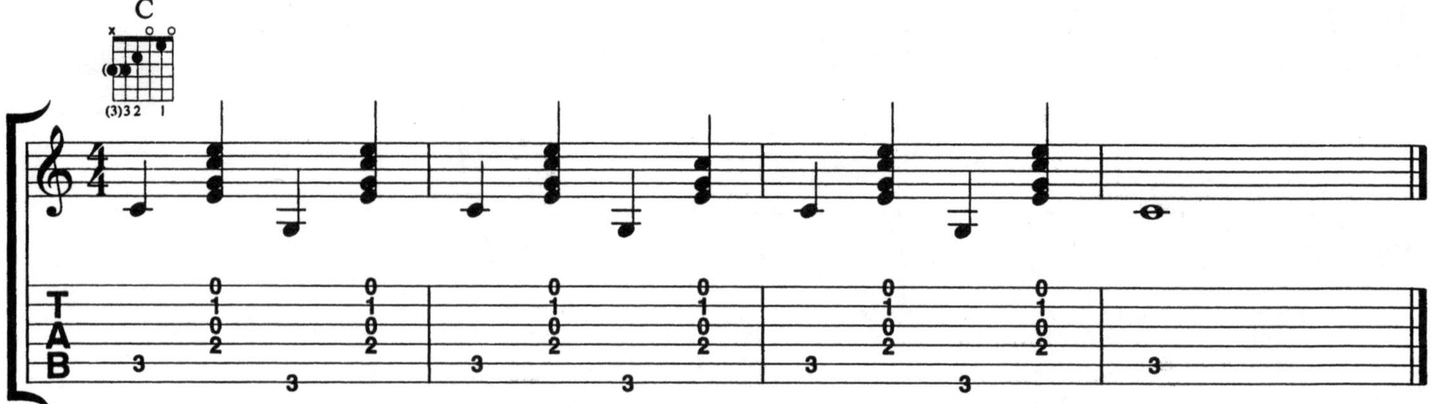

Example 22

We can apply the same type of patterns to the B7 chord. First try alternating between the 5th string B and the 4th string D♯.

Ex. 22A

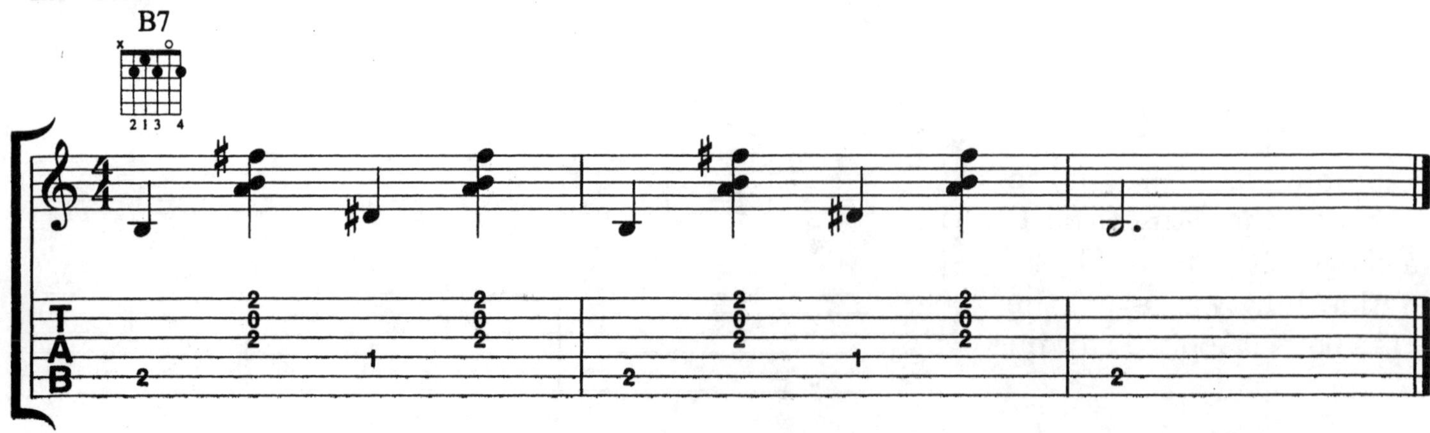

Example 22B uses the same type of finger shifting as you used with the C chord in Example 21B. Play the 5th string B, strum, then shift your 2nd finger from the B to the 6th string F♯, then strum again.

Example 23

This example combines all the chords you've learned with the alternating bass pattern.

E A

D G

C B7 E

Chord Categories

There are three categories of chords: Major, Minor and Dominant 7th. With these three types of chords you can play basically any pop or rock song. You already know five basic open position major chords: E, D, C, A and G.

Minor Chords: Minor chords differ from major chords by only one note: the 3rd. (To find the "3rd" count up three from the root (1). By lowering the 3rd of any major chord one fret it becomes a minor chord.

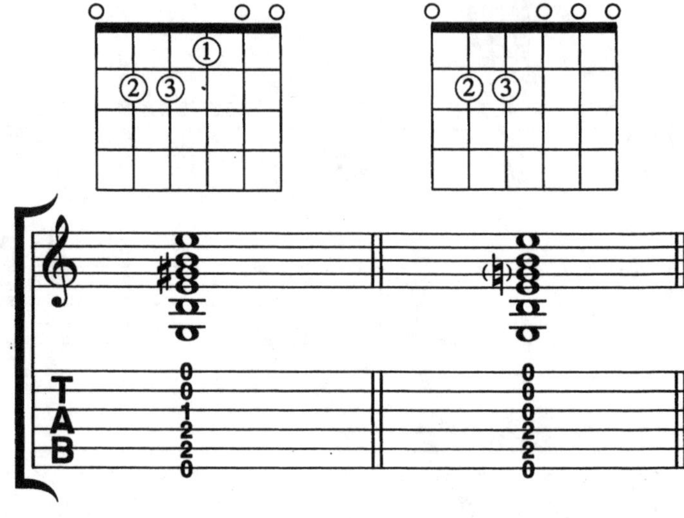

Example 24

Play back and forth between the E and Em chords:

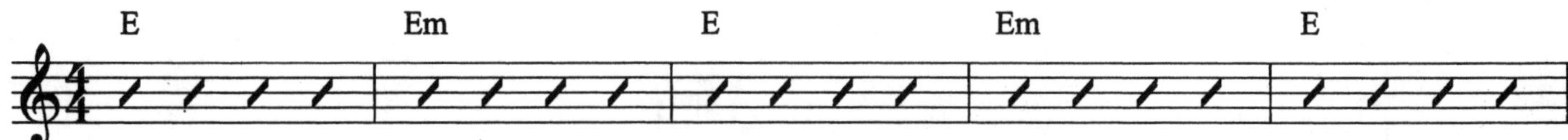

Notice again that the difference between the A and Am, and D and Dm chords is only one note (the 3rd).

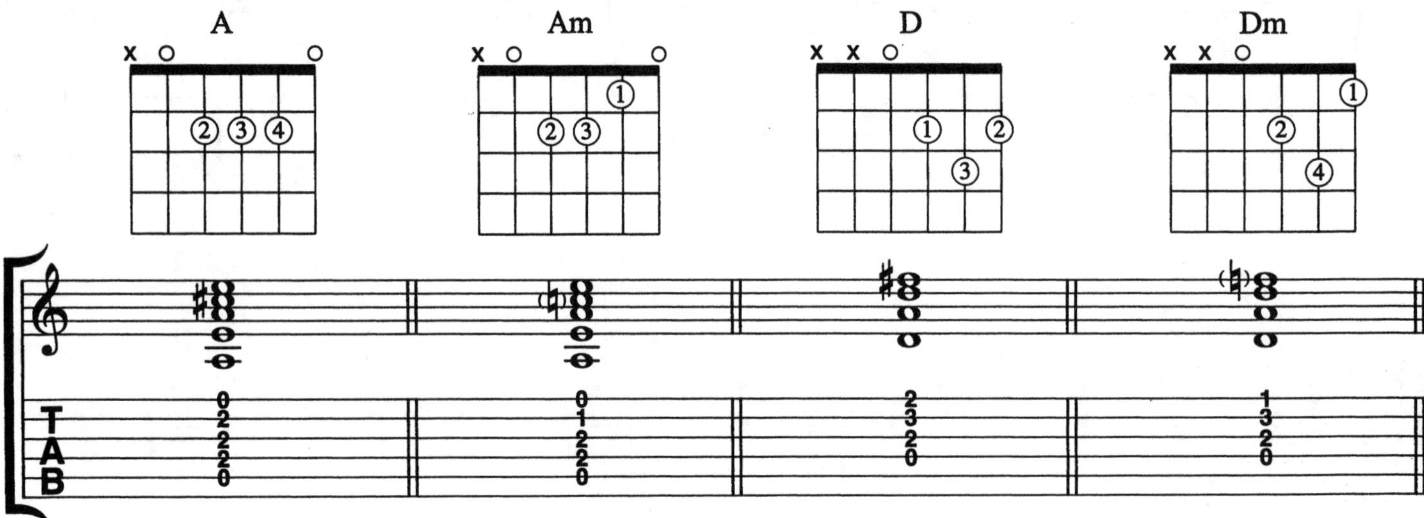

Example 25

Play back and forth between the A and Am chords:

Example 26

Play back and forth between the D and Dm chords:

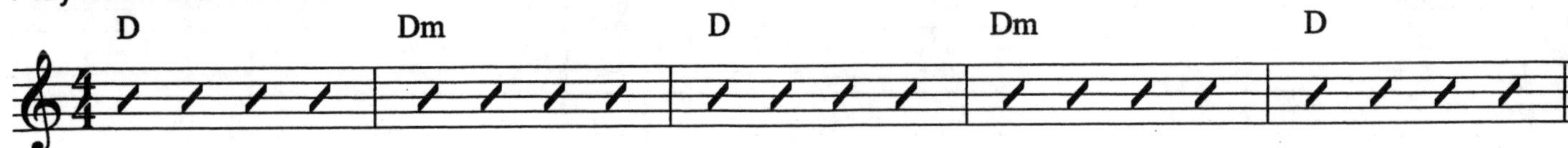

Dominant Chords: Dominant chords differ from major chords by the addition of one note: the 7th. (To find the "7th " count up seven from the root (1)). Adding the 7th to a major chord makes it a dominant 7th chord.

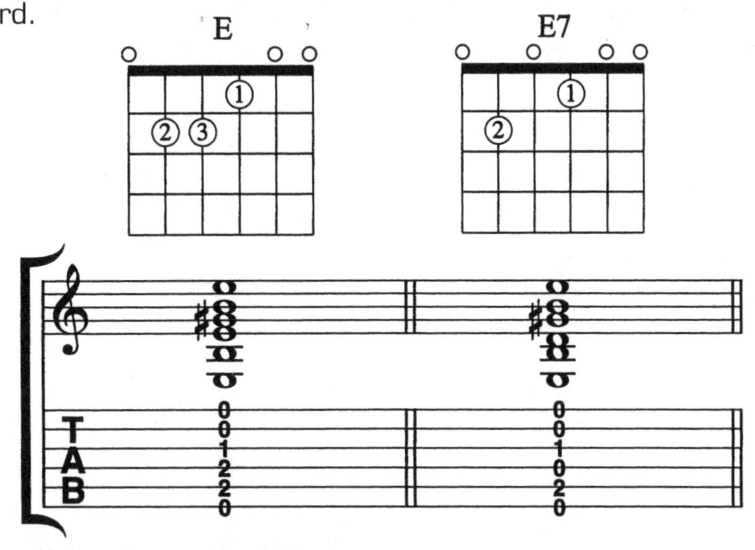

Example 27

Play back and forth between the E and E7 chords. Listen closely to the difference in sound the one new note makes:

The difference between the A and A7, and D and D7 chords is again the addition of one note: the 7th.

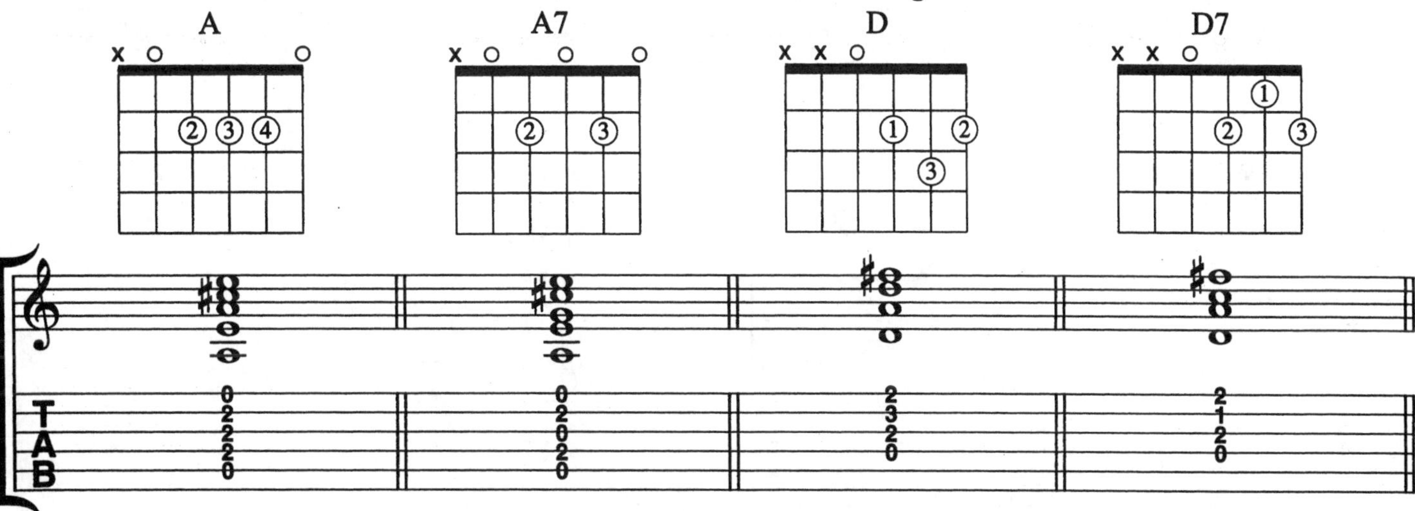

Example 28

Play back and forth between the A and A7 chords:

Example 29

Play back and forth between the D and D7 chords:

The open position G chord can be converted to a dominant chord as shown here. Try fingering the G chord with your 2nd, 3rd and 4th fingers. This will make the change to G7 easier.

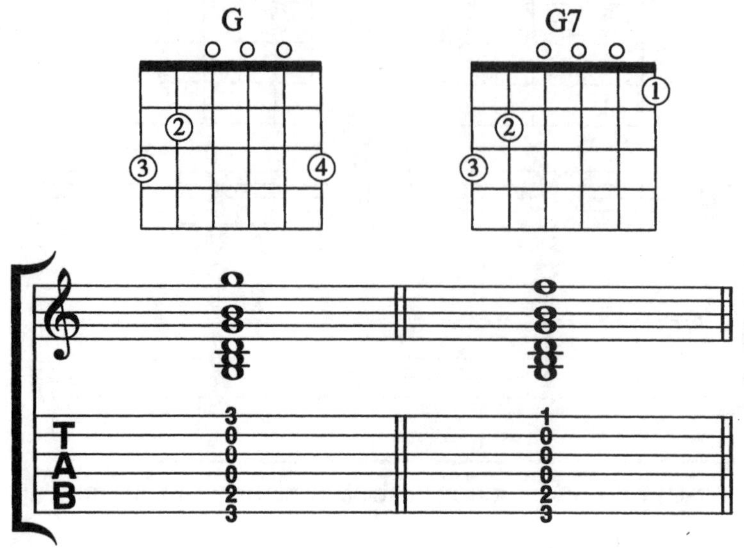

Example 30

Play back and forth between the G and G7 chords:

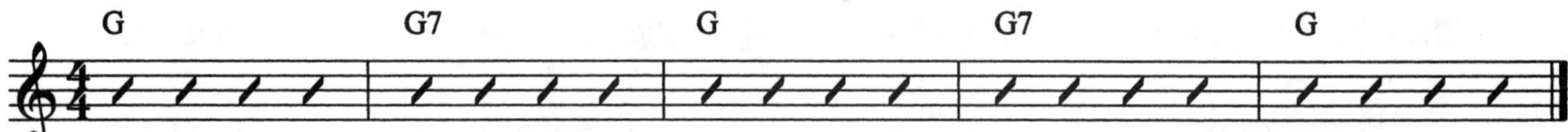

Now try converting the C to a C7. This is done by adding the 4th finger to the 3rd string.

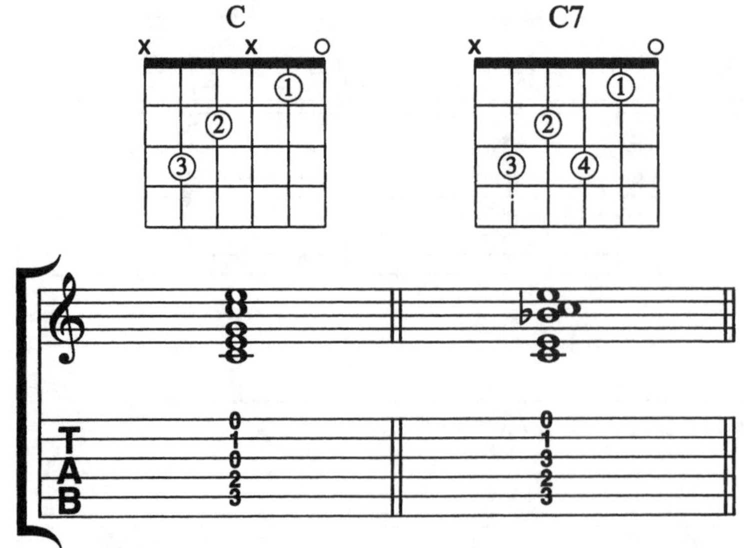

Example 31

Play back and forth between the C and C7 chords:

Fingerpicking

So far, all the music in this book has been playable with either a pick or your thumb. Fingerpicking involves using the thumb and fingers independently of one another. This gives you the ability to play separate bass lines and melodies, all at the same time.

Example 32

Hold an E chord. With your thumb play an alternating bass from the 6th string E to the 4th string E. Gently rest your index finger on the high E string while playing the steady quarter-note alternating bass with your thumb.

Example 33

Continue to hold the E chord while playing the alternating bass with your thumb. Play the high E string with an upstroke of your index finger. The up-stroke of your index finer should happen at the same time as the down-stroke of your thumb. Notice that the bass notes (thumb) are written stems down and the melody notes (index finger) are written stems up.

Example 34

Now trying plucking the high E string with your index finger in-between the thumb strokes. This is a little tricky at first. Keep playing this example until it feels easy and natural.

Example 35

The real beauty of this technique becomes apparent when you begin developing patterns that mix plucking on the beat (with the bass note) and plucking off the beat (in-between the bass notes). Practice this example until the alternating thumb becomes automatic—as if it is functioning independently of your fingers.

Example 36

Now try applying the same pattern to an A chord. Begin with just the alternating thumb, then add the index finger on the beat, then with the index finger in-between the beats and then the complete pattern as in the previous example.

Example 37

Now apply the fingerpicking pattern to a G chord. As you begin to feel comfortable with these fingerpicking patterns, it would be a good idea to begin substituting your right-hand middle finger and then your ring finger for your index finger on the top string. Eventually you will want to use all three fingers in varying combinations.

Example 38

In Example 19 we began using an alternate bass note for the D chord: the 5th string A below the 4th string D. In this fingerpicking example your thumb will alternate between the 4th string D and both the 3rd and 5th string A notes. Practice just the thumb movement until it feels natural (Example 38A). Then add your index finger (Example 38B).

Example 39

For the C chord your thumb will alternate between the 5th string C, the 4th string E and the 6th string G. As in Example 21B you will have to shift your 3rd finger back and forth from C to G. Practice just the thumb movement until it feels natural (Example 39A). Then add your index finger (Example 39B).

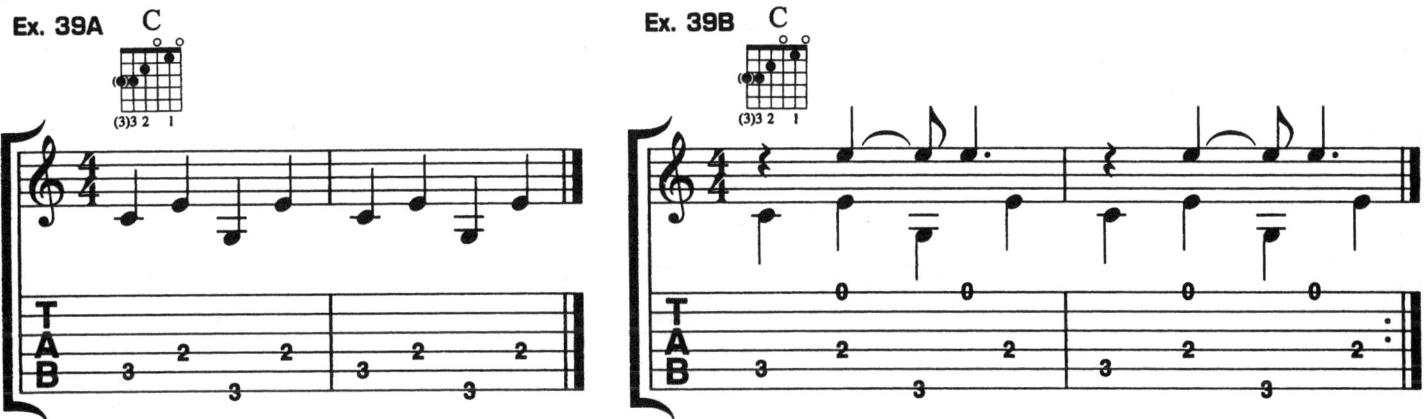

Example 40

Now apply the previous pattern to the B7 chord. You will have to shift your 2nd finger back and forth from the 5th to the 6th strings (see Example 22B). Again, practice just the thumb movement until it feels natural (Example 40A). Then add your index finger (Example 40B).

Example 41

This example combines the fingerpicking patterns with a complete chord progression.

Once the alternating thumb begins to feel "automatic" you'll be able to begin developing many variations on this pattern. Experiment with adding your middle and ring fingers in developing new patterns.

Hammer-Ons and Pull-Offs with Chords

One way to add new sounds and make your chords more interesting is to add and subtract certain notes from the chords as you play. We will use two different slurring techniques to add and subtract these notes:

1) A **hammer-on** is when you push (or "hammer") a left-hand finger onto a string with enough force to sound the note without using your picking hand.

2) A **pull-off** is when you release a left-hand finger from the string with a slight downward motion—actually plucking the string with the tip of your left-hand finger; again, sounding the note without using your picking hand.

Example 42

We can add a note to the E chord by "hammering" the 4th finger down on the 3rd string. This changes the chord from an E major to an E suspended.

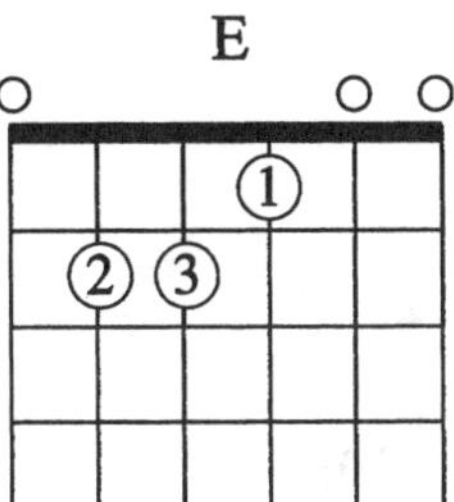

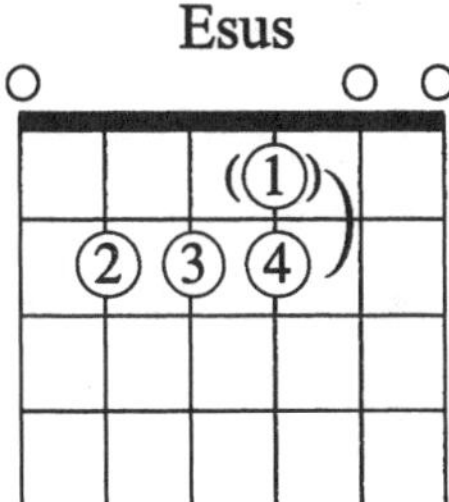

Play along with the recording. Then try making up some of your own patterns, switching between the E and Esus chords.

Example 43

We can add other notes to the E chord. These diagrams indicate an added note on the 2nd string. This changes the chord from an E major to an E6. The next two diagrams show an added note on the 1st string. This alters the chord from an E major to an Eadd9. The notes are "added" using the hammer-on technique, and released using the pull-off technique.

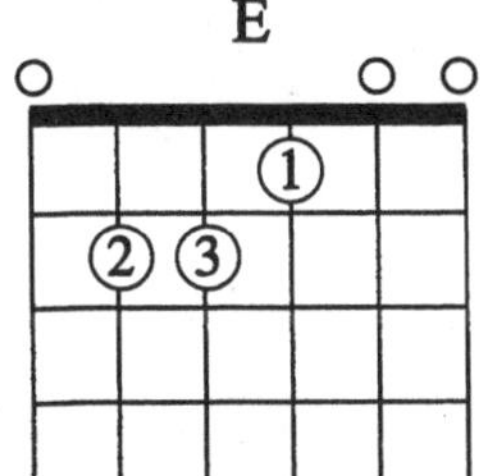

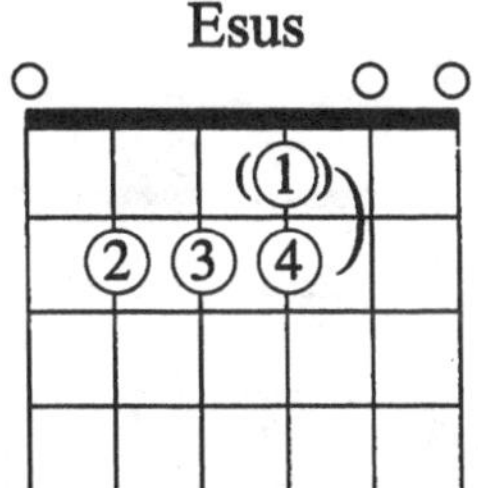

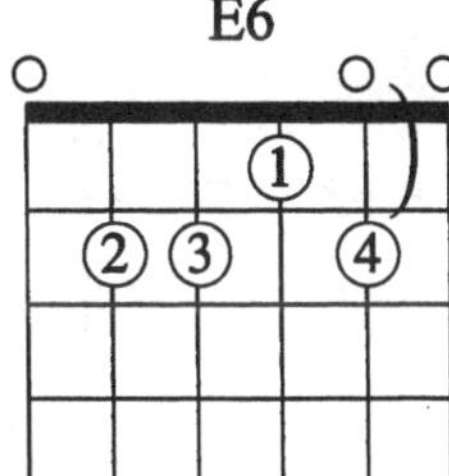

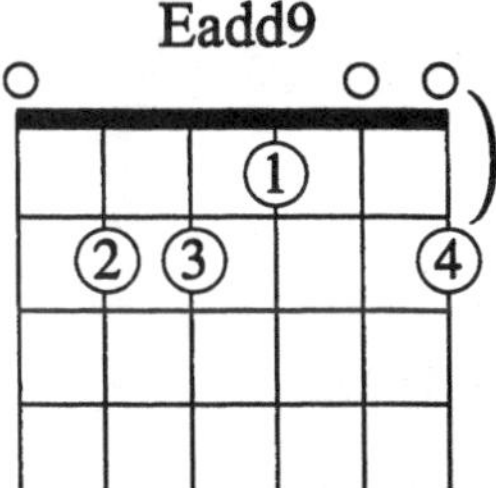

Again, play along with the recording. Then try making up some of your own patterns switching between the E/E6 and E/Eadd9 chords.

Example 44

By moving your 4th finger up one fret you can add a "D" note to the A chord forming a Dsus. By lifting your 4th finger off the 2nd string you form an Asus2 chord.

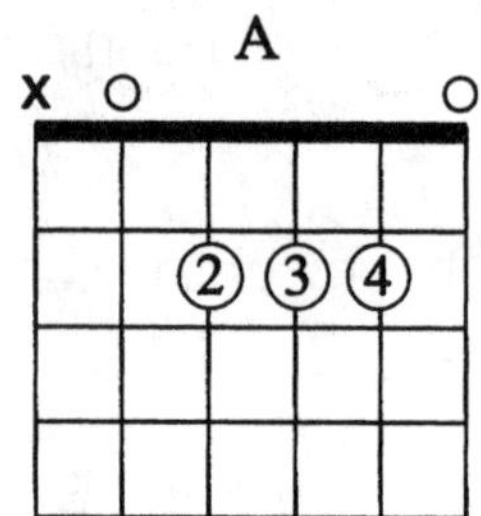

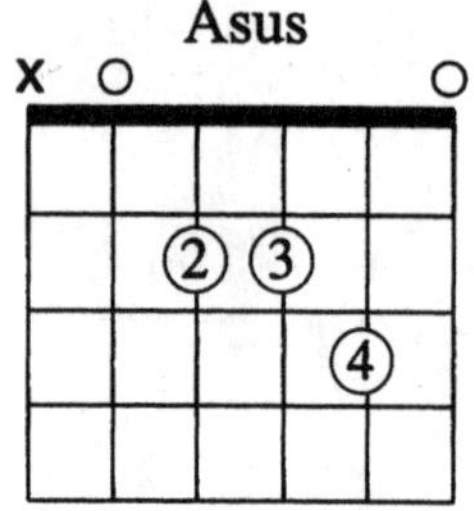

Again, play along with the recording. Then try making up some of your own patterns, switching between the A, Asus and Asus2 chords.

Example 45

By "hammering" your 4th finger on the 1st string G you can change the D chord to Dsus and by "pulling-off" your 2nd finger you can form Dsus2.

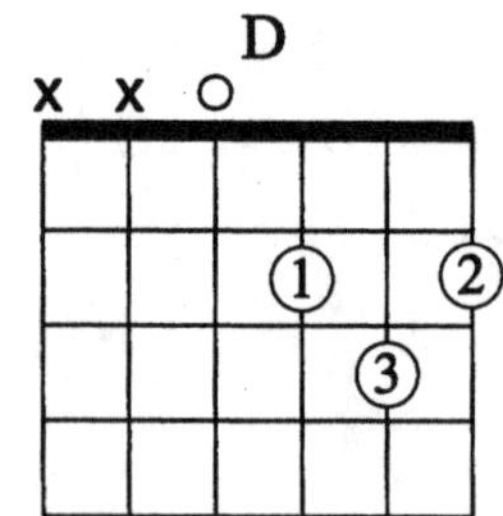

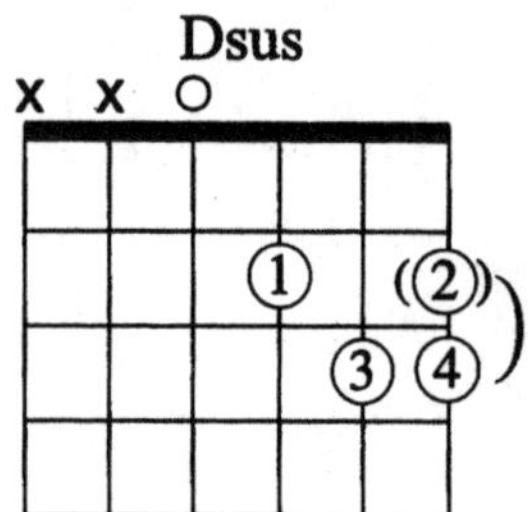

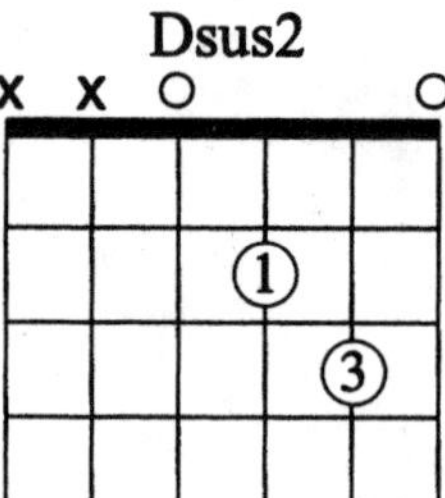

Again, play along with the recording. Then try making up some of your own patterns switching between the D, Dsus and Dsus2.

Example 46

If you finger the G chord with your 2nd, 3rd and 4th fingers your 1st finger will then be available for use on the 2nd string to form the Gsus chord.

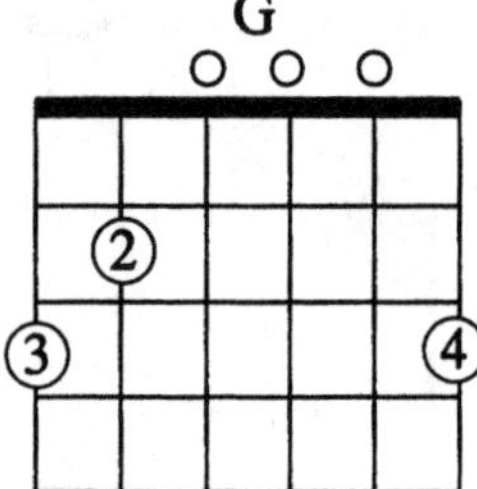

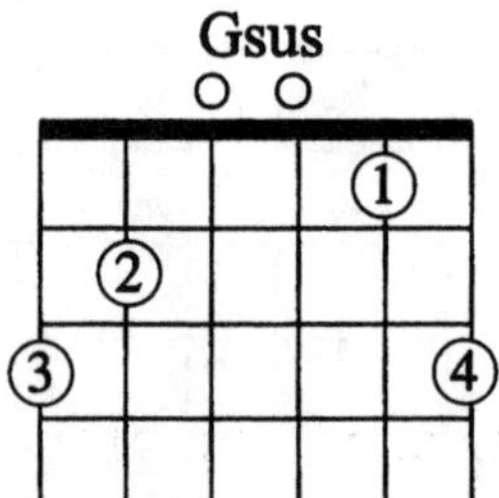

Example 47

For the C chord, the 4th finger can be hammered on to the 4th string to form a Csus chord. The 3rd finger can be pulled-off the 4th string to form a Csus2.

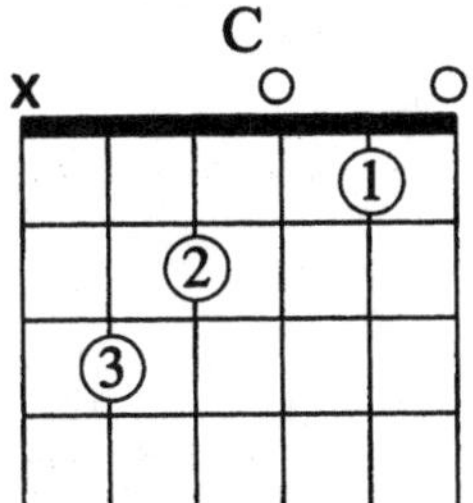

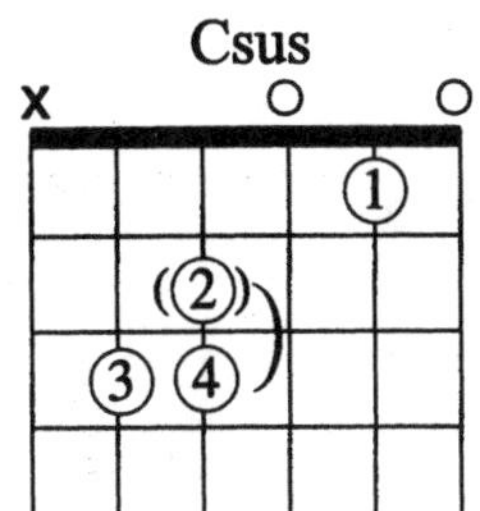

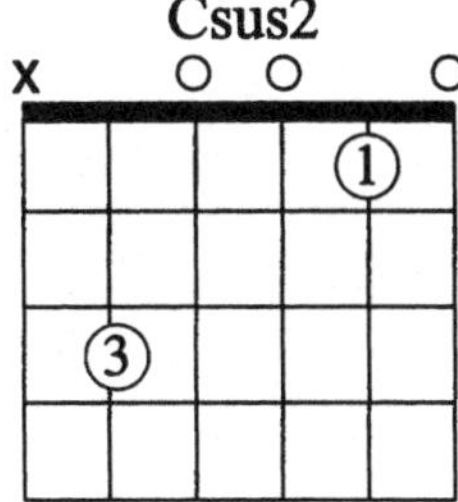

Example 48

Minor chords can be embellished in the same way as major chords—by adding and subtracting notes, usually using the hammer-on and pull-off slurring techniques.

For A minor, adding the 4th finger on the 2nd string changes A minor to Asus. Pulling-off the 1st finger forms an Asus2.

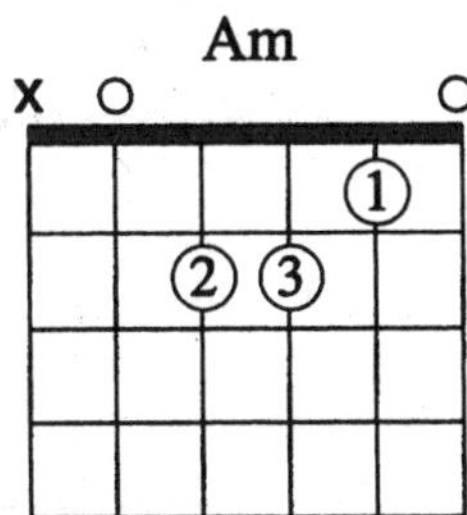

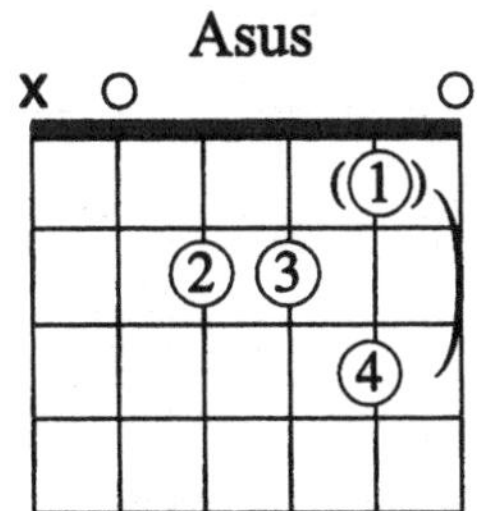

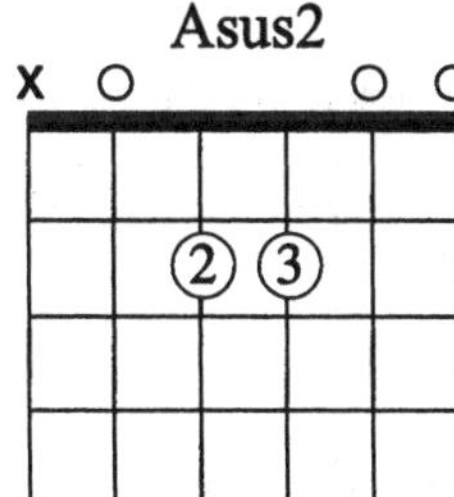

For D minor, adding the 4th finger on the 1st string changes D minor to Dsus. Pulling-off the 1st finger forms a Dsus2.

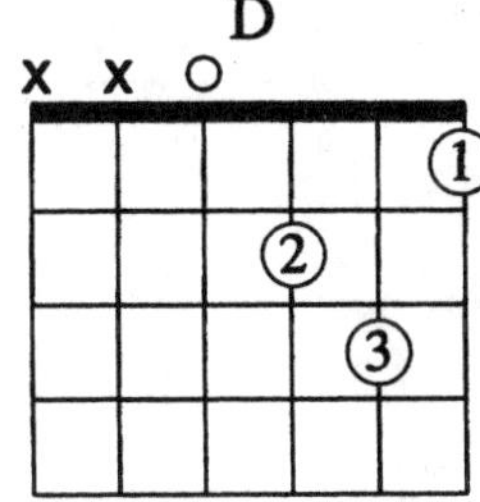

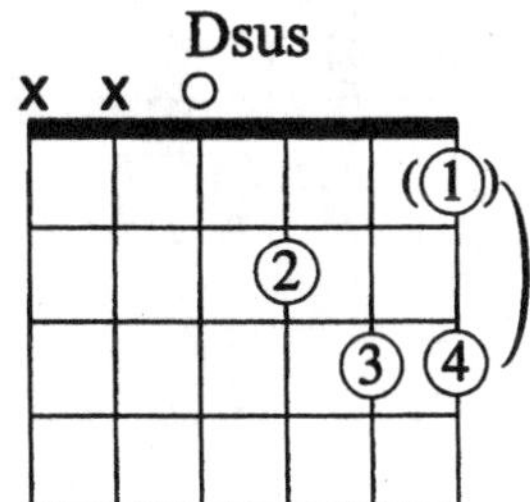

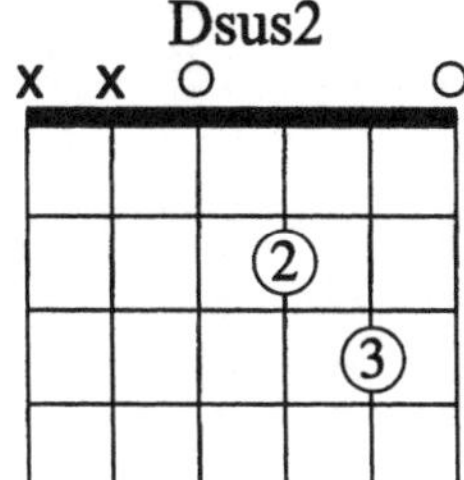

Again, play along with the recording. Then try making up some of your own patterns, switching between the various chords and their "colorations."

The Capo

So far, all of the chords you've learned have been first position "open" string chord voicings. Using just these chords you are well on your way towards playing many popular songs in the keys of C, G, D, A and E.

Example 49

With a capo you can transpose these chord fingerings to work in almost any key. For example, if you place the capo at the 3rd fret, all of the open string notes will be transposed up three frets. So if you then finger an E chord it will sound as a G chord, an A chord will sound as a C chord, etc.

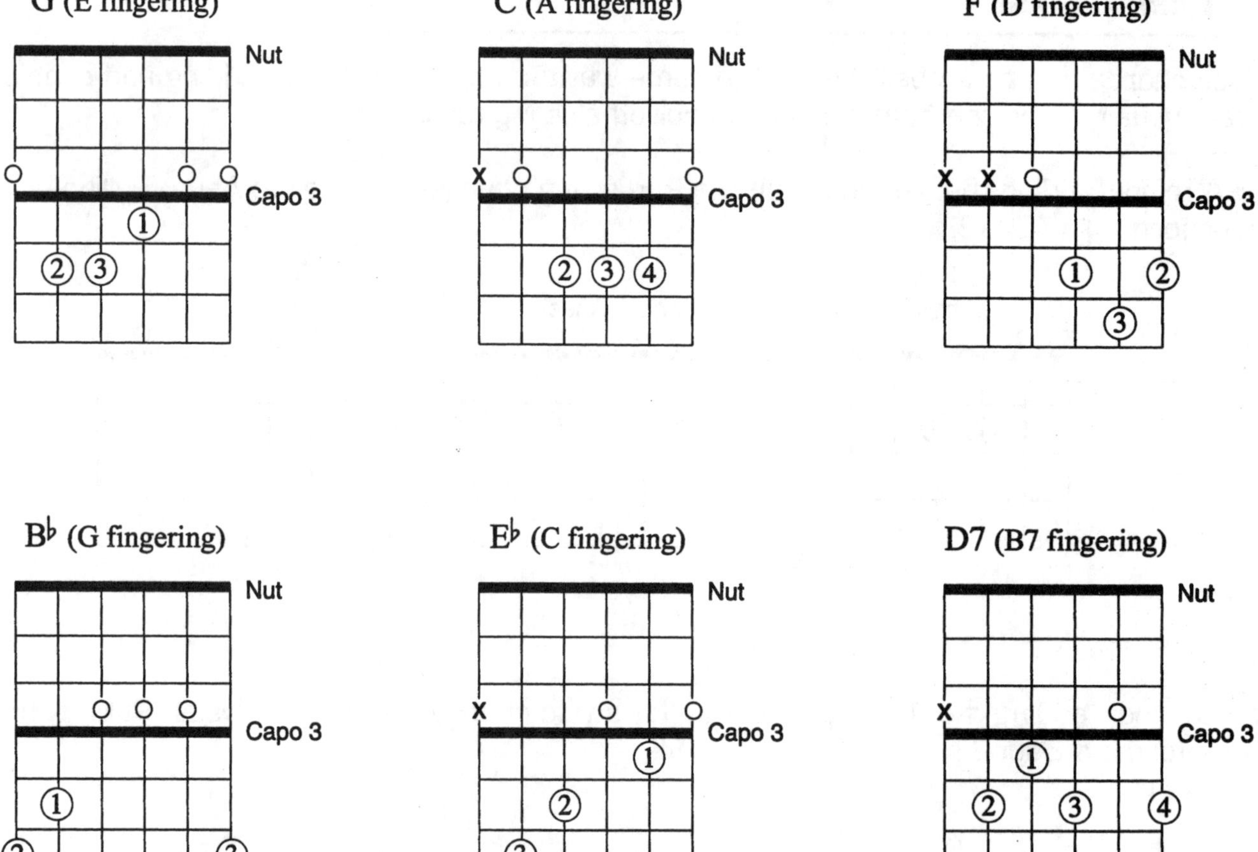

The capo is especially handy when you want to accompany a singer (or yourself). When the key of a song is too low, you can always bring it up higher by using the capo.

It is usually best to think of the song in the "fingering" key, locating the capo at whichever fret places the chords at a good pitch for the singer.

Barre Chords

There are two types of barre chords: those with their root on the 6th string and those with their root on the 5th string. Before we learn the barre chords lets first learn the notes on those two strings.

Example 50

This diagram shows the location of the natural (no sharps or flats) notes on the 6th string. It is useful to remember that there is a whole step (two frets) between all adjacent natural notes except for "E - F" and "B - C" which are separated by a half-step (one fret).

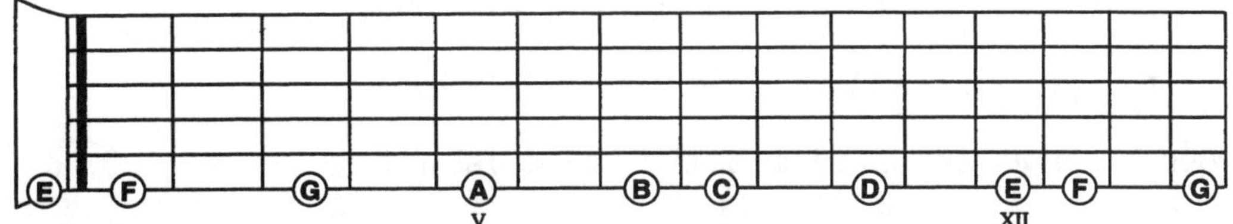

Here are the notes and tablature for the notes on the "E" string. Play these notes until they are memorized.

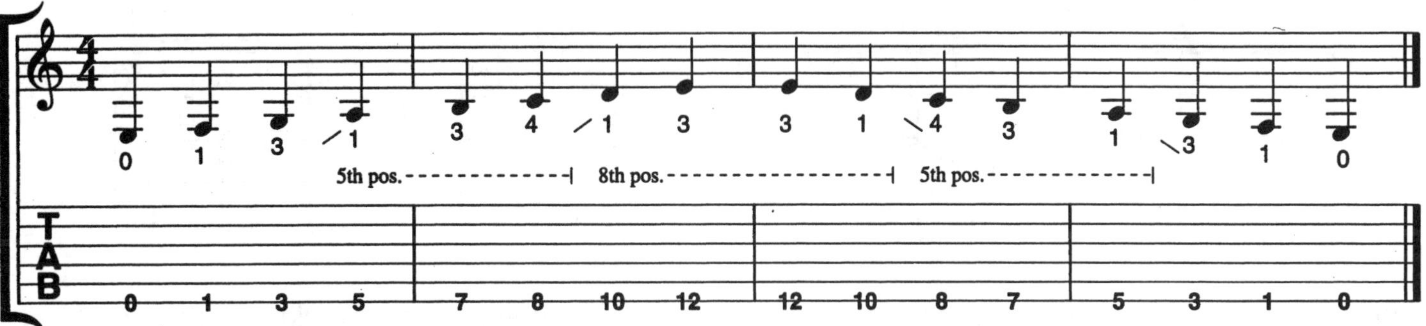

Example 51

This diagram shows the location of the natural (no sharps or flats) notes on the 5th string. Again, remember that there is a whole-step (two frets) between all adjacent natural notes except for "E - F" and "B - C" which are separated by a half-step (one fret).

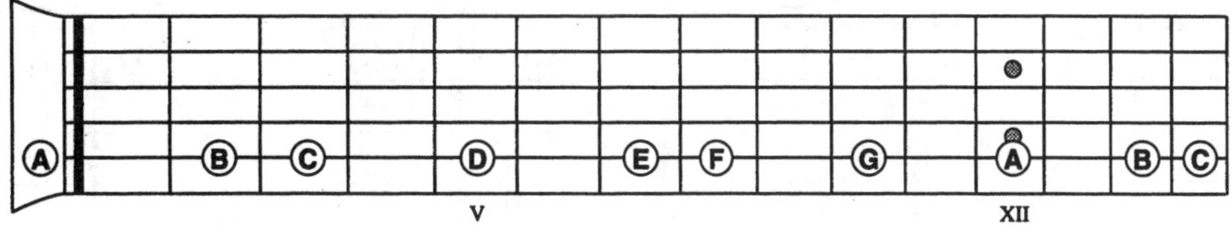

Here are the notes and tablature for the notes on the "A" string. Play these notes until they are memorized.

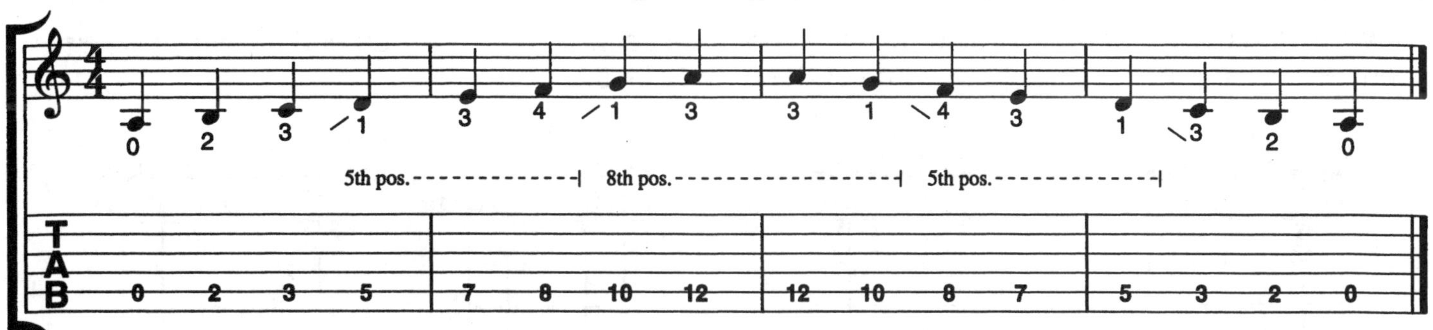

The "E" Type Barre Chord

So far we've only worked on open position chords. With barre chords you can leave the open position and play all around the neck.

Barre Chords: A barre chord is a chord in which two or more of the strings are played by one finger laying across those strings forming a "barre."

Example 52

The most popular type of barre chord is based on the common E chord. To form the barre chord:

1) Re-finger the E chord with your 2nd, 3rd and 4th fingers.

2) Shift your fingers up one fret.

3) Lay your 1st finger across all six strings at the 1st fret.

Practice each of the following chords, then try moving the barre chord to each fret on the neck and saying the name of the chord aloud.

E

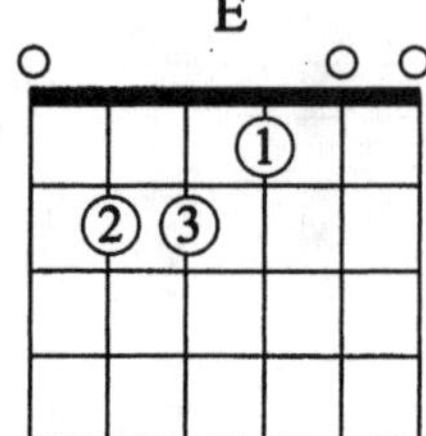

F

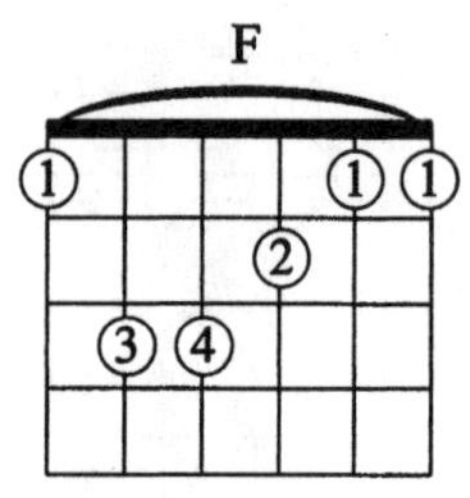

G

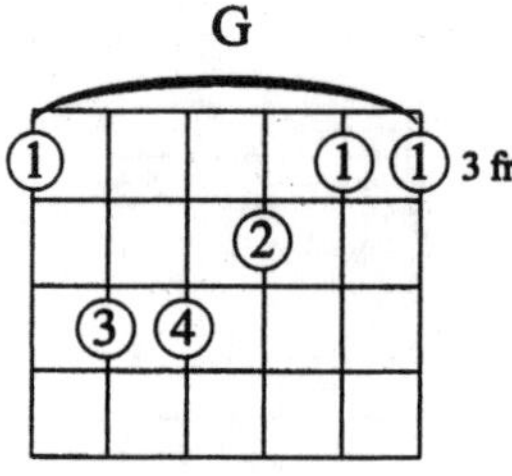

A

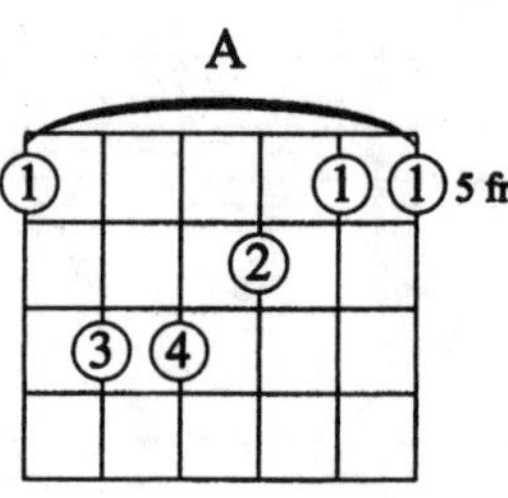

Tip: To add strength to your index finger barre, turn that finger slightly to the side so that the hard outside edge of the finger forms the barre; not the soft, fleshy part on the inside.

Example 53

Now convert the E minor to a barre chord. Again, practice each of these chords and then try playing them all over the neck, saying the name of the chord aloud.

Em

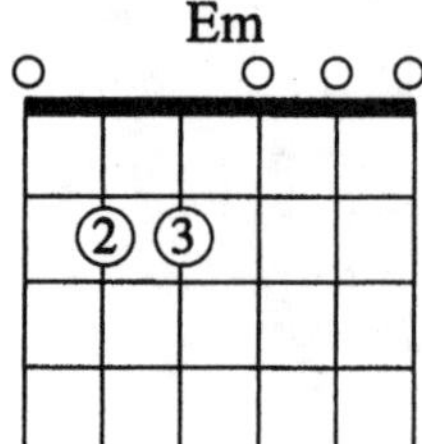

Fm

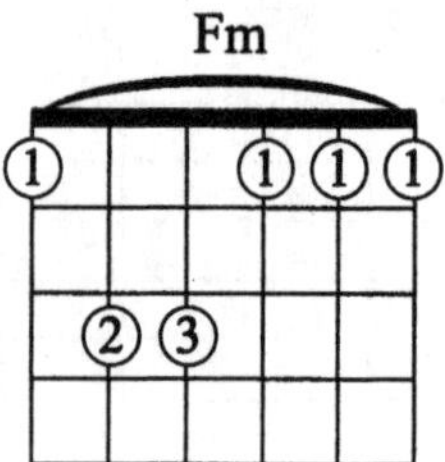

Gm

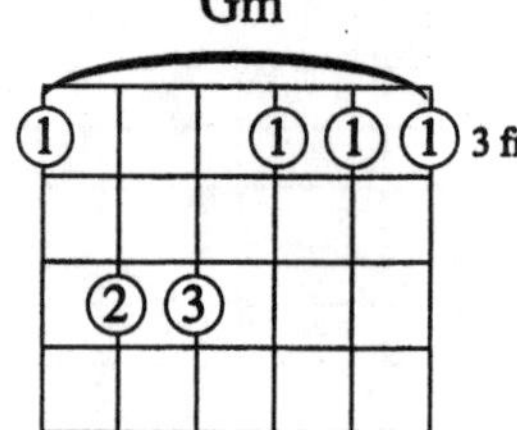

Am

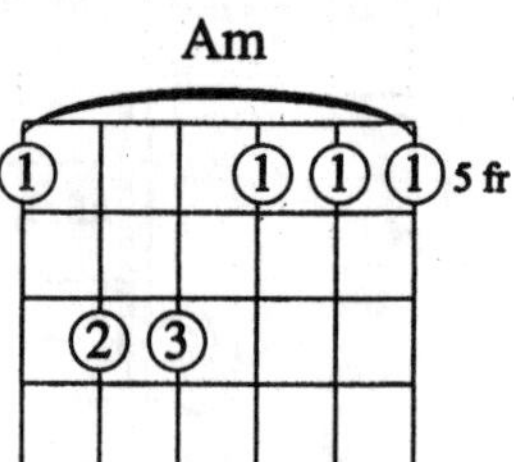

Example 54

Now convert the E7 to a barre chord. Again, practice each of these chords and then try playing them all over the neck, saying the name of the chord aloud.

E7

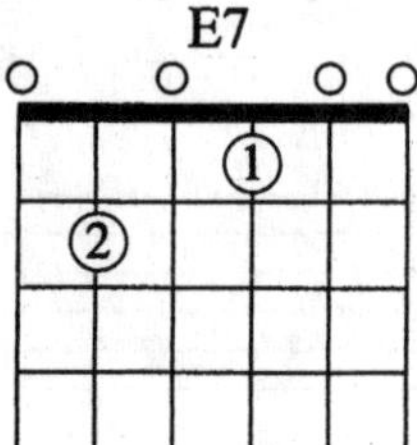

F7

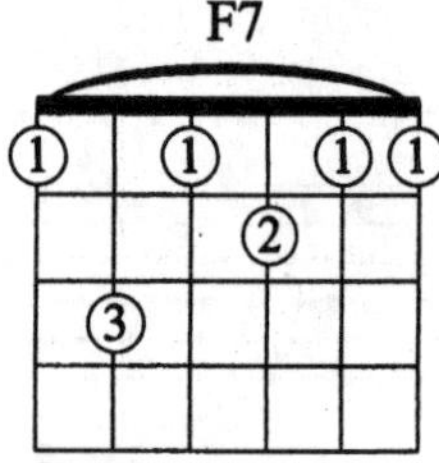

G7

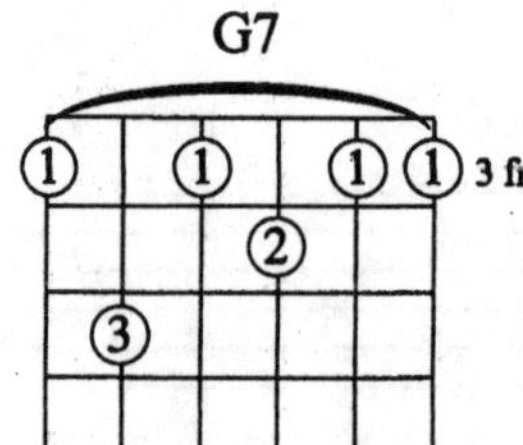

A7

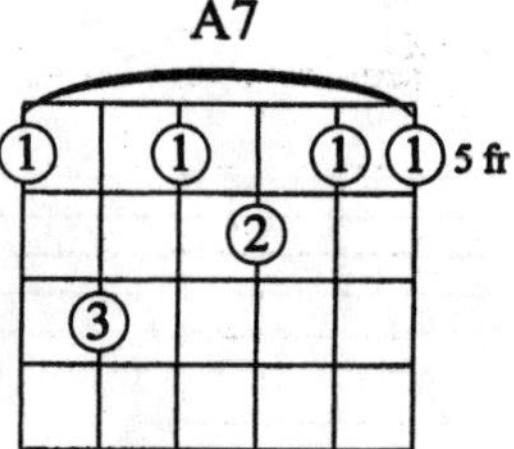

The "A" Type Barre Chord

The next most popular type of barre chord is based on the common A chord. To form the "A" type barre chord:

1) Shift your 2nd, 3rd and 4th fingers up one fret.

2) Lay your 1st finger across the top five strings at the 1st fret.

Example 55

Practice each of the following chords, then try moving the barre chord to each fret and saying the name of the chord aloud. Notice the optional fingering which requires a 3rd finger barre across the middle strings. When using this optional fingering you'll probably mute the 1st string with your 3rd finger. Practice both fingerings and see which works best for you.

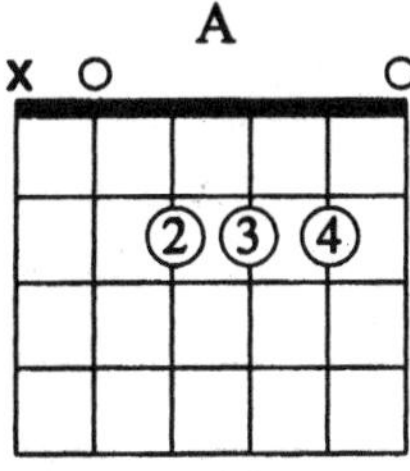

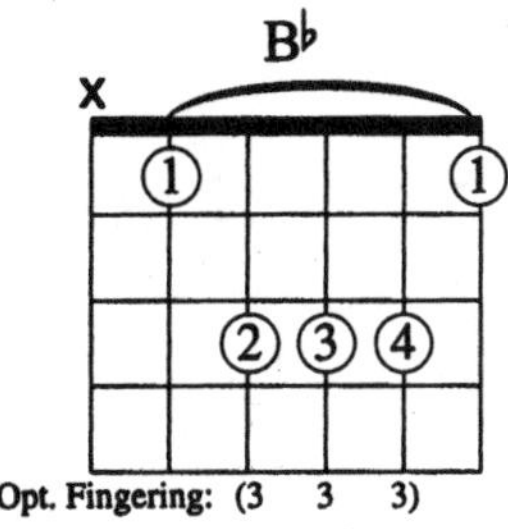

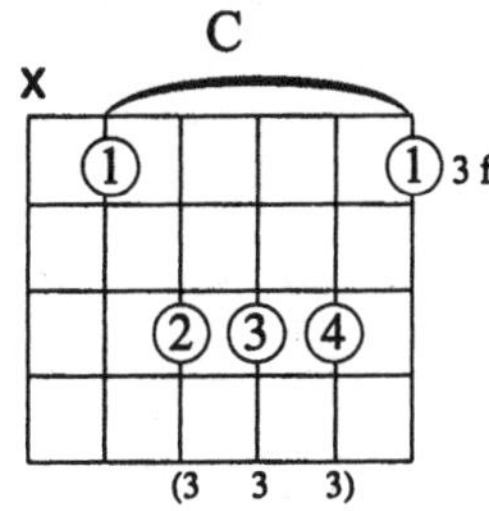

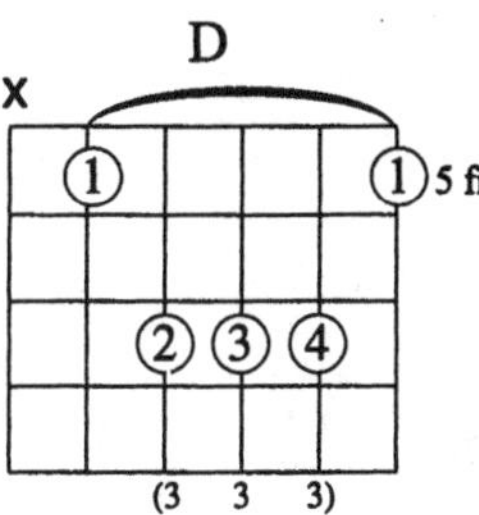

Example 56

Now convert the A minor to a barre chord. Again, practice each of these chords and then try playing them all over the neck, saying the name of the chord aloud.

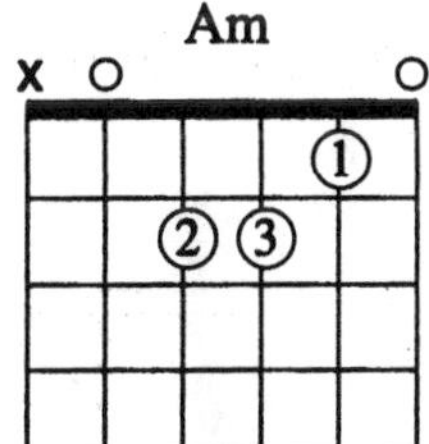

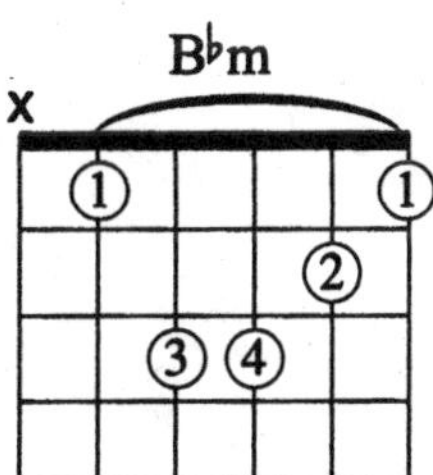

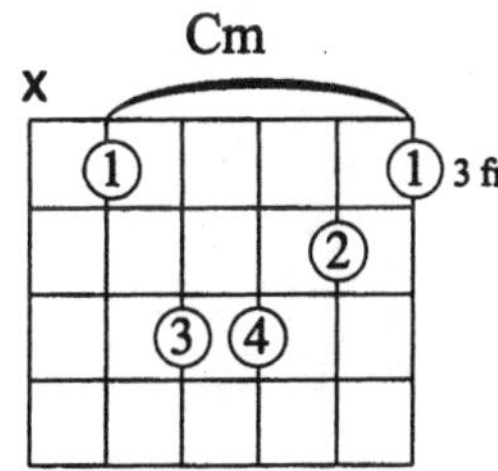

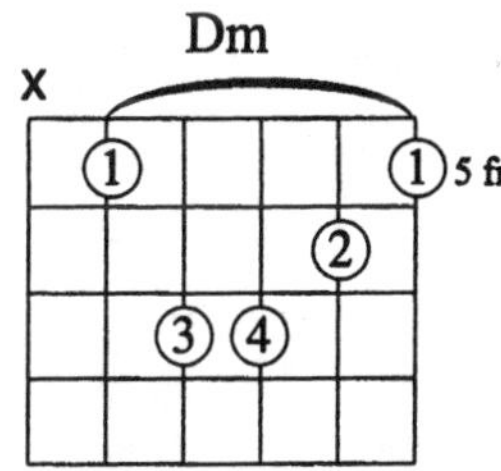

Example 57

Now convert the A7 to a barre chord. Again, practice each of these chords and then try playing them all over the neck, saying the name of the chord aloud.

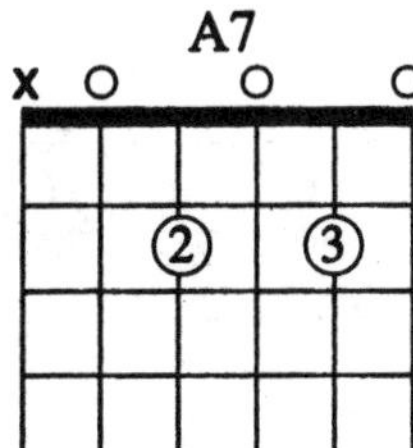

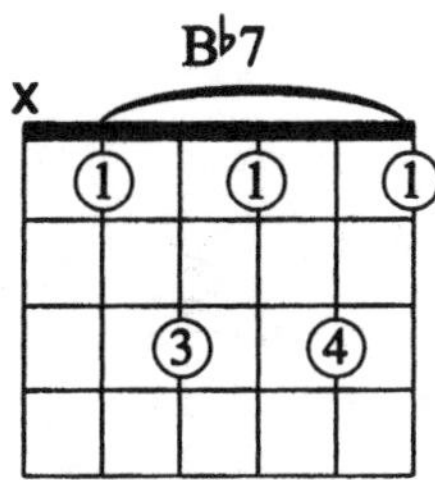

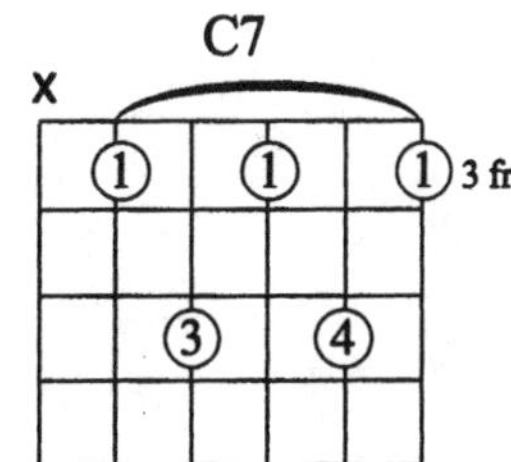

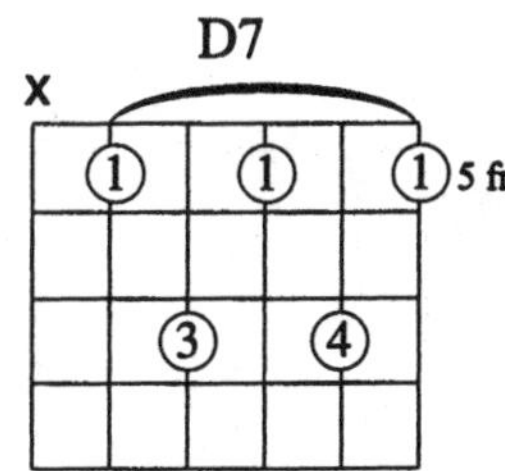

BLUES GUITAR

REVIEW: OPEN POSITION CHORDS

Acoustic guitar players, in any style, spend most of their time in open position (close to the nut) to make use of the open strings. The open strings resonate more than fretted notes and bring out the richness of the instrument.

Example 58: The E Chord

The first chord is an E major chord and is a triad because there are only three *different* notes in the chord:

E:	**E**	**G♯**	**B**
Major Triad:	1	3	5

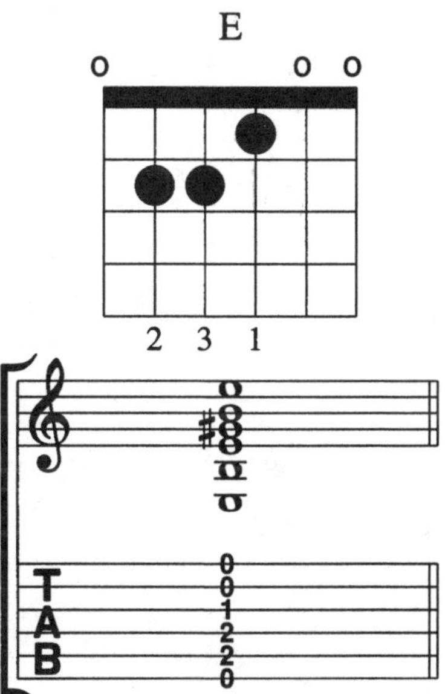

Make sure that all strings are ringing clearly by placing the fingertips right against the fret. Be careful not to touch the open strings. Do not push so hard that you are cramping your hand. The more developed your calluses are, the less you will need to push to get the right sound.

Example 59: The E7 Chord

In blues, a fourth note is added to the basic triad to create a **dominant 7** chord (indicated as E7). The fourth note is D, which is the ♭7 interval of E.

E7: E G♯ B D
Dominant 7: 1 3 5 ♭7

The following fingerings are the most common E7 fingerings that apply to the blues:

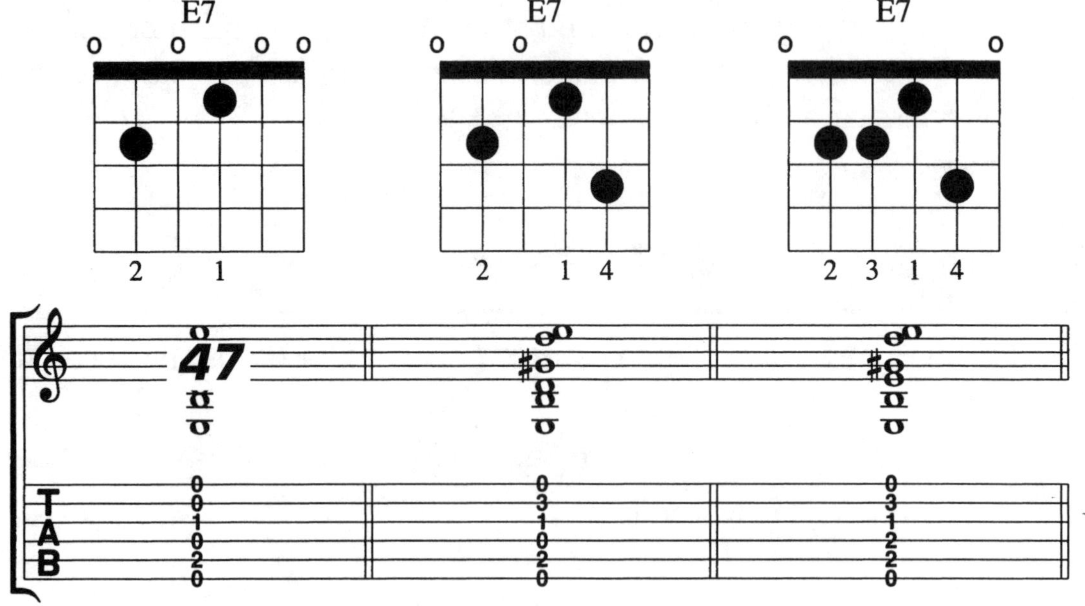

Example 60: The A Chord

The following are different fingerings for the A chord. Even though the notes are the same, the choice of fingerings is different.

A: A C♯ E
Major Triad: 1 3 5

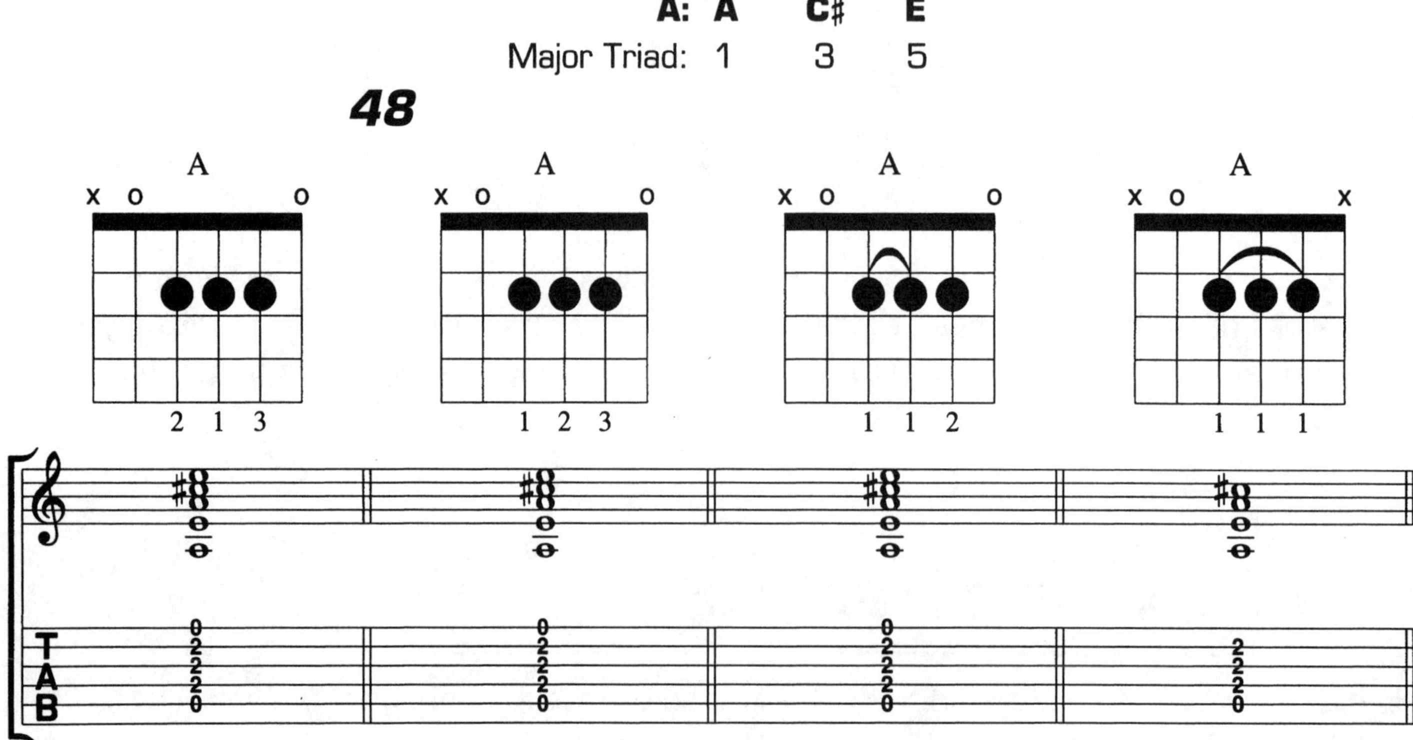

Example 61: The A7 Chord

To turn the A chord into a dominant 7th chord, add the G (♭7). There are two places to add a G to the open A chord: either take a finger off the 3rd string to expose the open G, or add the G to the first string.

A7:	**A**	**C♯**	**E**	**G**
Dominant 7:	1	3	5	♭7

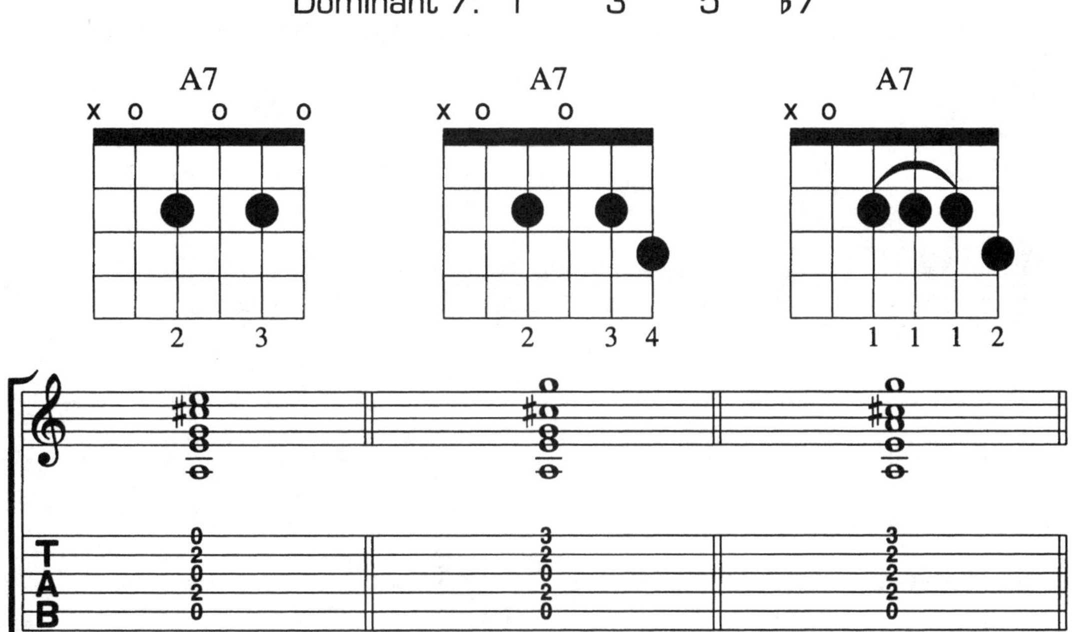

Example 62: The B7 Chord

There is one primary fingering used in acoustic blues:

B7:	**B**	**D♯**	**F♯**	**A**
Dominant 7:	1	3	5	♭7

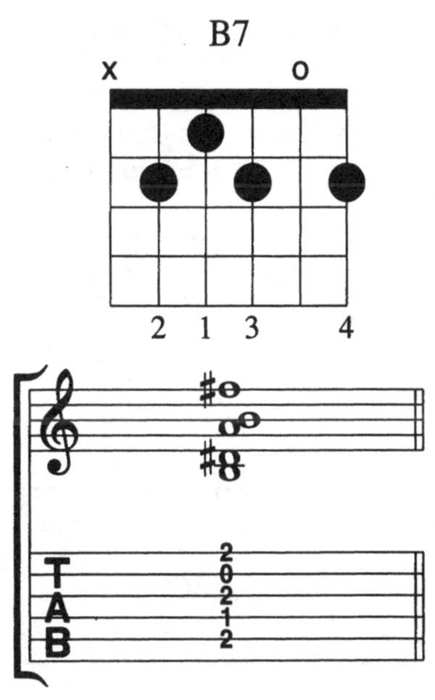

Example 63: Combine All Three Chords

Now that we have three chords, we can play a blues. Practice changing from one chord to the other to get used to making the transitions. Later, we will be learning some rhythm patterns that involve these chords.

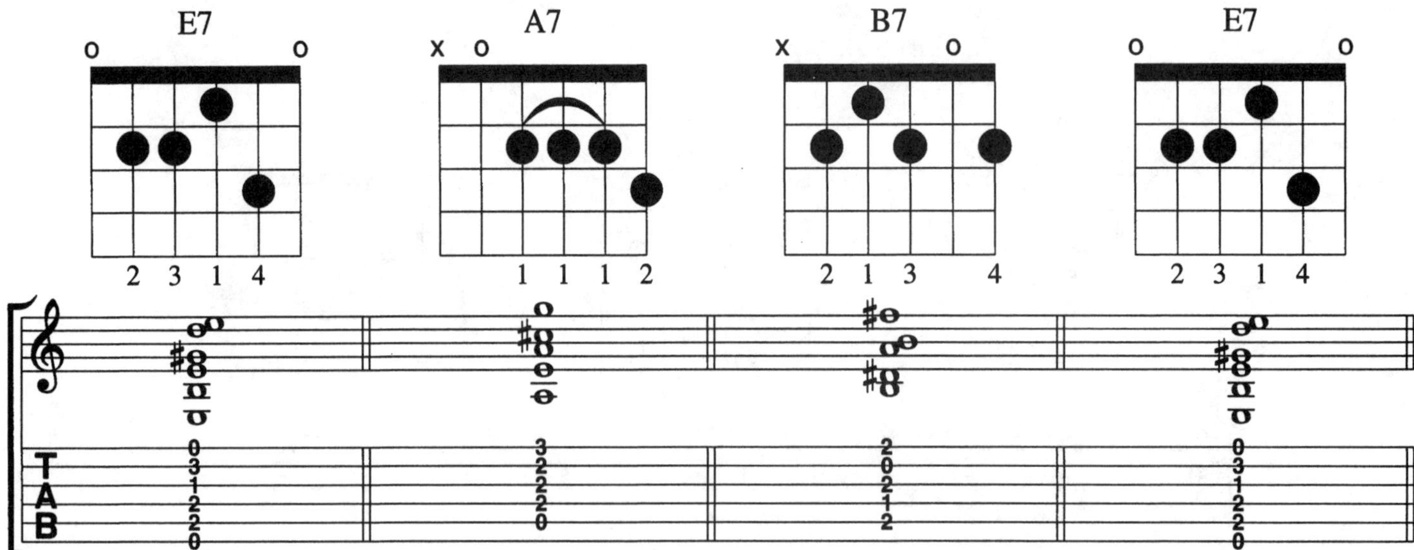

The **blues progression** is a specific pattern of chords that relate to a key. If you play a blues in the key of E, the I chord will be the E7. Two other chords, A7 and B7, are the IV and V chord of the key of E. The Roman numerals I, IV and V identify the relationship of the chords to the notes of the major scale:

E	F♯	G♯	A	B	C♯	D♯	E
I	II	III	IV	V	VI	VII	I

The I chord is built on the first note, or root, of the major scale. The A is the IV chord of E because it is built on the 4th note of the E major scale, and B7 is the V chord because it is built on the 5th note of E major.

There are several different blues progressions that are popular, but the one that's the most popular is the "12-bar" blues. The I, IV and V chords are always arranged in the same sequence within these twelve bars.

E BLUES

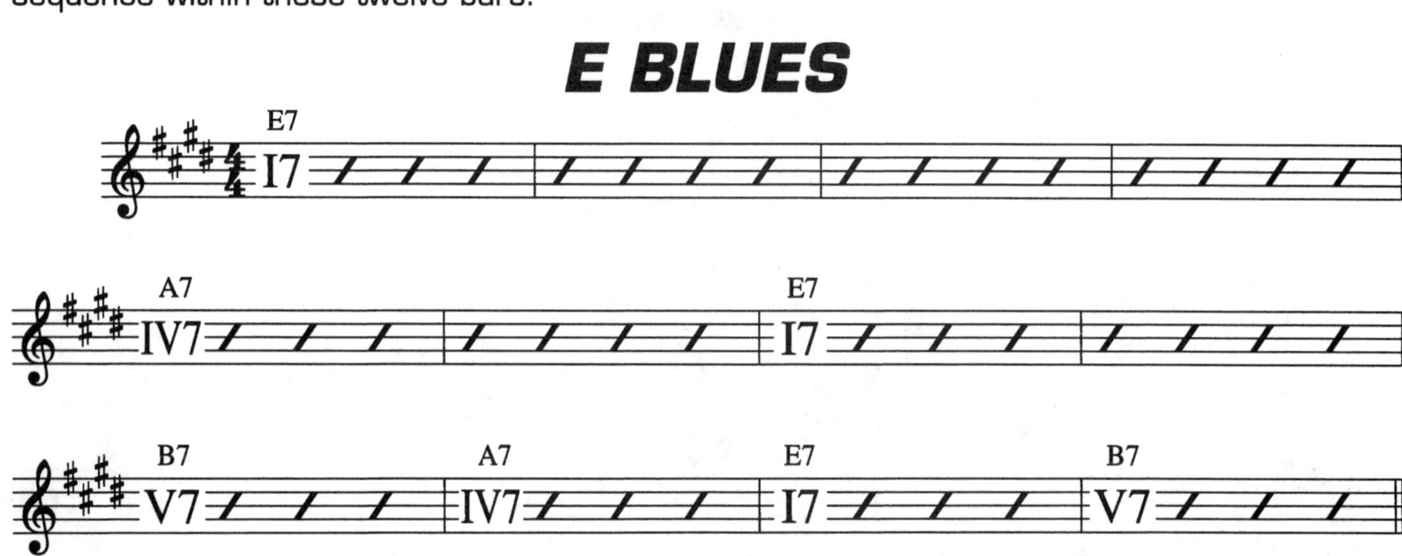

The Key of A

The other common keys that you hear on the acoustic guitar are the "open keys," so called because they use a lot of open strings. The second most common open key is the key of A. The I, IV and V chords in an A blues are A7, D7 and E7. You already know how to play both the A7 and the E7, so the only new chord is D7. You get a D7 by taking an open D triad and lowering the higher octave D to a C:

Example 64: D and D7 Chords

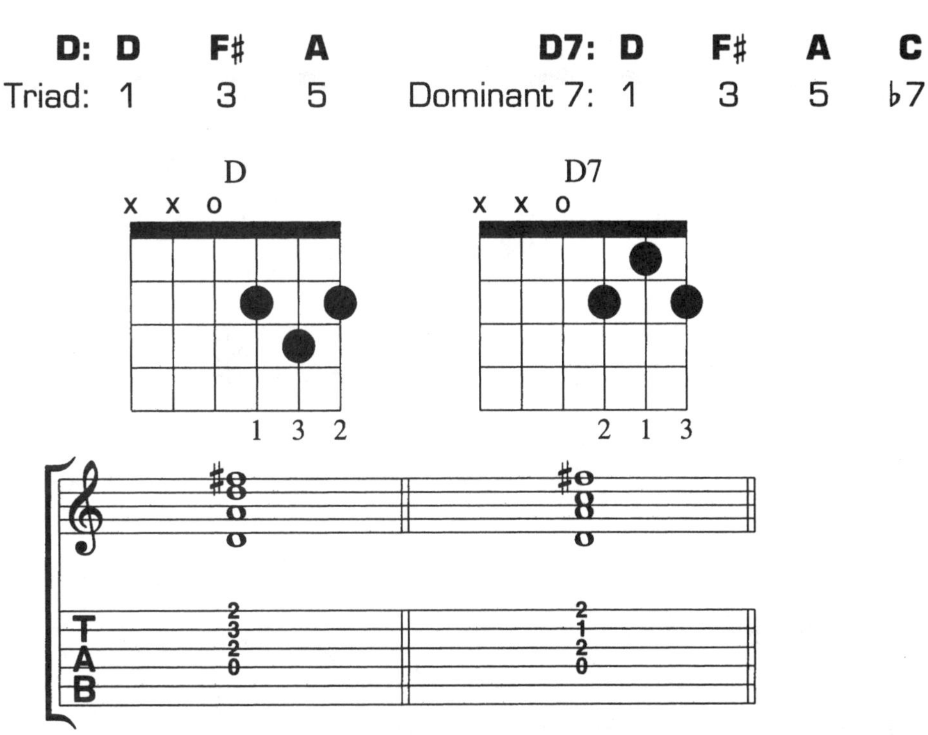

Memorize the blues in A using chord symbols and Roman numerals.

A BLUES

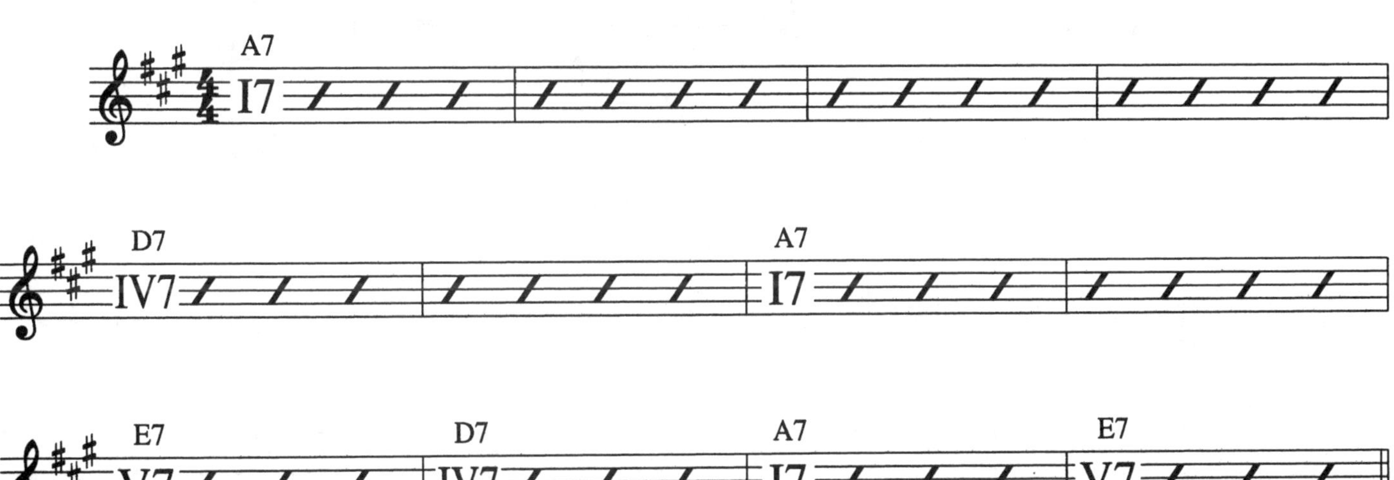

The Key of C

Another common open position key on the guitar is the key of C. The I, IV and V chords in a C blues are: C7, F7 and G7.

Example 65: C7

The C7 is a C triad with a B♭ added to the third string:

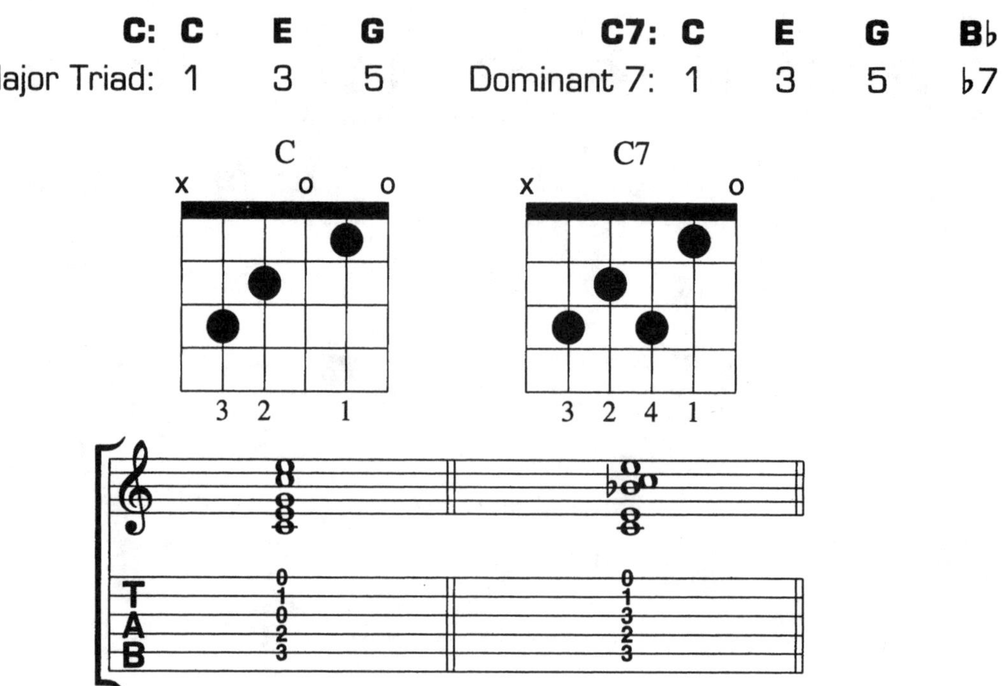

Example 66: F7

The F7 is an F triad with an E♭ added to the second string:

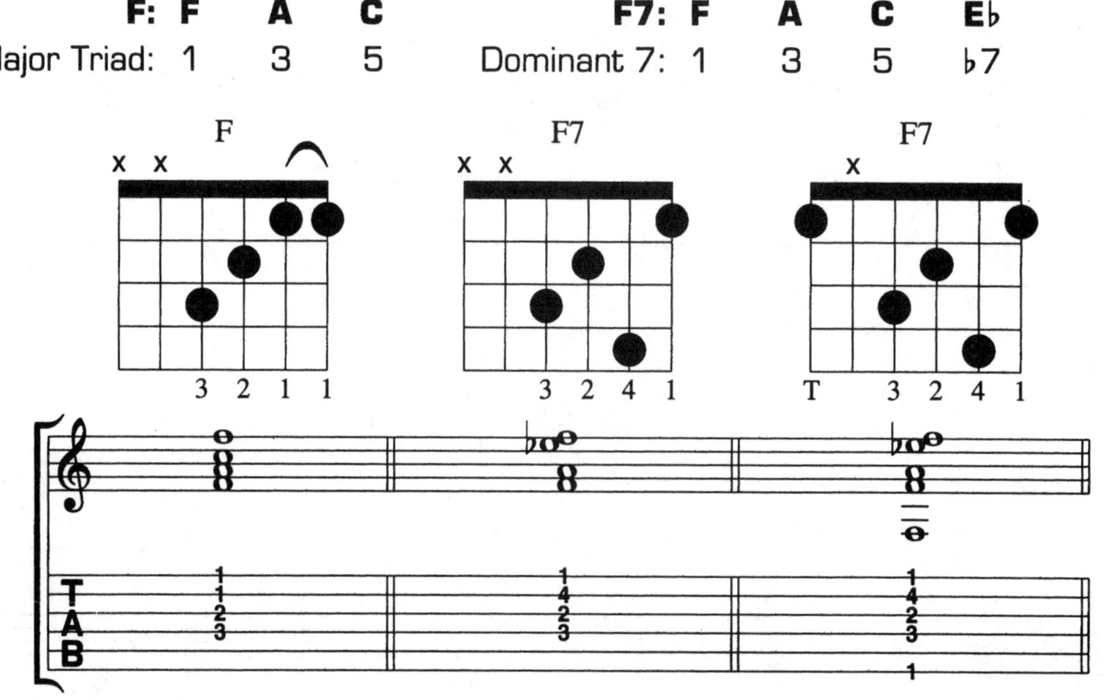

Example 67: G and G7 Chords

There are two common fingerings for G:

G:	**G**	**B**	**D**
Major Triad:	1	3	5

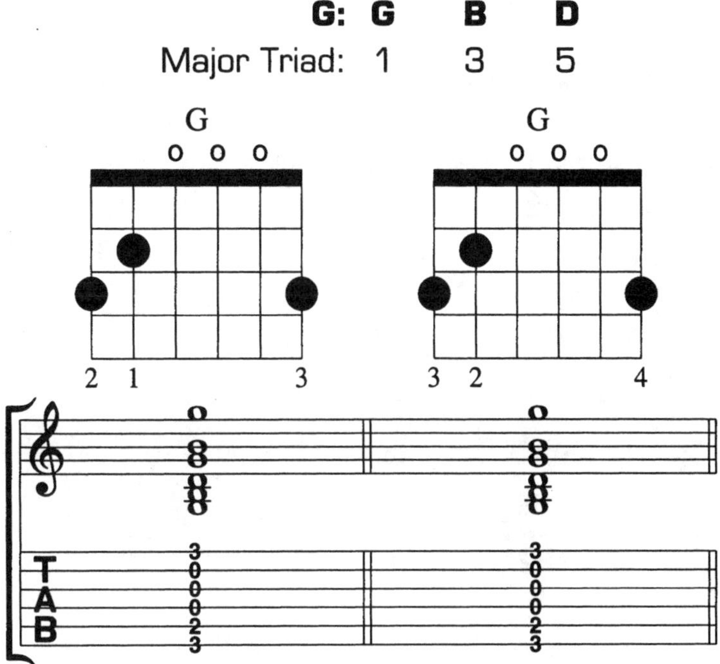

The second example makes it easier to turn the G into a G7. The G7 is a G triad with the first string root lowered to an F:

G7:	**G**	**B**	**D**	**F**
Dominant 7:	1	3	5	♭7

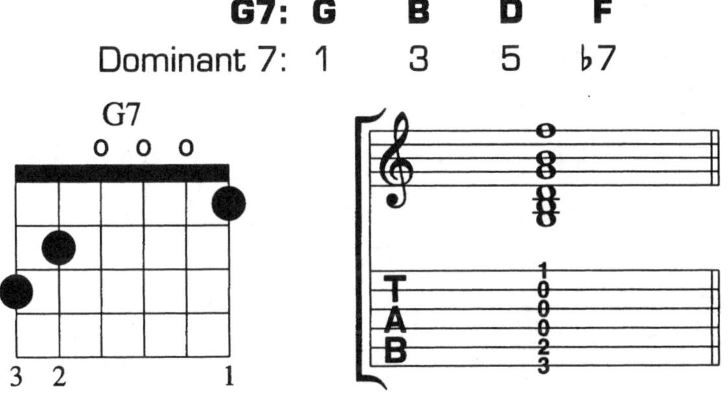

Memorize the following blues in C the same way you memorized the other keys. At this point you should be able to hear the similarity between the keys.

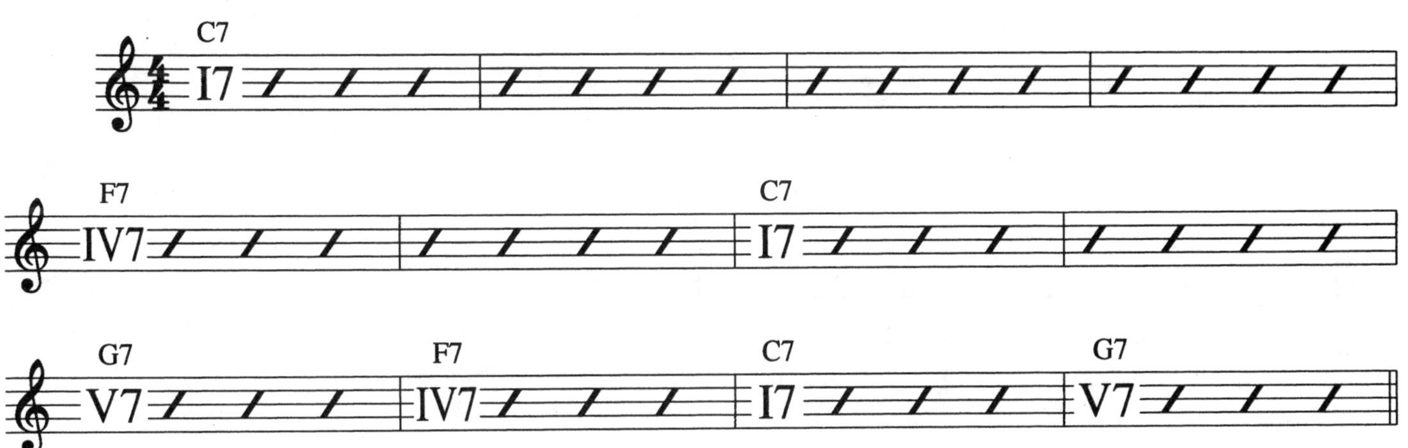

BLUES PROGRESSIONS

Example 68: Bass-Chord Pattern

This example is a 12-bar blues in E. The rhythm pattern is called bass-chord accompaniment because you alternate between bass notes and full chords. There are two benefits to this pattern: it brings out the full sound of the instrument and is easier to move from one chord shape to another. Since you only have to play one or two notes for the bass, you have more time to finger the rest of the chord shape resulting in a smooth sounding transition.

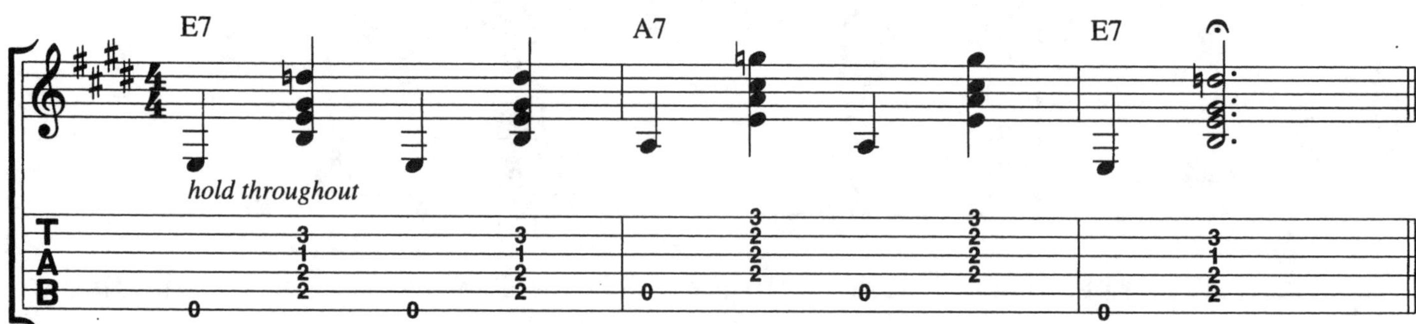

Example 69: Blues Progression in E

Play the following blues in E with the recording while employing the bass-chord pattern.

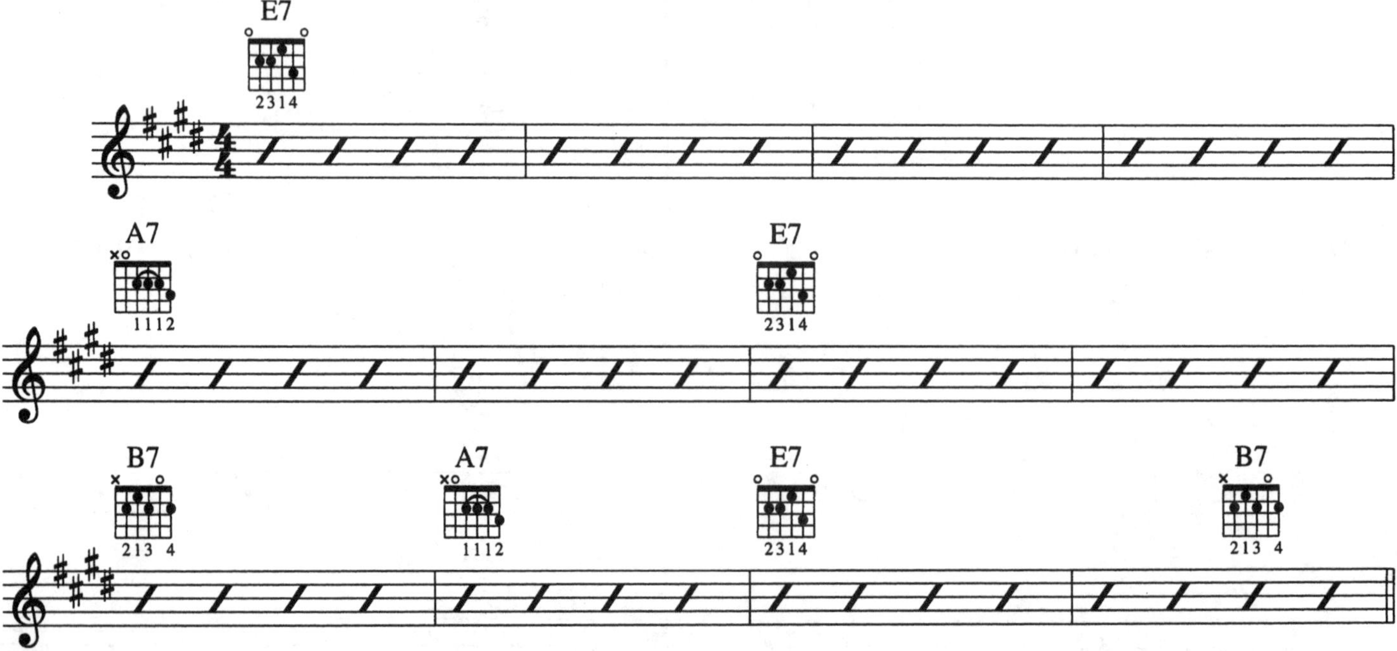

Notice the last chord, B7, is only played on the last two beats of the last measure while all of the other chords have at least one full bar each. This part of the progression is called the *turnaround* because, as the word implies, it turns the progression "around," back to the beginning.

Example 70: Blues in A

This is the same progression as the previous example but transposed to the key of A. Review the A7, D7 and E7 chords and apply the bass-chord pattern to the following progression. Notice that this example uses the I chord to end the progression. In the previous examples, the V chord was used to "turnaround" the progression back to the beginning.

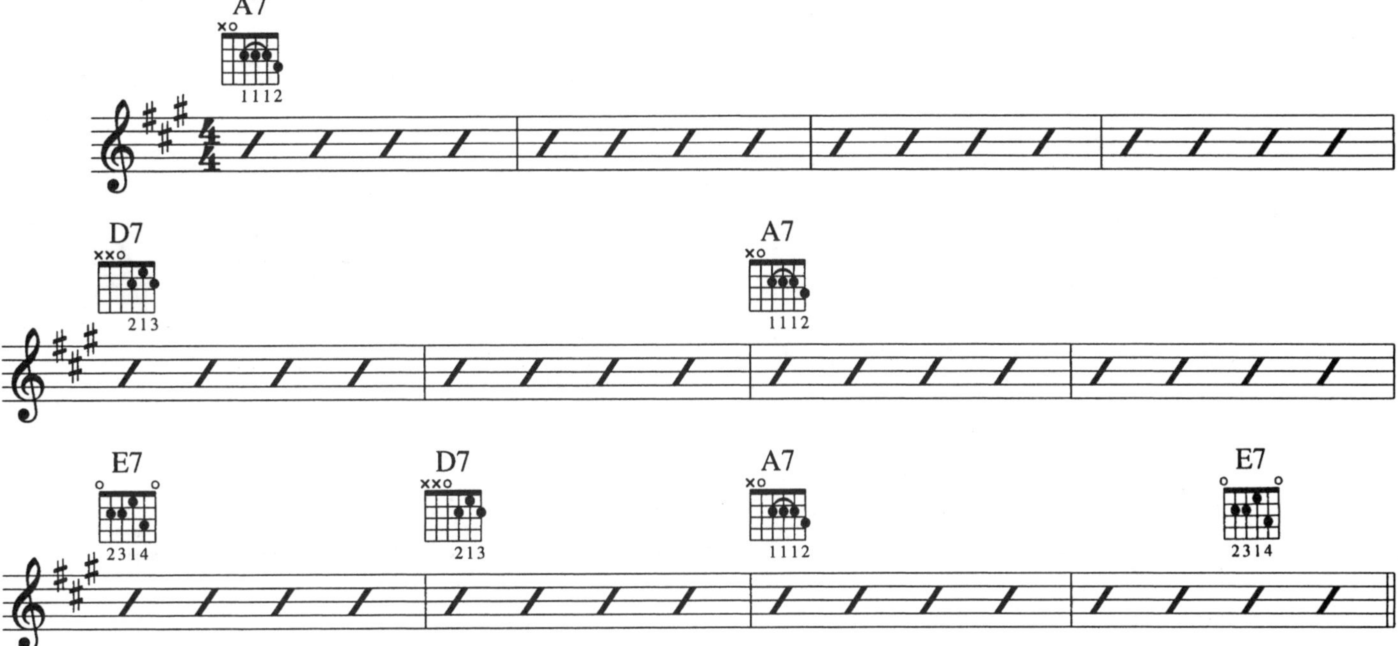

Example 71: Blues in C

To transpose the blues progression to the key of C, start by reviewing the C7, F7 and the G7 chords. Now play the following progression using the same bass-chord pattern as the previous examples.

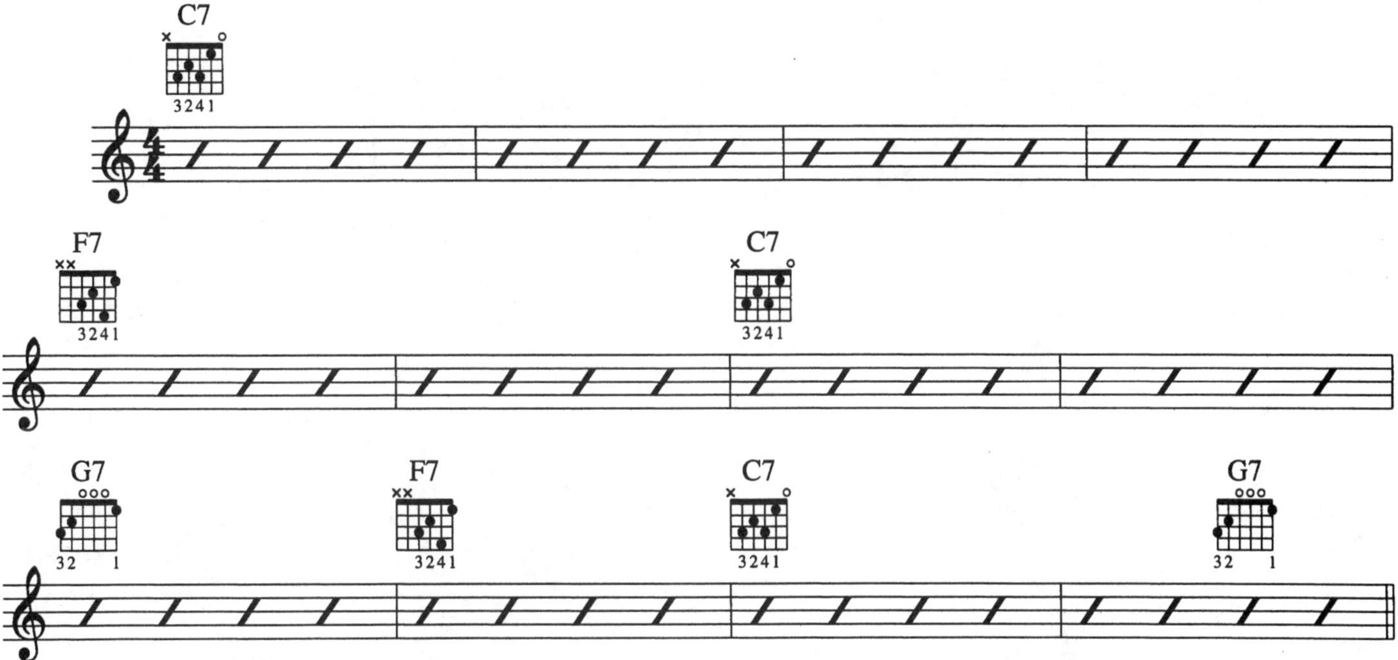

Example 72: The Quick-Change Progression

The previous examples start off with four bars of the I chord. This is called the "slow-change" blues. A variation on this progression, the "quick-change," is to replace the second bar with the IV chord and return to the I chord in the third bar. The rest of the progression remains unchanged.

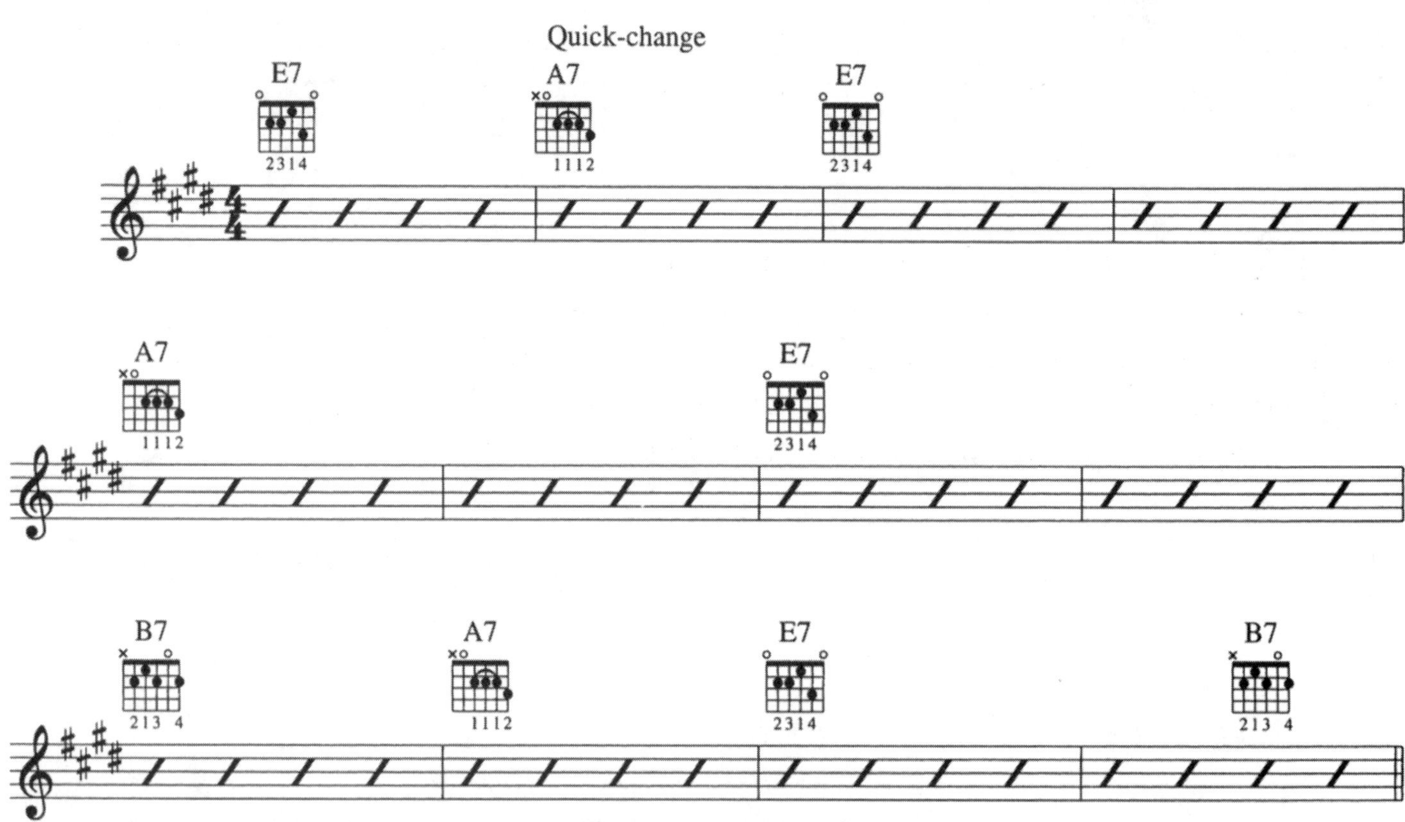

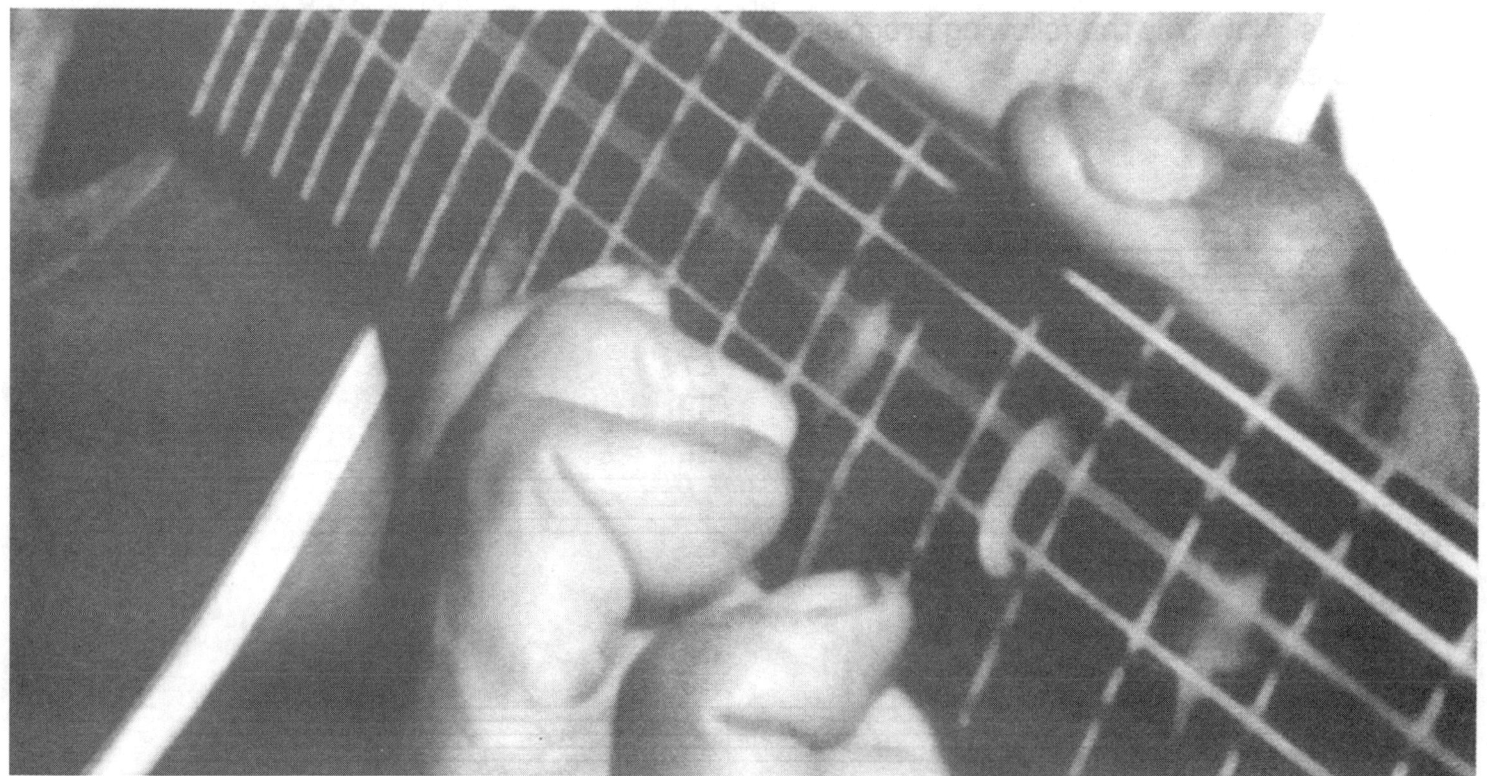

RHYTHM

It's amazing what a little bit of rhythm will do to make those chords sound good; changing the right-hand rhythm pattern while playing the same exact chords covered in the previous chapter. This is how you can start building your rhythm patterns, starting with the full chord shape and breaking them down, bit by bit, to find the melodies.

Example 73: The Shuffle Groove

The rhythm patterns demonstrated throughout this book are called *shuffle grooves.* The shuffle groove is fundamental to blues. The shuffle is a triplet, but played only on the first and third part of the beat, giving it an uneven, lopsided effect.

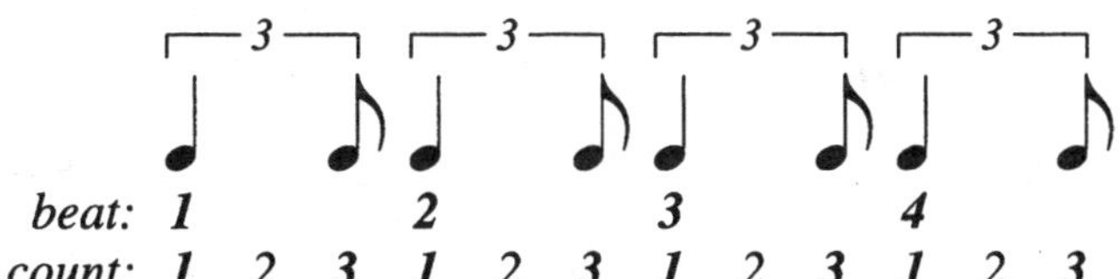

It is very important to emphasize the **down beat** (the first part of the beat) to give the groove more depth.

A shuffle is usually written in straight eighth notes, and it is left to the player to interpret the feel to have the first half of the beat to be longer than the second.

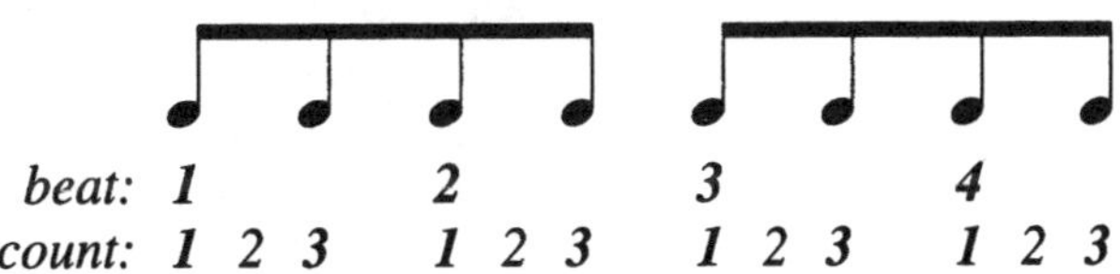

At the beginning of most songs, you will see an indication such as "shuffle" or "blues feel," or you will see this symbol which tells you to interpret eighth notes with a triplet or "shuffle" feel:

Example 74: Left-Hand Embellishments

When you embellish a chord by adding or removing notes, you are adding some melodic movement. The following example is an E7 embellished by adding the ♭7th (D) to the 2nd string with the 4th finger to create a melody. This, combined with the shuffle groove and the bass-chord strum pattern, can make a simple open chord shape sound like the blues.

Example 75: A7 Embellishment

The following example embellishes the A7 chord by creating a melody with the E, F♯ and G notes on the 1st string. Continue to use the shuffle groove and the bass-chord pattern.

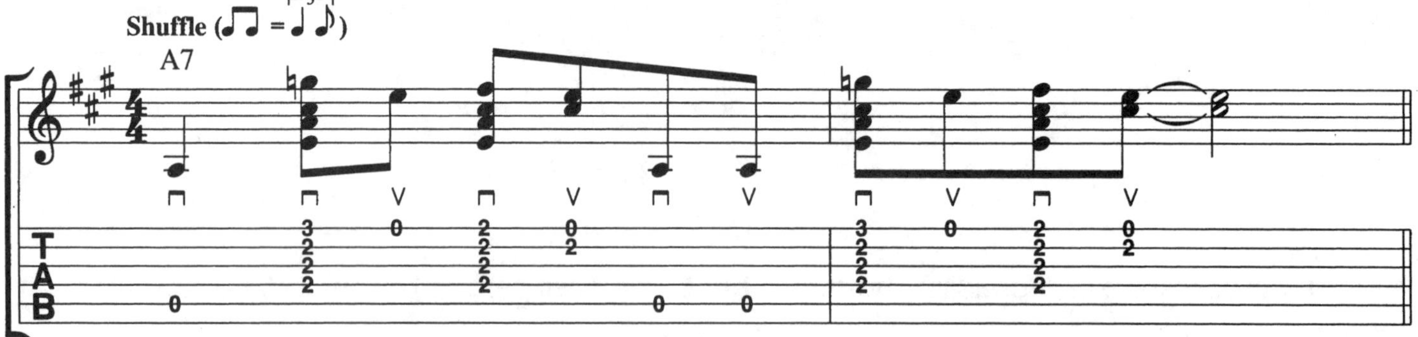

Example 76: Whole Progression

The following blues in E incorporates left-hand embellishment and the bass-chord strum pattern. Remember to maintain the shuffle groove throughout.

Since the B7 chord only lasts for one bar, it will sound fine if you just maintain the bass-chord pattern.

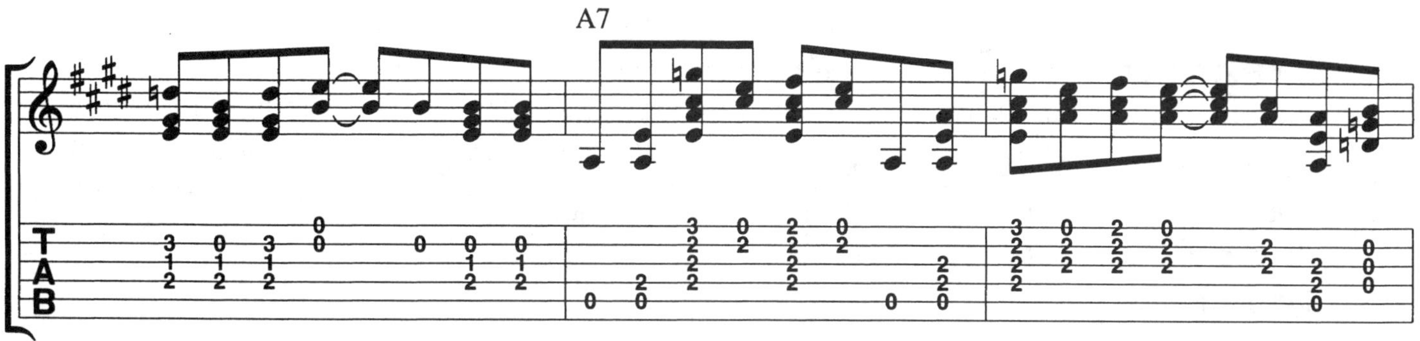

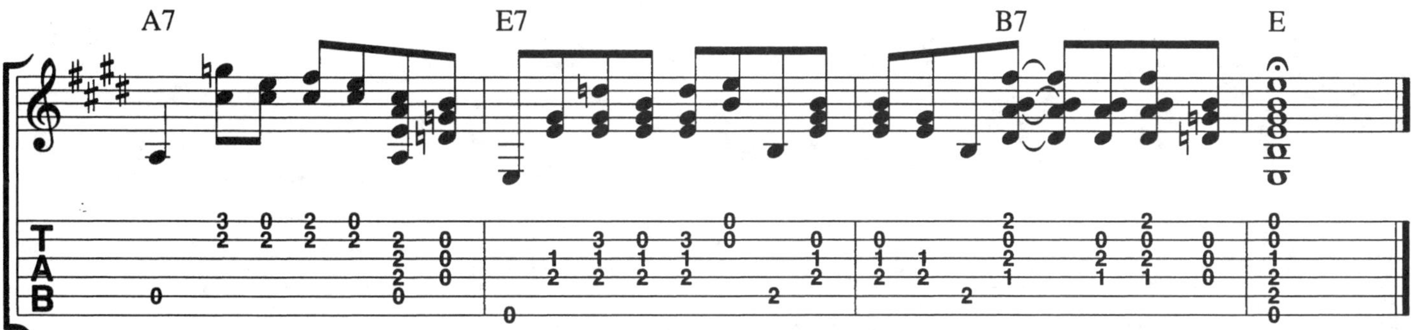

It should sound full, have some groove to it and feel relaxed. If you find yourself tightening up, your right hand struggling or your left hand struggling, just slow it down. Take your time and work on the fingerings.

Example 77: E7 Variation

This embellishment for E7 utilizes the same intervals as the previous A7 embellishment example: the 5th (B), 6th (C♯) and ♭7 (D) on the 2nd string.

Example 78: Quick-Change in E

Apply the previous E7 variation to a quick-change blues progression in E. While this progression can be used to accompany a vocalist or soloist, it can also stand alone as a full solo instrumental. It contains harmonic, rhythmic and melodic movement to provide a full musical statement.

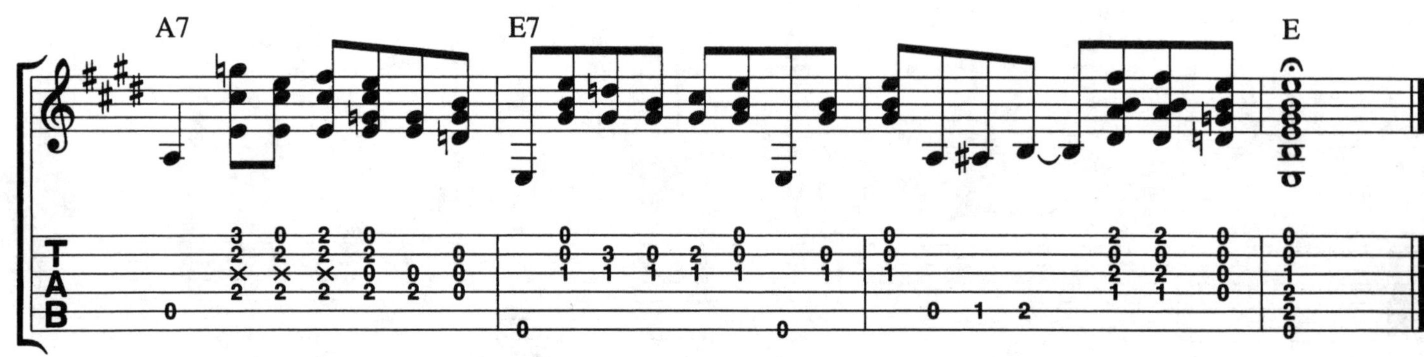

BASS-LINES

So far we have looked at chords using melody notes as embellishments. Another way to dress up the chords and link them together is with **bass-runs**. You can approach bass-runs as a variation to the bass-chord pattern by simply adding more bass notes.

Example 79A: E7 to A7 Bass-line

The bass-line should lead to the root of the next chord. Notice how the bass notes at the end of the E7 bar sound like they are "stepping up" to the A7 chord.

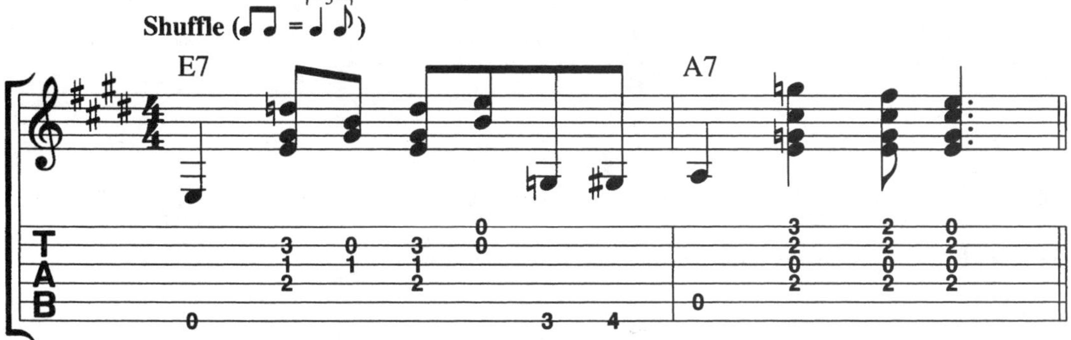

Example 79B: A7 to E7 Bass-line

There are a couple of choices for bass-lines that lead from A7 to E7. The first choice is to continue the upward movement and jump down to the low E at the beginning of the next bar.

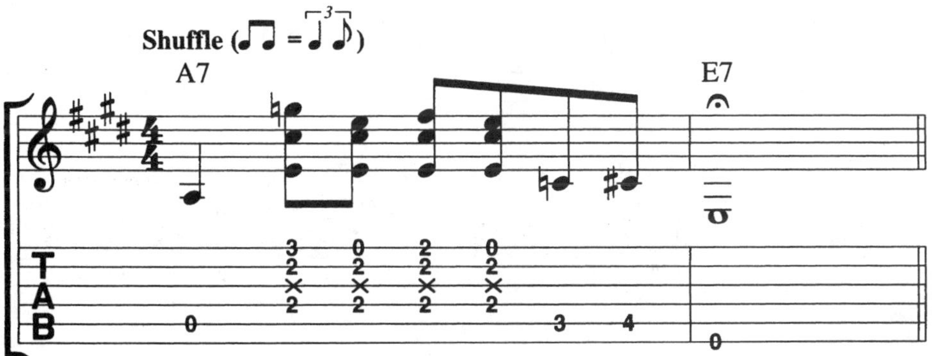

Example 79C: Another A7 to E7 Bass-line

You can also walk straight down from the A7 to the E7.

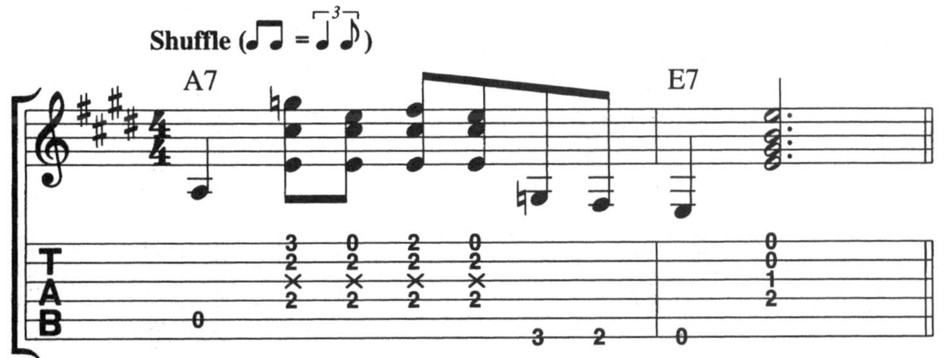

Example 79D: B7 to A7 Bass-line

You can walk up to the B7 from the open A by playing the note in between the open A and the second fret B. Then reverse the pattern from the B7 to the A7. This little walk-up to the B7 is a line you will hear in numerous blues songs.

Shuffle
E7
B7
A7
TAB

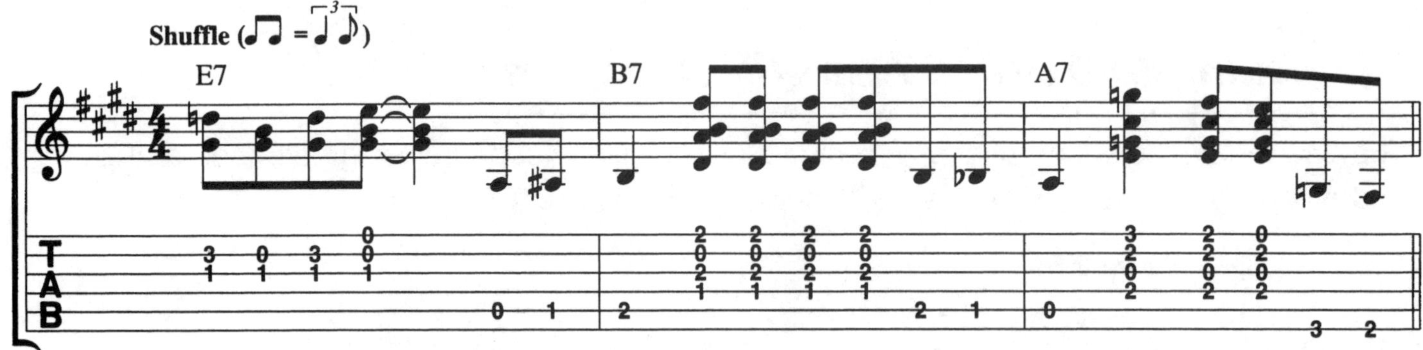

Example 79E: The Whole Bass-line Progression

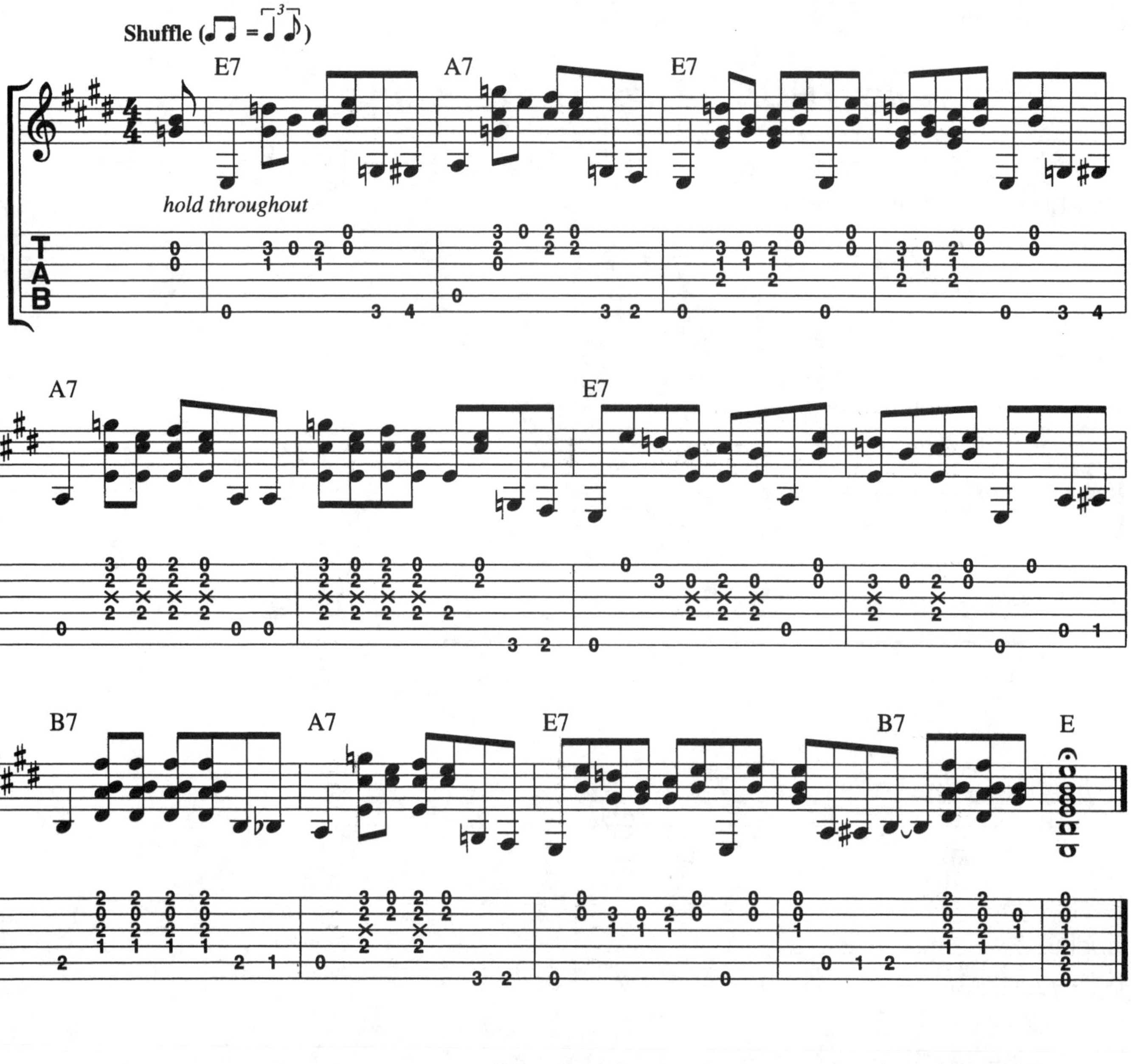

Shuffle
E7
A7
E7
hold throughout
TAB
A7
E7
B7
A7
E7
B7
E

Example 80: The Jimmy Reed Progression

A lot of people call this the "Jimmy Reed" pattern, named after the immortal Chicago blues guitarist. Jimmy Reed simultaneously played acoustic guitar and harmonica on a neck-rack, kind of a folk style, and wrote many fabulous, influential blues songs.

In spite of its acoustic roots, this pattern is actually the most basic that electric blues players learn today because it leaves room for vocals and other instruments. Play the blues in E with a shuffle groove and use all down strokes.

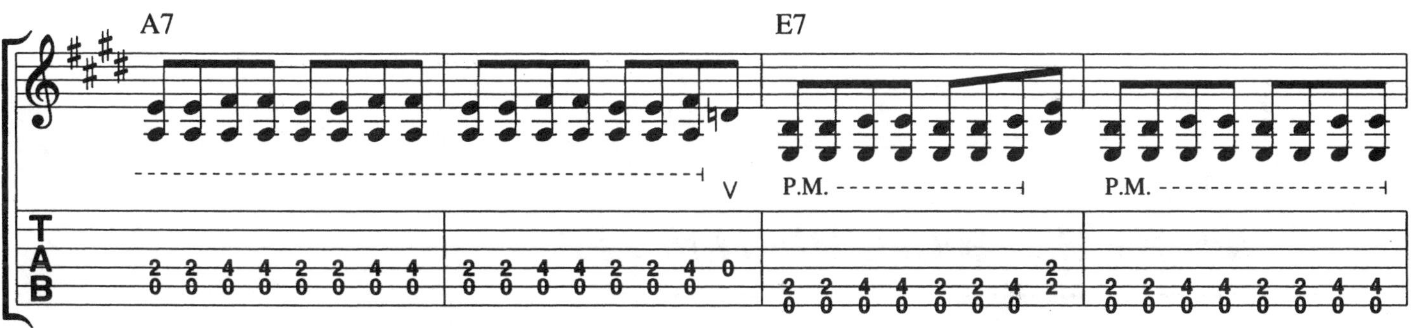

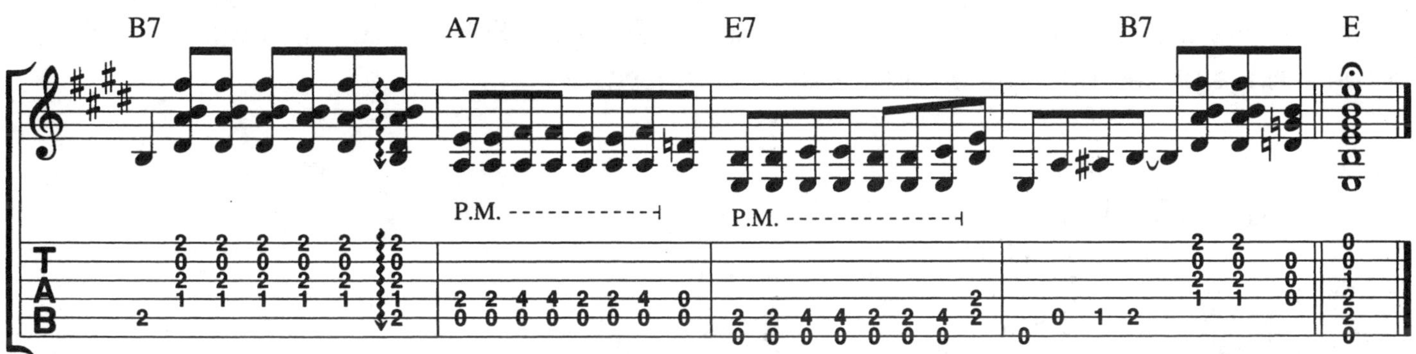

Notice how this pattern sounds more "compact and muted" compared to the big, open and ringing sound of the previous progressions. You can accomplish this by **muting** the strings with your right hand, placing it lightly against the strings near the bridge.

Example 81: Up-strokes and Accents

You can add rhythmic variety and flavor to the groove by occasionally throwing in accented up-strokes. These accents should not interrupt the groove or replace the accents on the down beat.

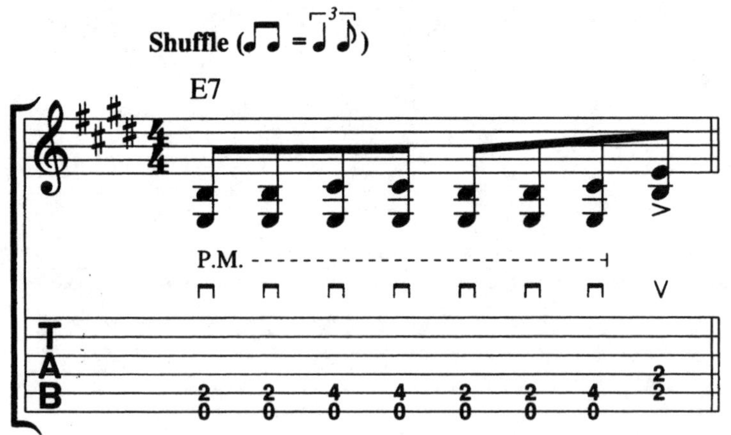

Example 82: Blues Rhythm Lick

This move is a common blues cliché. Technically, it is the IV chord being thrown in quickly to create more melodic movement. For the open E7 chord, add the A triad by laying your finger across the 2nd, 3rd and 4th strings at the 2nd fret. Follow this move with the same three strings played open, and finish with the E chord.

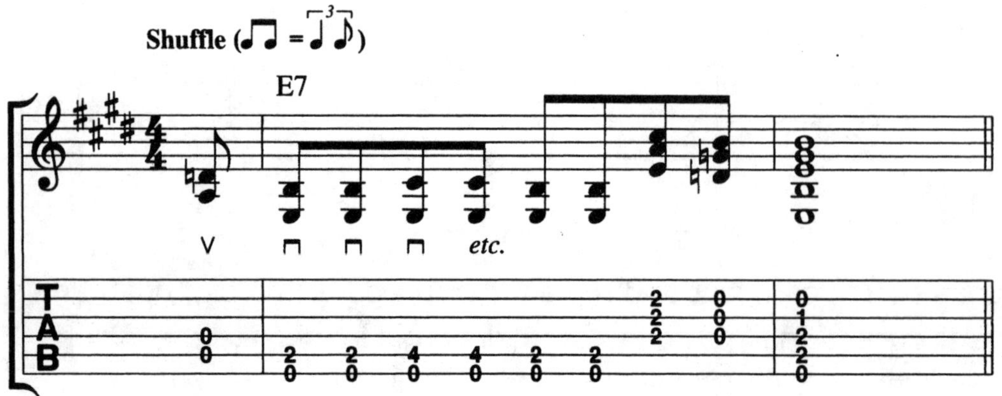

Example 83: Full Progression

Apply the previous examples to the following slow-change blues in E.

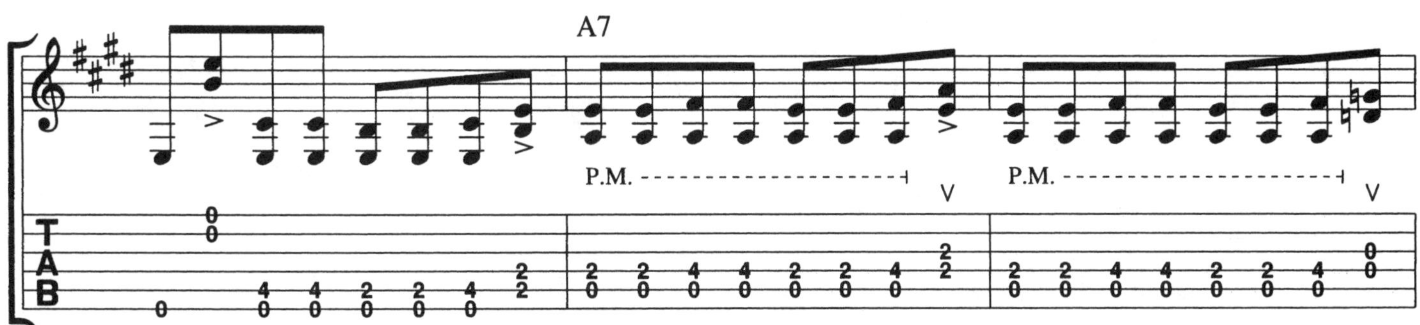

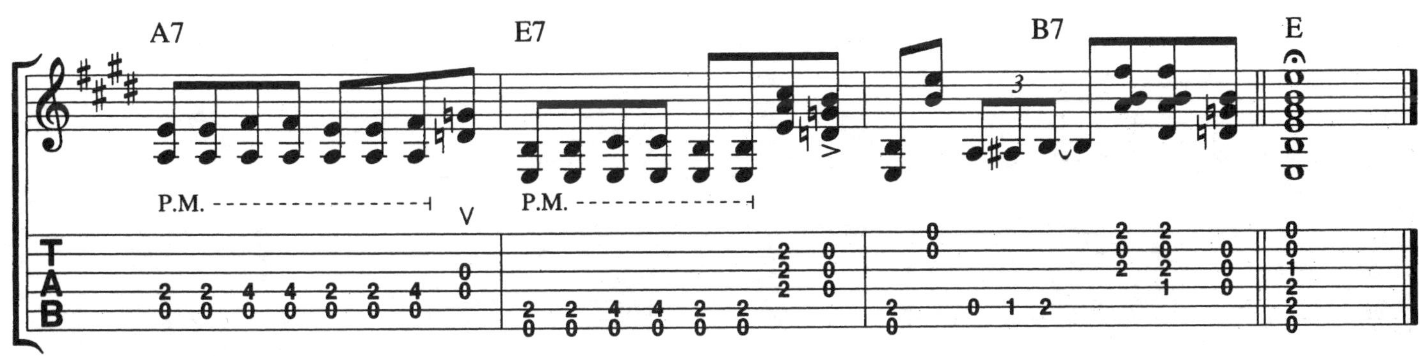

Example 84

Now add bass-lines.

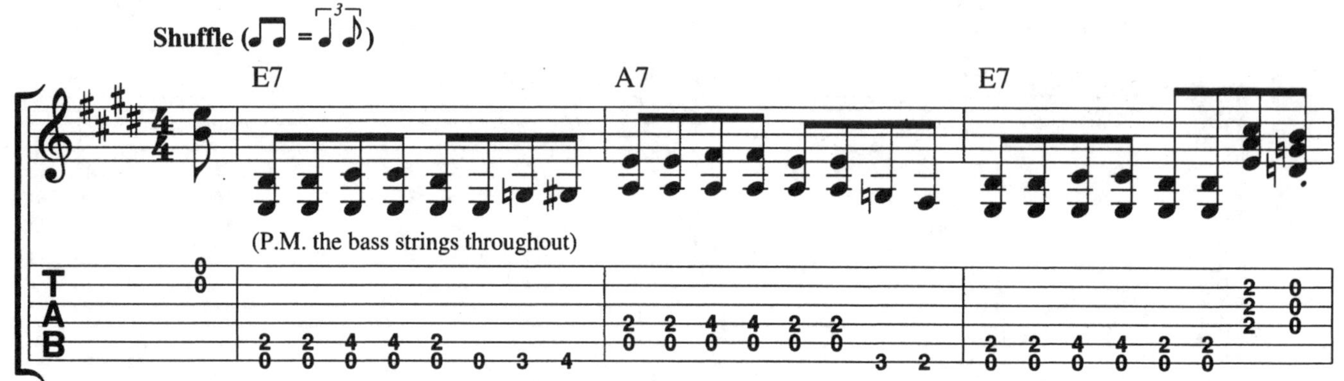

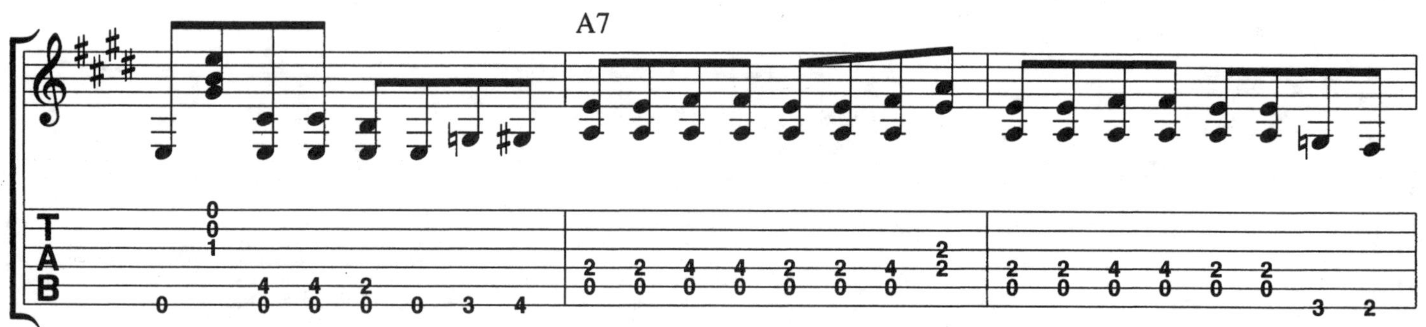

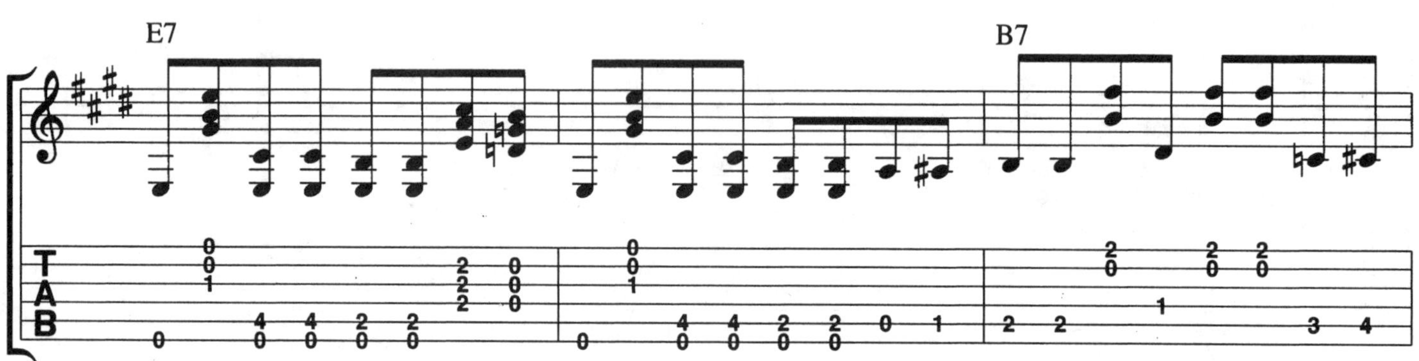

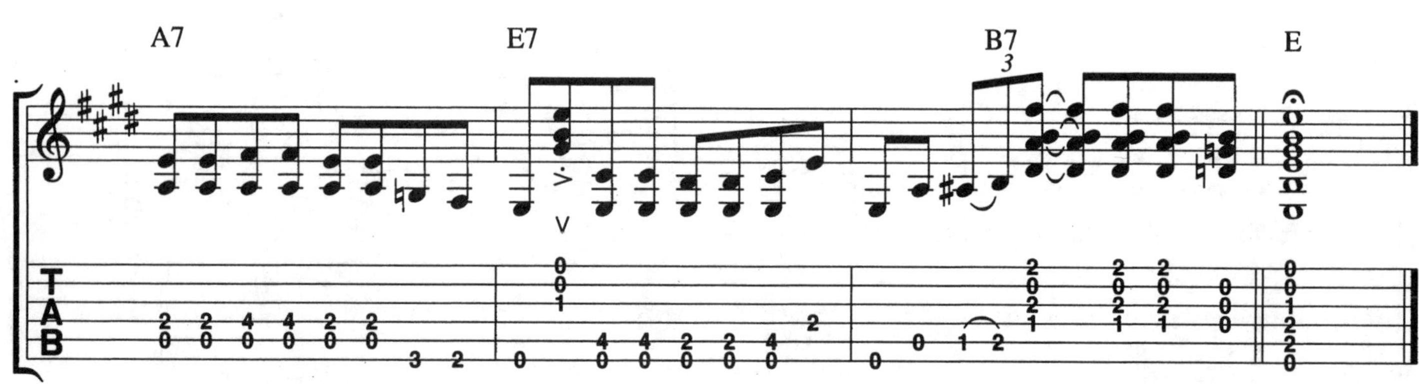

Example 85

This quick-change blues in E combines bass-lines to connect the chords and big chord embellishments.

Keep experimenting with each of the elements covered up to this point: chord shapes, progressions, rhythm patterns, melodic embellishments, bass-lines, muting and accents to come up with some of your own ideas. More importantly, you need to listen to other players to hear how they incorporate these ideas. You will notice how songs that might have seemed complicated to you in the past can now be broken down into simpler ideas.

Example 86: Blues in E Turnaround

So far we've been using one turnaround, a little bass-run up to the B7 chord in the last measure:

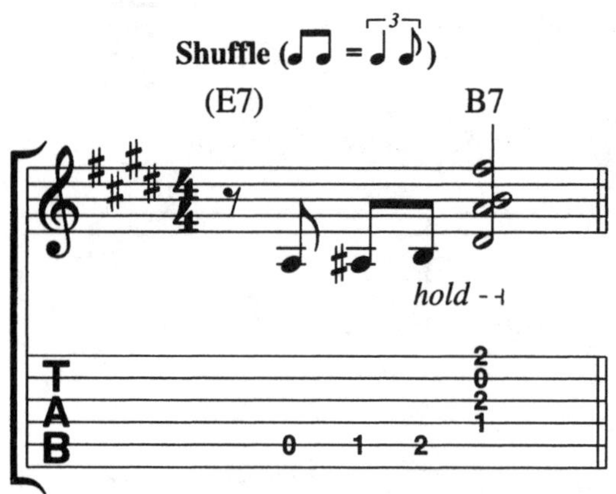

It is quite common to use variations on the last two bars to "turn the progression around" to the beginning. Memorize every turnaround as a lick that you can place at the end of a progression at will.

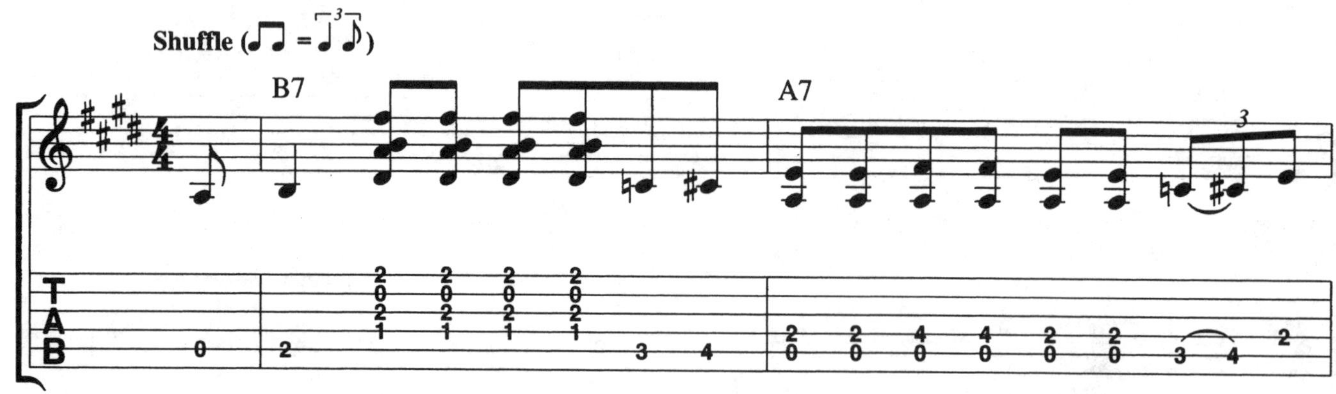

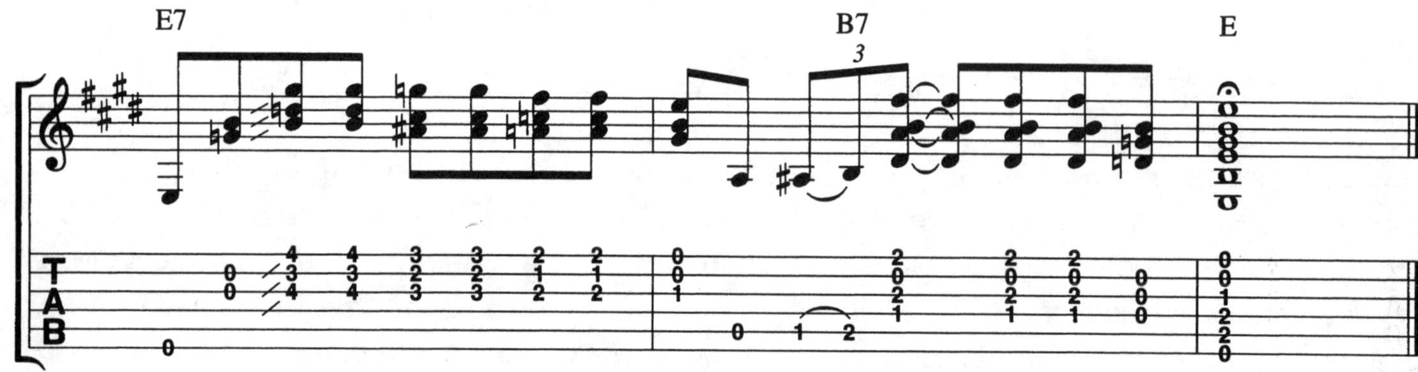

BLUES IN A

The key of A is probably the second most common guitar key for blues. Now experiment with the following embellishment ideas for both the A7 and D7 chord. The E7 will use the same embellishments used in the key of E.

Example 87A: A7 Embellishments

Hold the A7 fingering with the 1st and 2nd fingers and use the 3rd and 4th fingers to embellish the chord on the 4th and 5th frets of the first two strings.

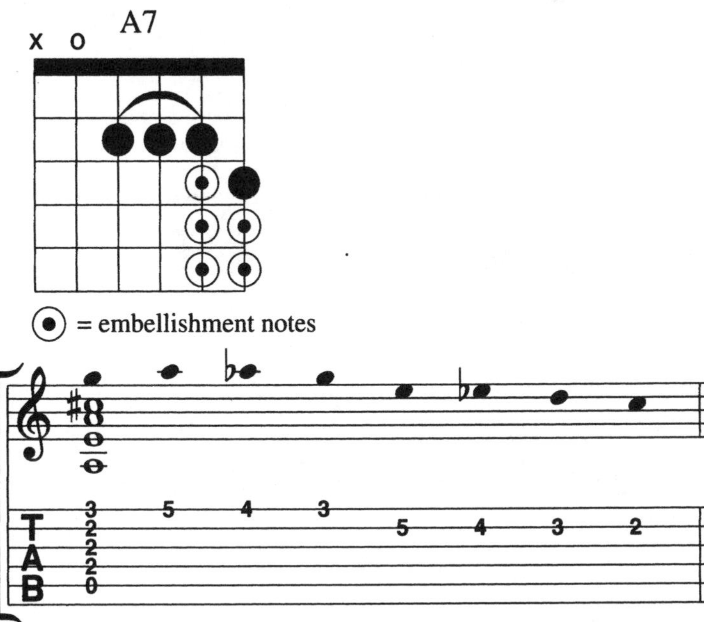

Example 87B: D7 Embellishments

A simple way to embellish the D7 is to barre the 1st fret on the first two strings with the 1st fingers.

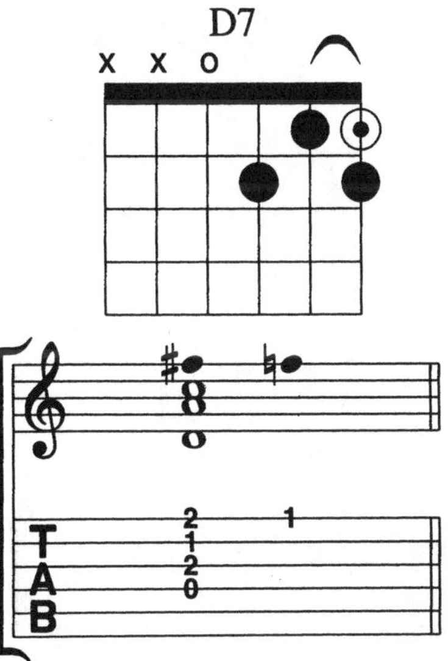

Example 87C: Blues in A

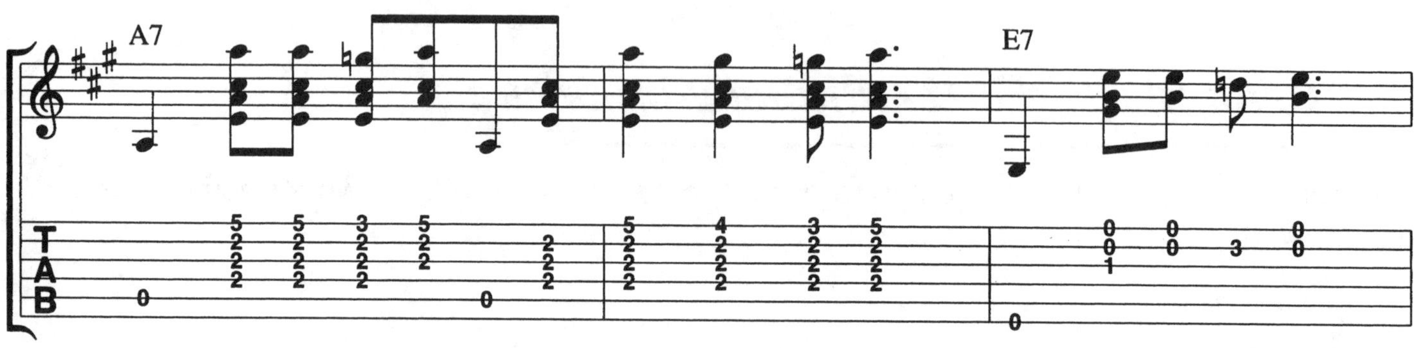

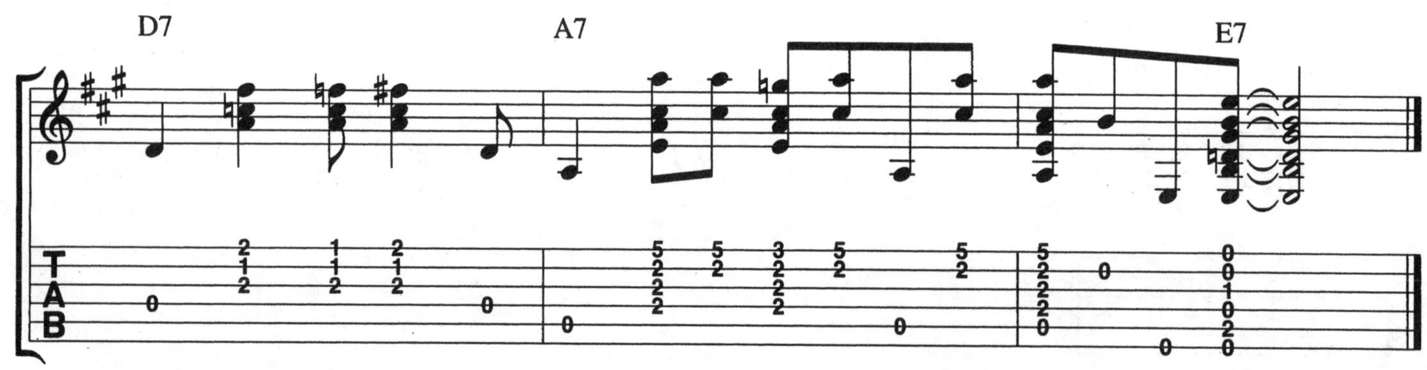

Example 87D: E7 to D7/F♯

There is a weak spot in the previous progression; the transition between the full sounding E7 and the thinner sounding D7. The lowest sounding D on the instrument is almost an octave higher than E, making the transition sound and feel more abrupt. As a solution, use the low F♯ in the bass of the D7 instead of the D. This will smooth the transition between the two chords by adding more fullness to the D7 chord and reducing the distance between the bass notes to a whole step.

While the F♯ is in the chord, it usually is not in the bass. When a note other than the root is in the bass, it is indicated in the chord symbol by placing a slash after the chord name, followed by the name of the bass note. So, for example, the D7 chord with an F♯ in the bass is indicated as D7/F♯.

Example 87E: Blues in A

Play the whole blues in A with a quick change progression incorporating the D7/F♯.

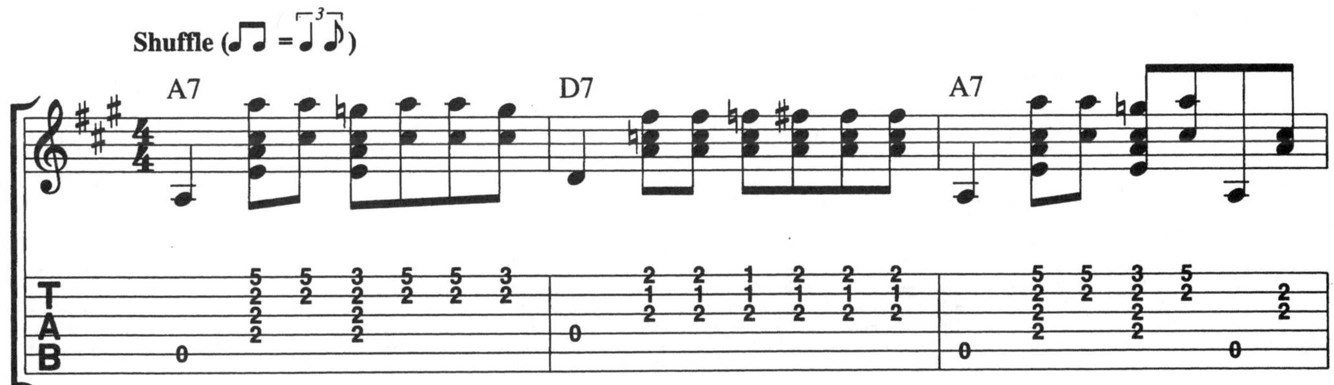

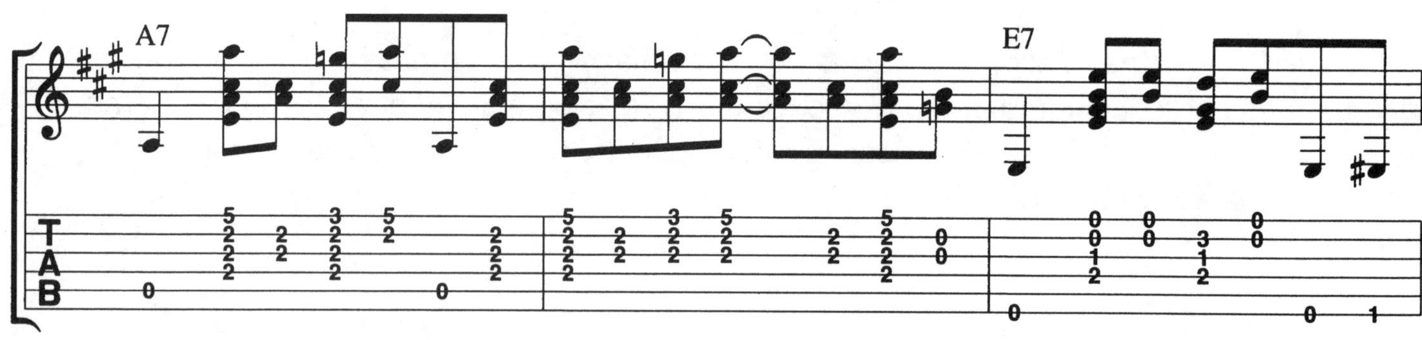

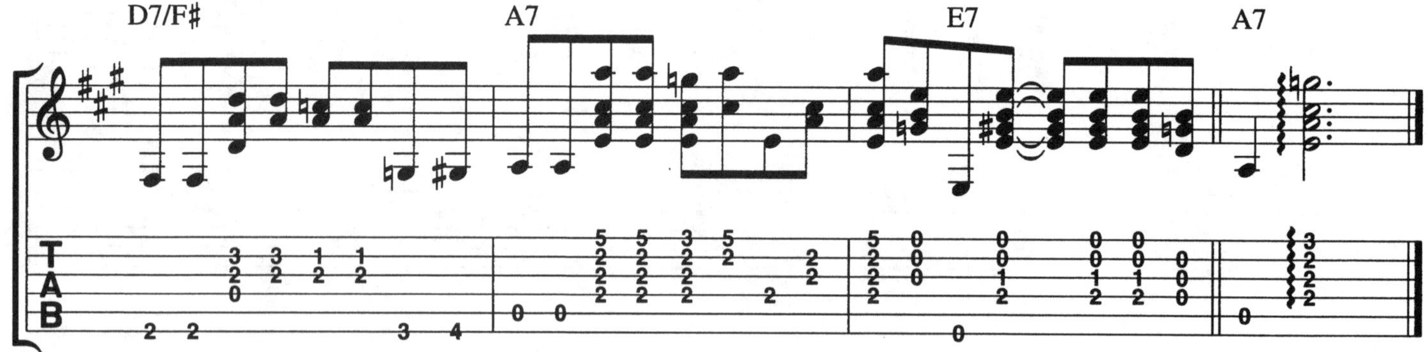

Example 88: Blues in A Turnaround

Here is a simple turnaround for the key of A. Start on the second beat and use the same fingering for each chord while shifting down one fret at a time.

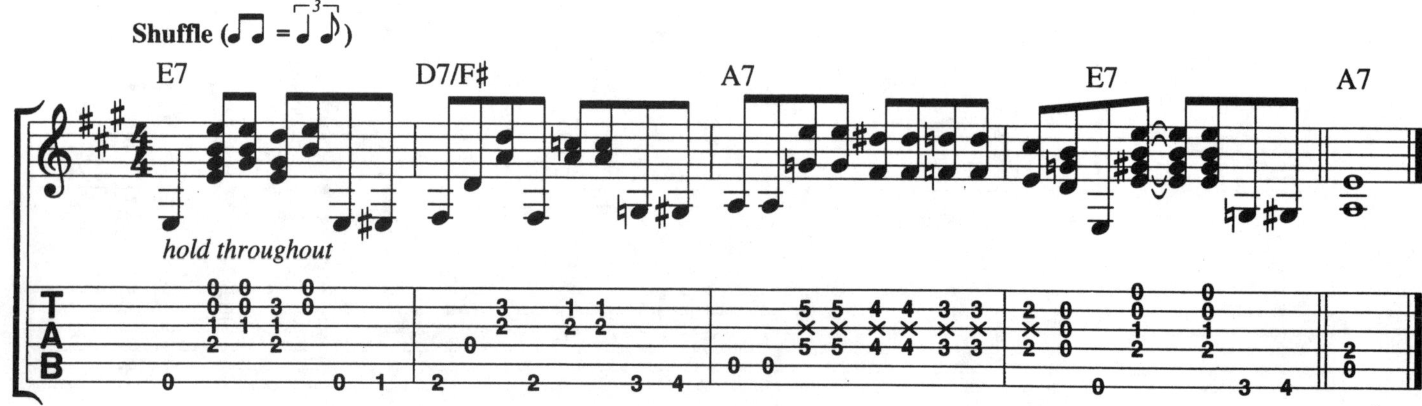

SOLO ACOUSTIC BLUES GUITAR

Solo blues guitar style is the art of playing unaccompanied blues guitar. You can use a flat pick for the bass notes and single-note leads, using your fingers to strike the chords and embellishments. This is called hybrid-picking. It's also okay to use a thumb-pick, finger-picks, or fingers without a pick.

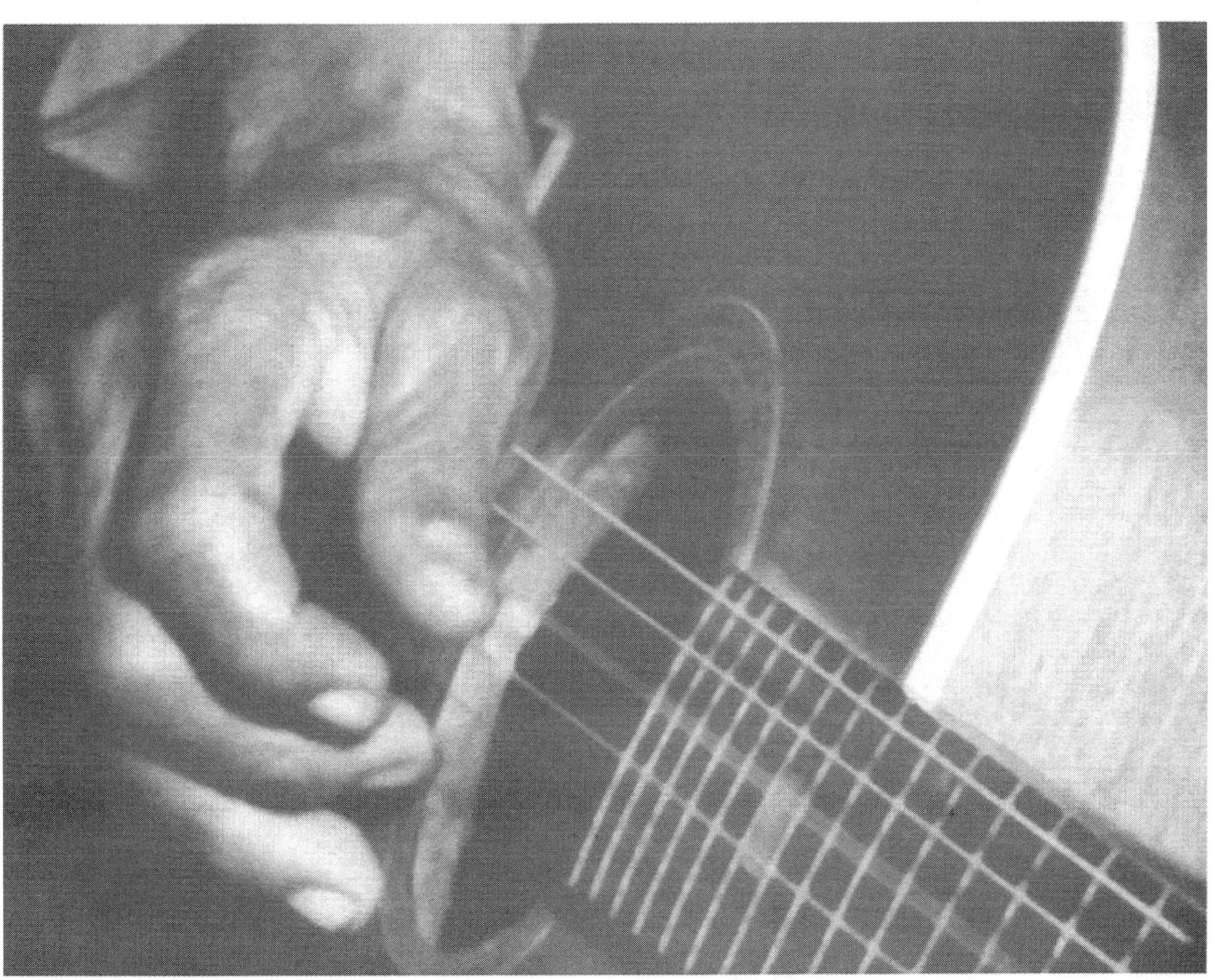

BLUES LICKS

A lot of the great single-line solos that you hear are really not as different from the chord parts as you might imagine. When we learn chords and we learn how to embellish chords, we are really creating melodies using notes that belong to the chord as well as notes built around the chord — *scale tones.* Rather than learn scale patterns up and down the neck, as is the custom when learning electric guitar, we will concentrate on the *chord tones* to find out what notes can be used for melody and soloing. The open chords are especially important because they bring out the rich, full character of the acoustic guitar.

Example 89A: E7 Blues Lick

If, for example, you want to play a melody or to solo against an E chord, instead of just playing an E scale, try looking at the notes of the chord to see what you can get out of it. The following lick is a very common blues pattern utilizing only the notes of an E7 chord. The trick is to hold the open E7 chord shape while making it sound like a single-note melody.

Example 89B: A7 Blues Lick

While this lick has the same selection of notes as the embellishment examples in the previous section, the technique is slightly different. It uses the open A7 chord shape plus embellishment notes, but it is played as a single-note lead pattern.

Notice the curved line between the third and fourth note. It is called a **slur** and it indicates that the F♯ on the 2nd fret is to be struck and then "pulled-off" to the open E. This technique adds some swing and phrasing to the lick. The best way to employ this technique is to strike the F♯ and pull across the string with your 2nd finger, sounding the open E string in the process.

Example 89C: B7 Blues Lick

At the B7 chord, notice the single-note pattern that utilizes the right hand only, while the left hand holds the chord shape.

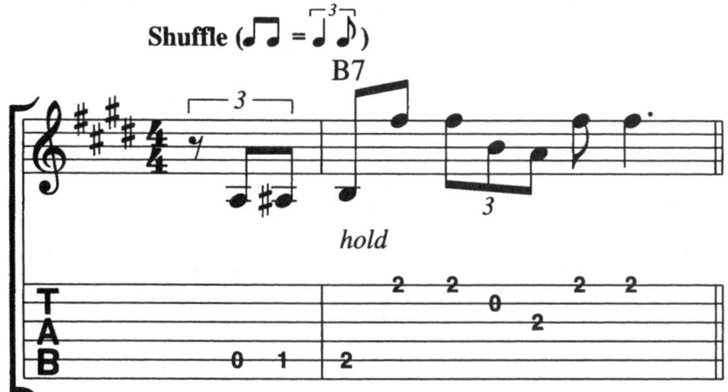

Example 89D: E7 Lick

One of the most notable stylistic blues trademarks you can get from a guitar is the bend. Bending is the technique of stretching the string to raise the pitch of a note. You stretch the string by pushing or pulling the string toward a neighboring string. Bending "in pitch" means the note is bent far enough to sound like an accurate note or pitch above the fretted note. In blues, it is also common to use quarter bends, which are only slight bends that add some spice to the fretted note instead of taking it all the way to the next note.

With the exception of the open E, this lick is the same as some of the previous A7 licks. This works because it starts with an E and finishes with E7 chord tones. Notice the quarter bend on the 3rd fret of the 1st string:

Example 89E: A7 Lick

This lick actually spells out an **A blues scale**. A single-note scale pattern by itself would normally sound too thin for solo style guitar. Starting the lick with an open A and allowing it to ring throughout makes this single-note pattern sound fuller.

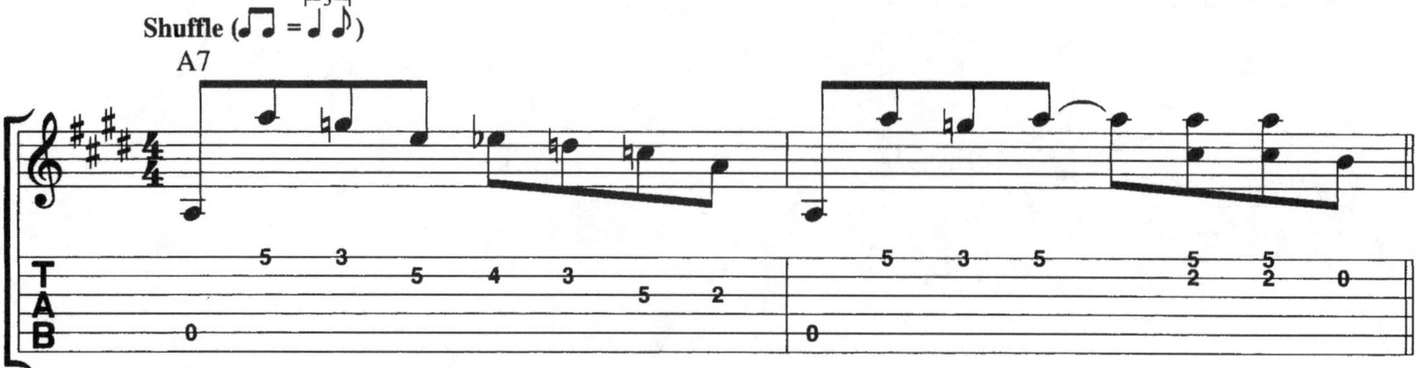

Example 89F: Turnaround Variation

This turnaround should look familiar, but there is one chord shape that is different from the open chords that we have been using. The primary reason for using a different chord shape like this is that this shape sounds higher and thinner than the open fingering. This allows for more melodic movement and variety. You can label these chords with different names when moving down the fretboard in half steps, but it really isn't necessary. By starting and ending on E, the chords in between sound more like a transition than a series of different chords. It is better to treat this movement as a melodic idea since it doesn't really change the overall chord progression.

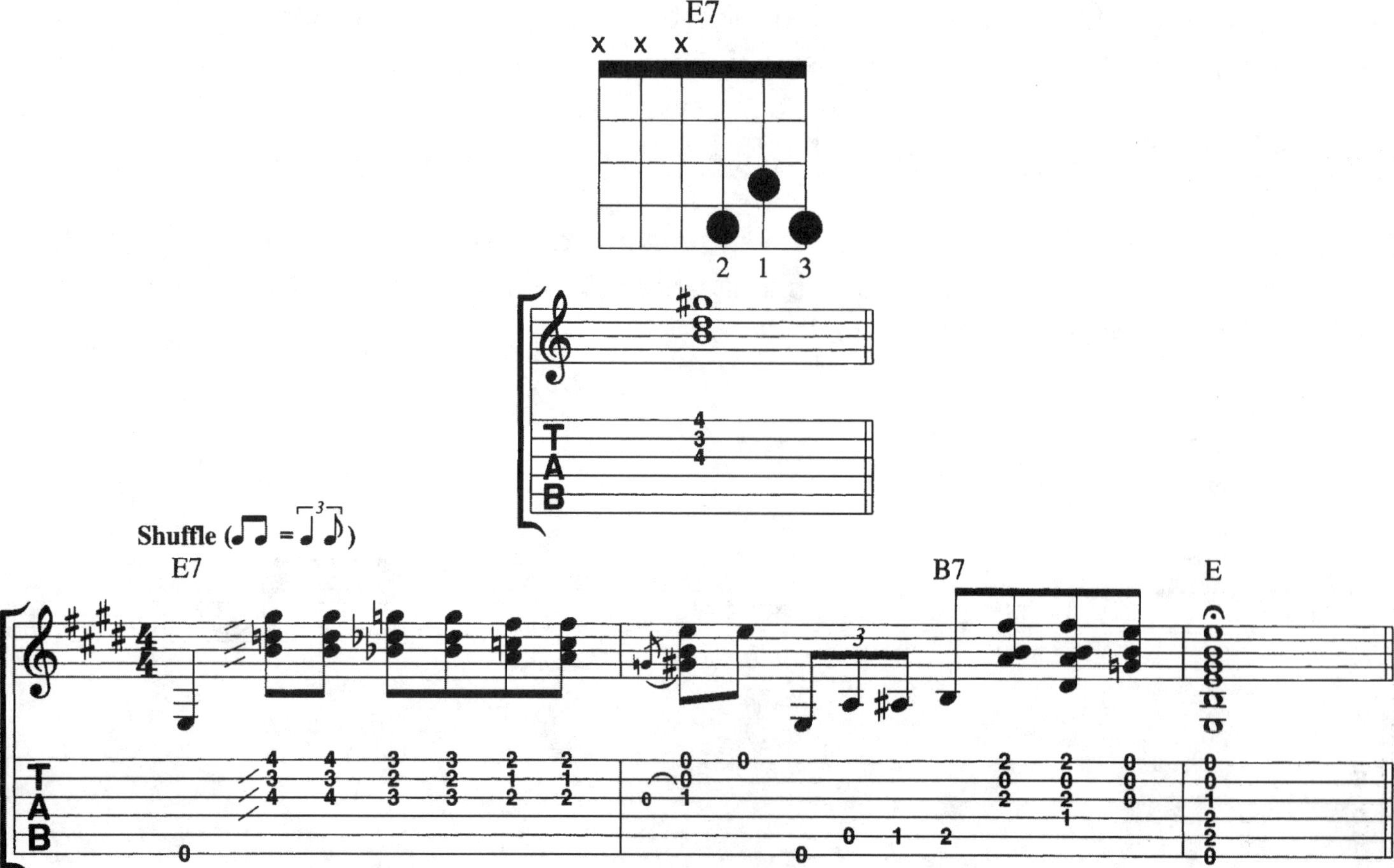

Example 89G: Whole Progression

Now let's put together all four of the previous licks to create a complete progression.

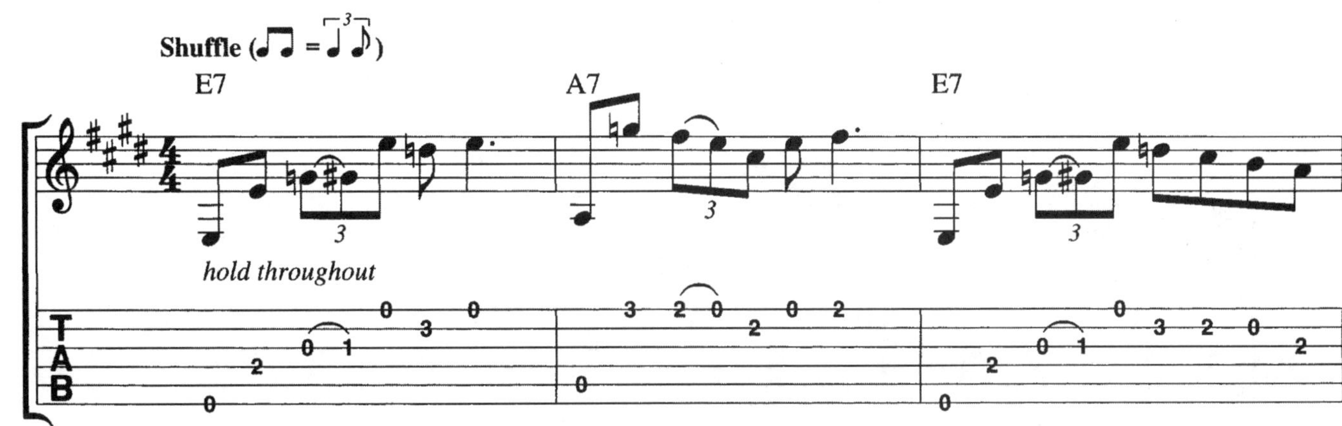

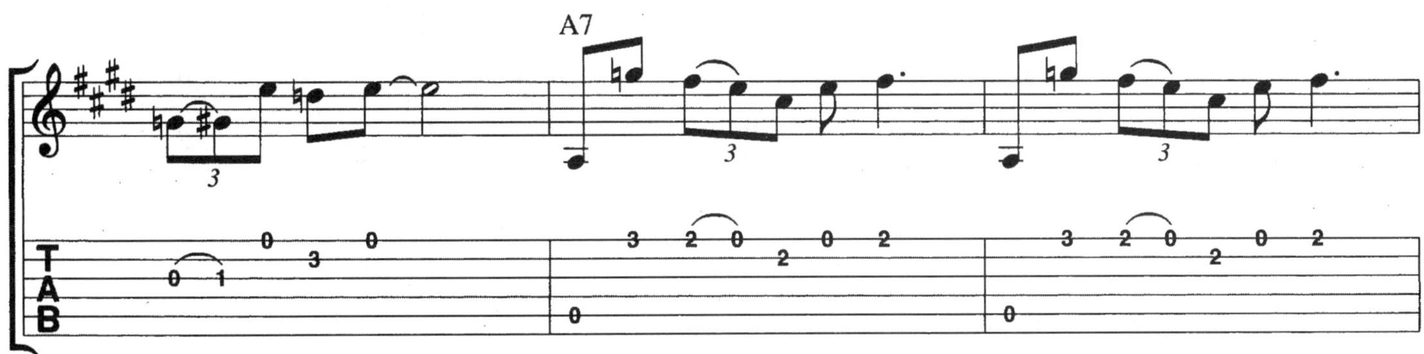

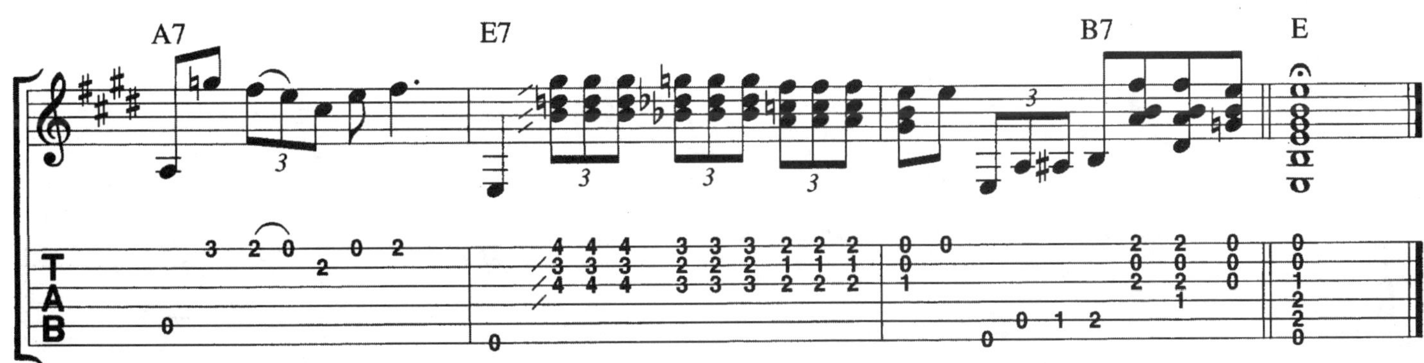

Example 90: More Blues Bass-lines

Even though the previous example sounds full harmonically and melodically, there is still some empty space. Here is another opportunity to apply bass runs to make it sound like a complete piece of music.

Shuffle
E7
A7
E7
A7
E7
B7
A7
E7
B7
E

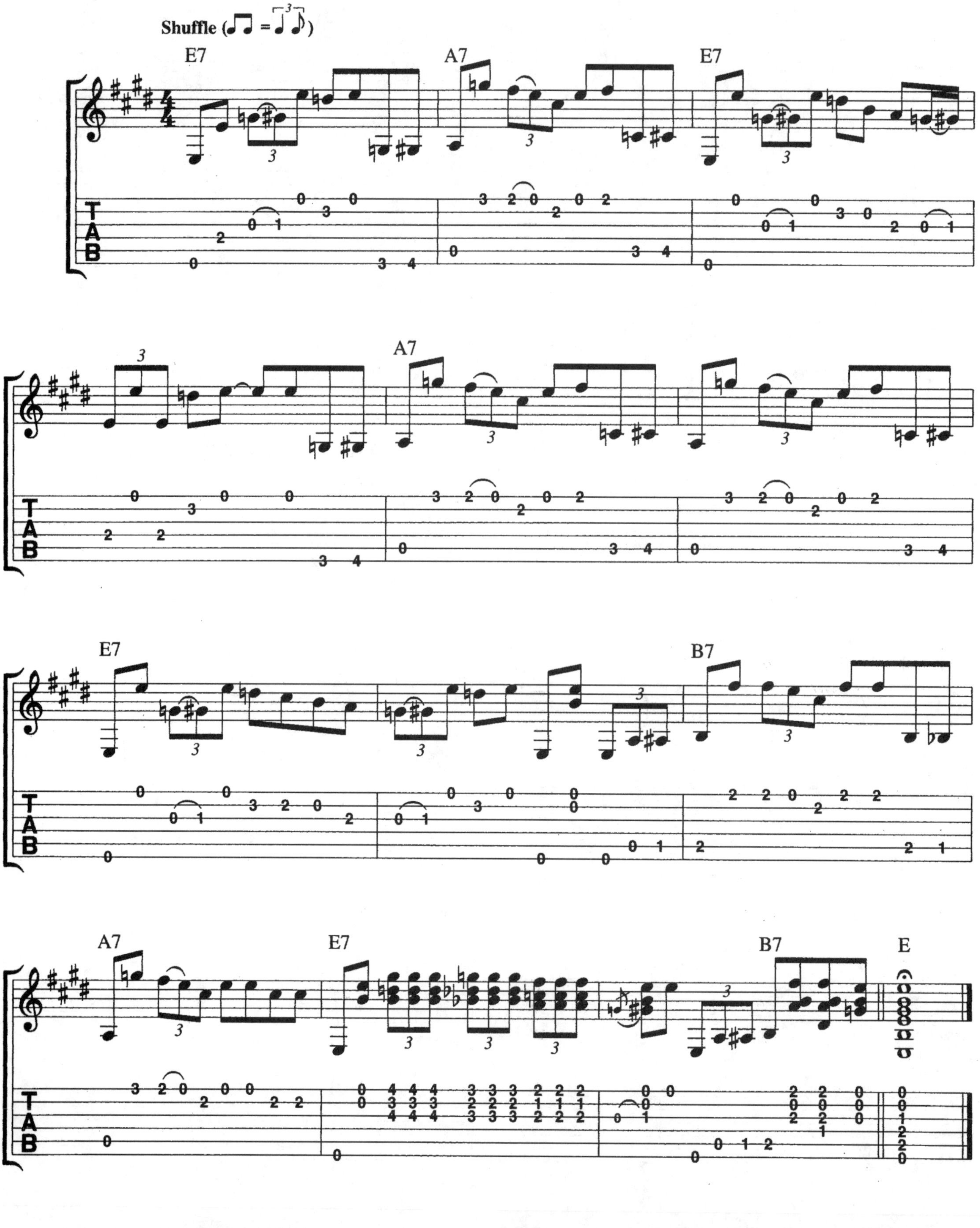

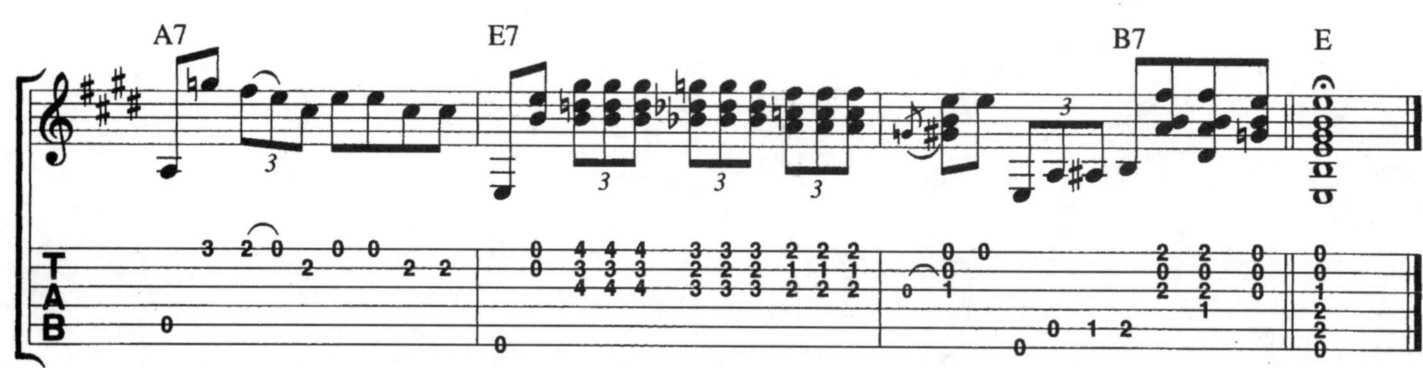

BLUES CHORD SOLOING

In order to master the powerful technique of soloing with chords, you need to memorize certain chord inversions. Chord inversions are not only a great way to add melodic movement to your chords, but they also provide valuable visual references that will help you to travel the fretboard.

When you invert a chord, you are actually re-arranging the same notes into a different order. By re-arranging the notes, different notes end up on top of the chords and on the bottom. For example, the order of the notes, from the low string to the high string, of the open E7 is **E-B-E-G♯-D-E**. The melody notes are either D or E. The order of the notes of the next inversion, at the 2nd postion, is **E-B-D-G♯**. This places G♯ in the melody.

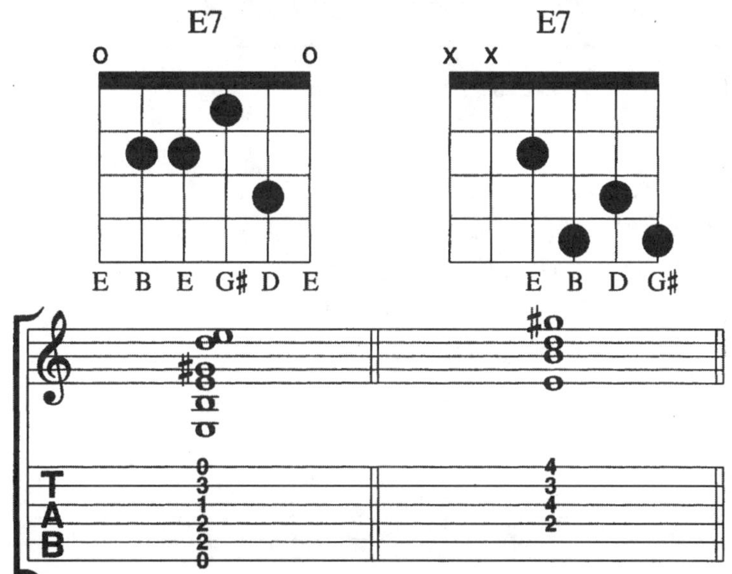

Example 91: E7 Inversions

Now take this a step further and learn the inversions that will place the remaining notes of the chord in the melody — B, D and the higher octave E. Play the following shapes forward and backward in the order that they occur and it will sound like a scale of chords.

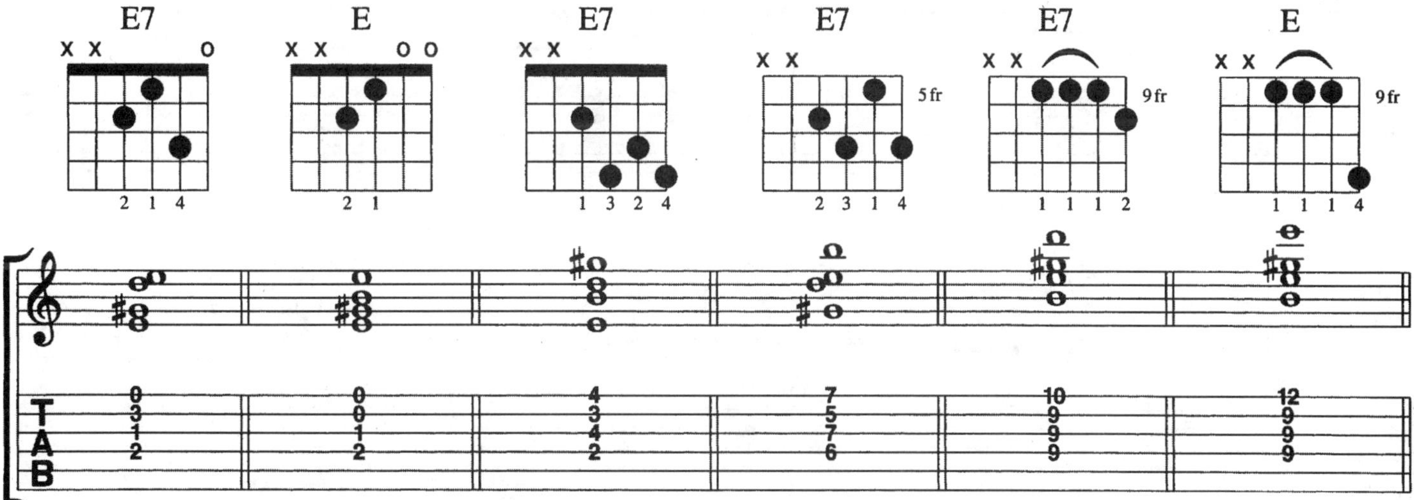

Example 92: Chromaticism

You can add more melodic options and more tension to dominant chord inversions by taking any inversion up or down a half step, as long as you return to the actual chord. This half step movement is often described as **chromatic movement** or **chromaticism**.

Descending
Ascending
E7

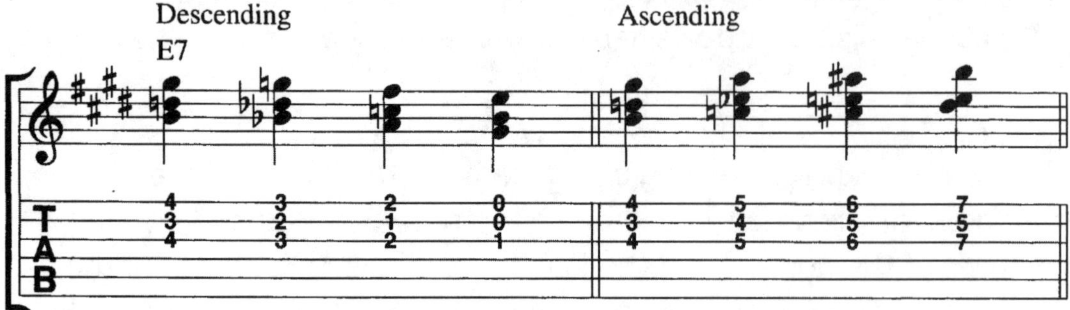

Example 93: Blues Chord Solo 1

This chordal technique is used by country blues guitar players to solo without losing the feel of the rhythm.

Notice how taking this E7 fingering down one fret to E♭7, for the second measure, implies a quick-change progression. Since this fingering omits the root (E♭), it does not clash with the E of the A7 chord. If you compare this E♭7 fingering to A7, you will find that there's only a one note difference; the B♭ instead of the A. The B♭ is compatible with the A7 chord, thus allowing the E♭7 chord to act as a **substitute**.

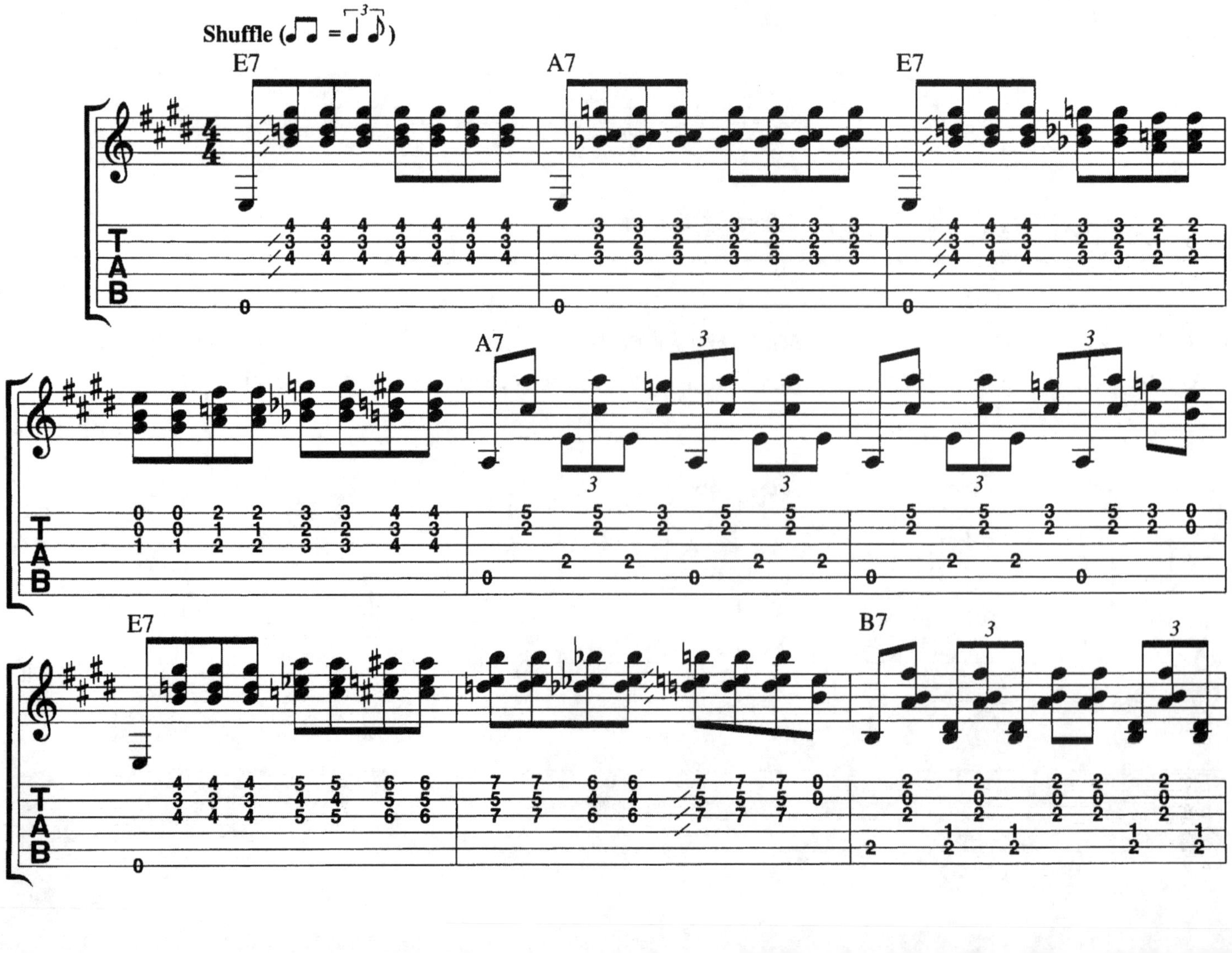
Shuffle
E7
A7
E7
A7
E7
B7

Example 94A: A7 Inversions

Now transpose E7 inversions to A7.

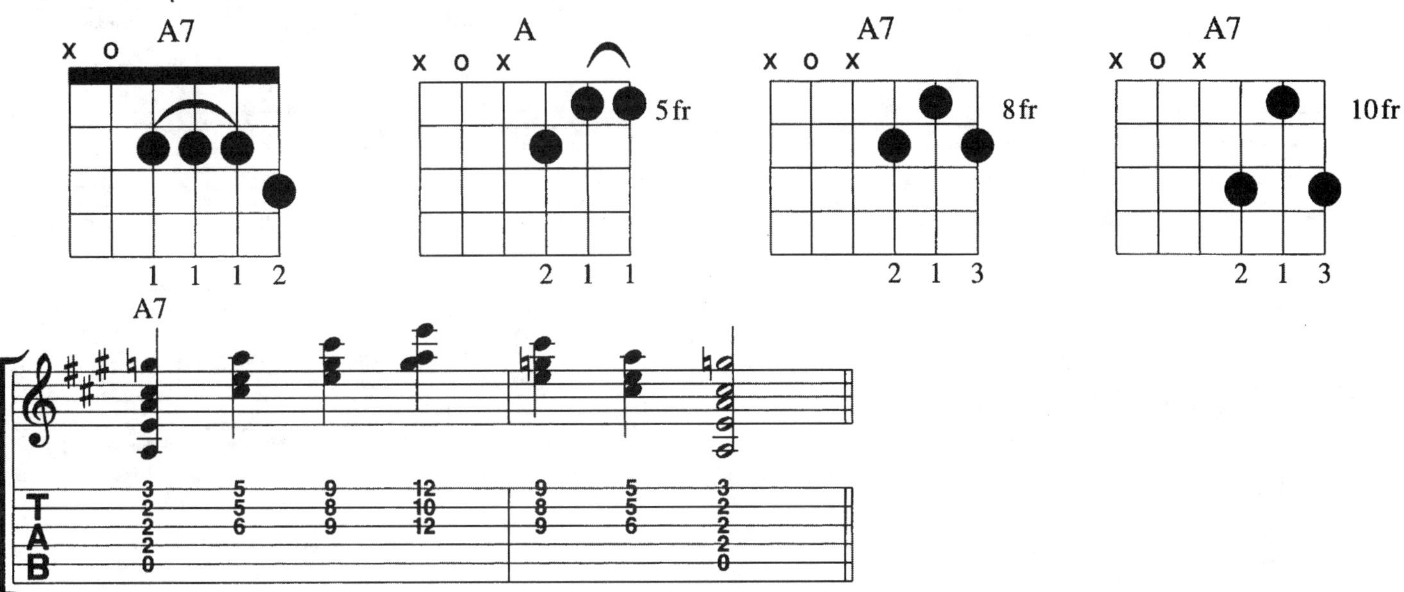

Example 94B: A7 Inversions with Chromatics

Example 94C: Chord Solo Turnaround

Apply inversions and chromaticism to a turnaround.

Example 94D: Blues Chord Solo 2

Notice how the ascending patterns that take you up the fretboard increase the tension and the excitement, while descending patterns tend to decrease the tension and excitement.

Example 94E: Blues Chord Solo 3

After learning Blues Chord Solos 1, 2 and 3, try combining them in exactly the same order. Chord Solo 3 spends the most time in the higher register of the neck. As a result, the first two solos will sound like they are building to a climax in Solo 3.

THE BLUES SCALE

In addition to using chord shapes, there is a more obvious source to help you choose notes that give you the blues sound, *the blues scale.* The blues scale has five notes and an extra note in it that people use a lot. The first five notes of the E blues scale are known as the E minor pentatonic: E-G-A-B-D. The extra note is B♭, which is technically described as the ♭5 or "blues" 5th.

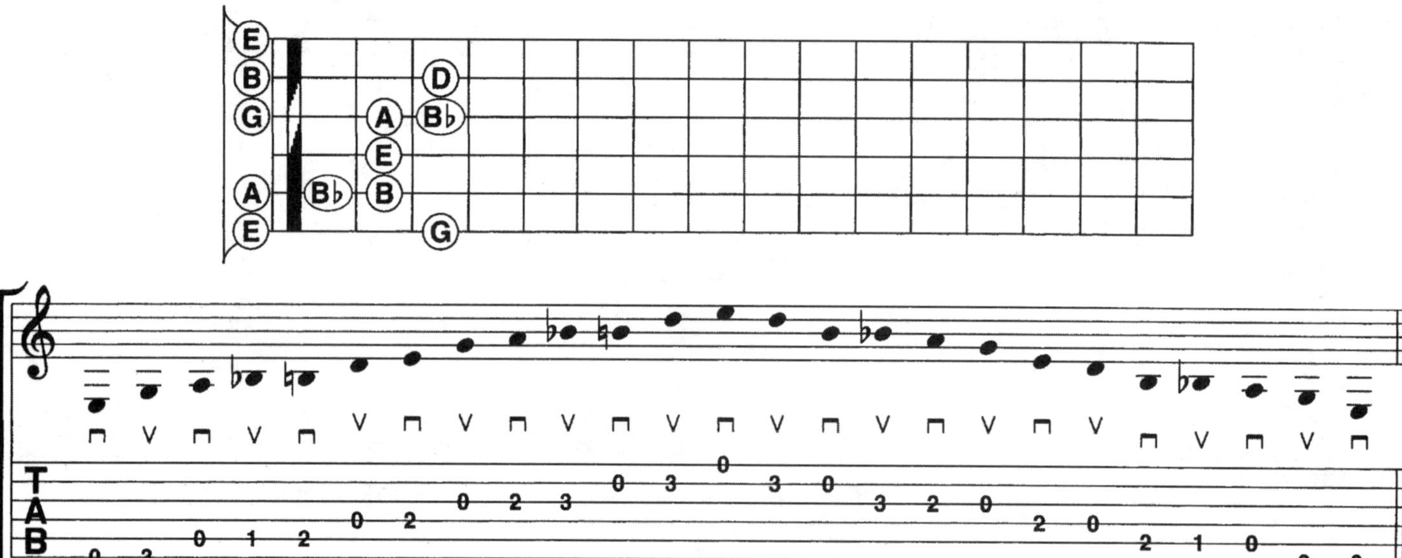

These notes can be found all over the fretboard, but in acoustic blues you will find that a thorough knowledge of the open position will be enough for the majority of your playing.

Example 95A: E Blues Lick 1

Notice the effect of the bends and the shuffle groove, which can be enough to change an otherwise dry sounding scale into a musical statement.

Example 95B: E Blues Lick 2

The combination of hammer-ons and pull-offs give this lick a lot of spice.

Example 95C: E Blues Lick 3

Each slide should be accented "on the beat" to give it more drive.

Example 95D: E Blues Lick 4

Combine the previous licks.

Example 95E: E Blues Lick 5

The next two licks, played in the low register, are in the style of Chicago blues players like Muddy Waters.

Example 95F: E Blues Lick 6

Example 95G: E Blues Lick 7

You can use the combination of low-note and high-note melodies to create a **call-and-response** effect that is often refered to as **question-and-answer phrasing**.

Example 95H: Double-Stop Turnaround

The "double-stop" bend during the A7 lick is a little tricky. You need to keep your first finger on the 1st string while the second finger bends the 2nd string slightly. There's a famous tune that uses this lick in the intro called "That's Alright," and it was written by Muddy Waters' guitar player, Jimmy Rogers.

Example 95I: A Progression Of Licks

At this point, you should be able to see how the E blues scale can fit an E7 chord. When playing through a blues progression, you now have to deal with relating the scale to two other chords; in this case, the A7 and the B7. The beauty of the blues scale is that you do not have to play a different scale for each chord.

FINGERSTYLE BLUES

Fingerpicking is a great way to keep "time" for yourself with bass notes while simultaneously playing the melody notes. When done correctly, it should almost sound as if two people are playing instead of one.

Make sure you practice every pattern very slowly at first, then gradually increase the speed. You should mute the bass notes to contrast the ringing melody notes.

The best way to learn the independence that is necessary for this technique is to start with an even bass pattern and add each melody note one at a time. You will find that the melody notes are either played at the *same time* as a bass note or *in between* the bass notes.

As you are memorizing the patterns, make sure you memorize which notes are played on the beat and which ones are not.

Example 96A

Start with a single-note shuffle in the bass using the open E. Emphasize the down beat, and use the **palm mute** technique by placing the right-hand palm lightly against the strings near the bridge. Do not push so hard that you stop the notes from ringing, just hard enough to get a muffled sound. Later, when you begin adding melody notes to the pattern, the muted bass notes will contrast the ringing melody notes in such a way as to create the illusion that more than one instrument is playing at the same time.

Example 96B

Now add a melody note on the first and third beats of each measure. You will have to strike the first string with your middle finger while striking the bass note with the pick. This movement is often described as a **pinch**. Be careful not to break tempo, and remember to maintain the palm mute.

Example 96C

Play a melody note on every beat. This pattern alternates between pinching the bass and melody notes on every beat and playing a bass note in between each pinch.

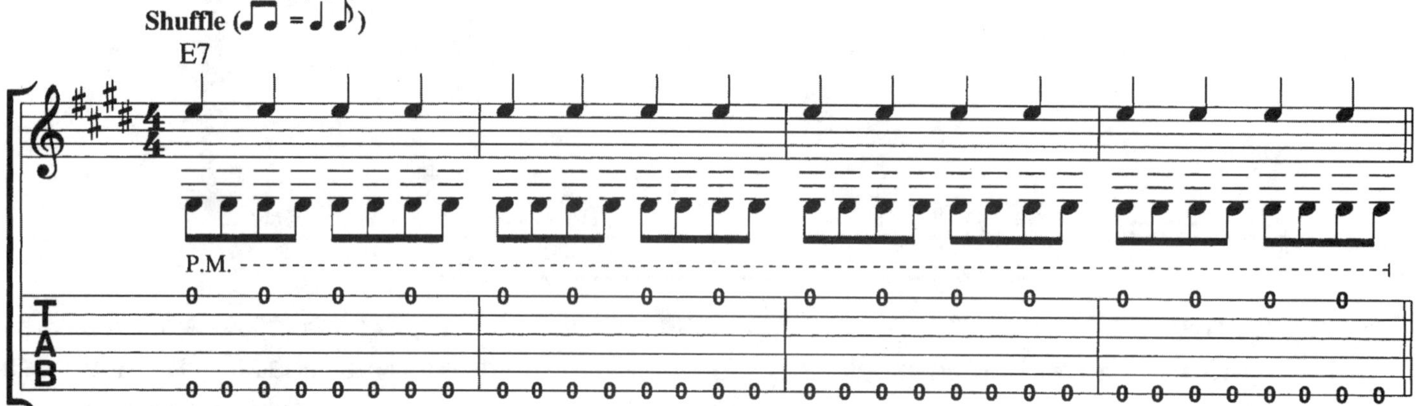

Example 96D

Now play the melody in sync with the bass notes by playing the exact same shuffle in the melody that is in the bass. This is a great exercise of pinches throughout.

Example 96E

Play the melody note on the opposite part of the beat as the bass notes. When played correctly, placing a melody note in between the uneven bass notes will sound like a solid triplet.

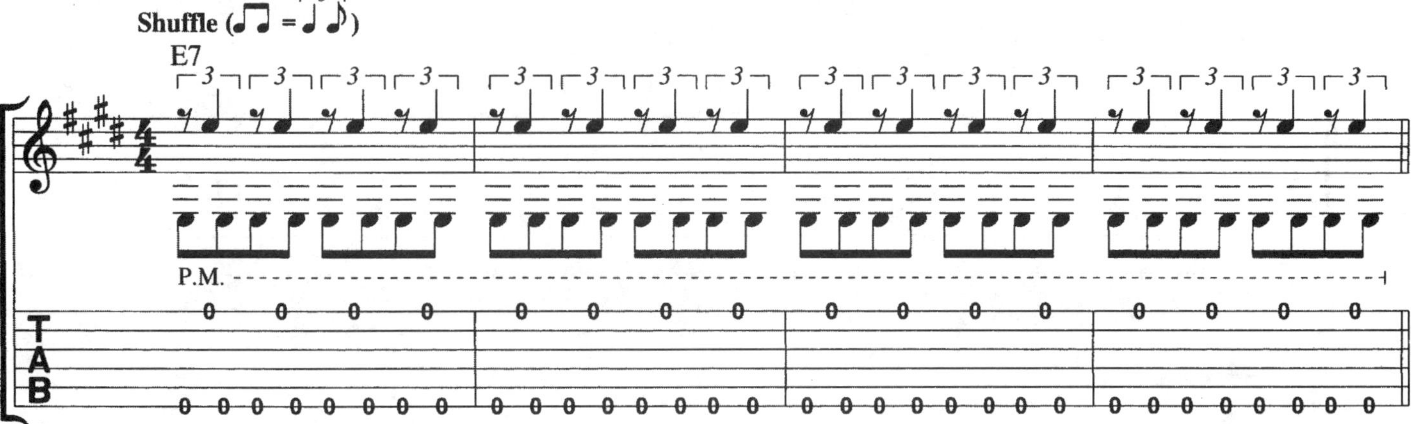

Example 96F

Alternate between placing melody notes *on the beat* with the bass notes and *off the beat* in between the bass notes.

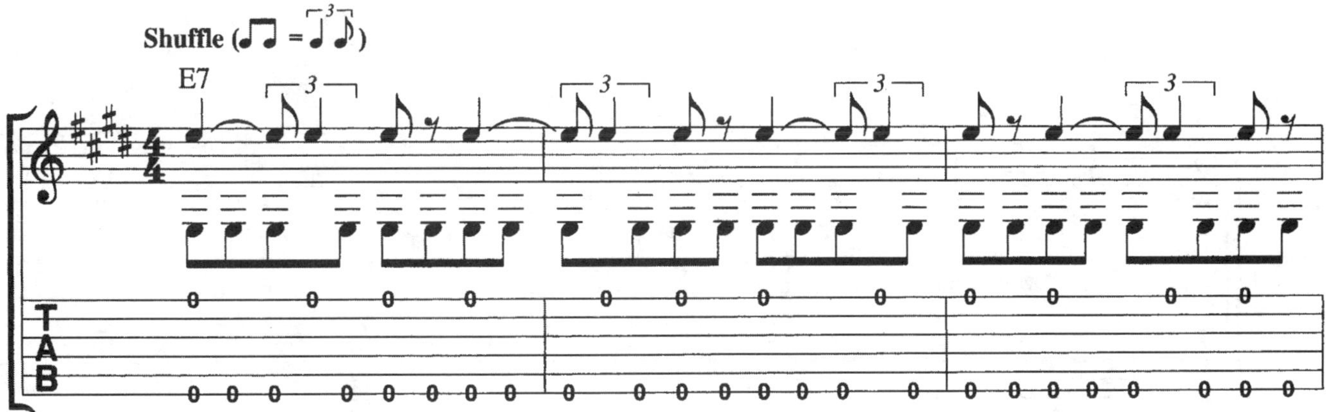

Example 96G

Now let's replace the one-note pattern in the melody with an E blues scale in open position.

Shuffle (♫ = ♩♪)

E7

Example 96H

Gradually incorporate the E blues licks you just learned.

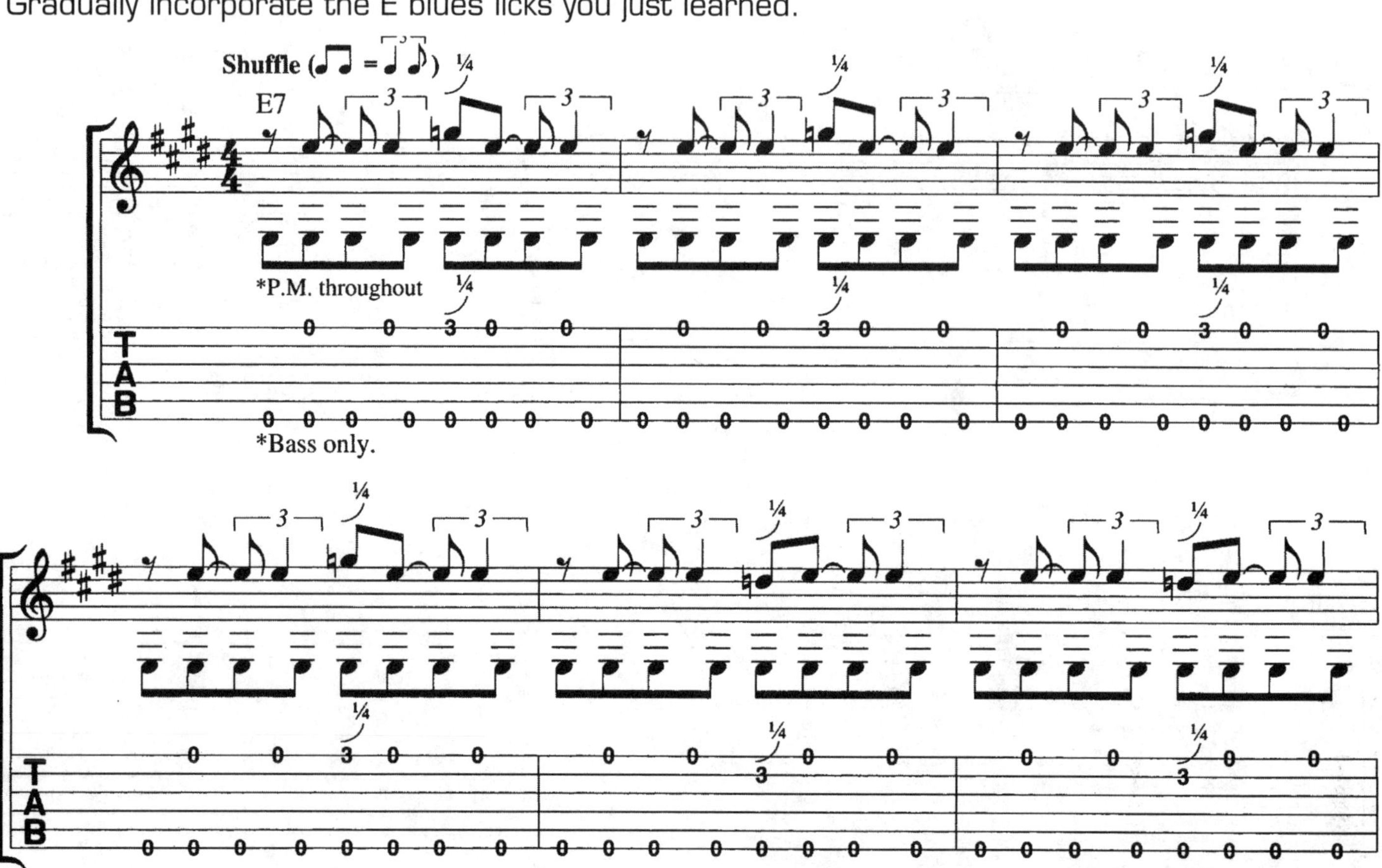

Example 96I: Muddy Waters Progression

A great way to sum it all up is with this "Muddy Waters-style" progression. While Muddy Waters didn't invent this style, he did popularize it. Make sure you practice this progression very slowly to memorize which melody notes are on the beat and which notes are in between.

E7

B7 A7

E7

Example 96J: Muddy Waters Turnaround

All this progression needs is a great turnaround like this:

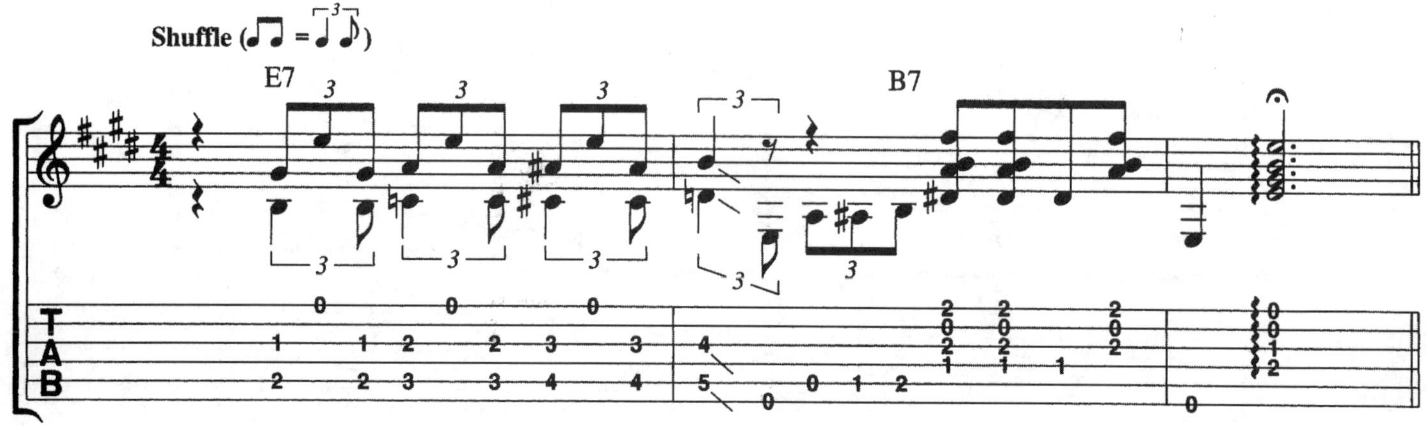

PUTTING IT ALL TOGETHER

It is important to finish by using progressions to apply the ideas and concepts that have been discussed throughout this book: the shuffle groove, bass/chord patterns, embellishments, bass-lines, accents, muting and turnarounds.

Example 97

This progression is a quick-change blues in E. Fullness will come from emphasizing the bass-line. Remember to hold the chord shapes as you play the melody. Do not try to finger the melody-line one note at a time. Notice the variations between the two choruses (repeats). These variations are improvisations that will keep the progressions interesting.

A7
E7
B7
E7
A7
E7
A7
E7
B7
A7
E7
rit.

Example 98

This example is a lick-oriented blues in A. It starts off with a two bar intro that is actually a turnaround. It is very common to use a turnaround for the intro since the turnaround's main function is to lead to the beginning of the progression.

The shuffle feel in this example should be very strong. At first it will be a little tricky to maintain the shuffle, since there is a variety of rhythms found in both the bass and melody. Make sure you play the example slowly at first. Do not increase the speed until you are certain that you are playing the correct rhythm for each note.

The intro lick in the first measure is based on the same blues scale fingering covered earlier, except it is played in the key of A. In the key of E, open strings are an important part of the fingering. In the key of A, your first finger has to play all the notes that you originally learned to play as open:

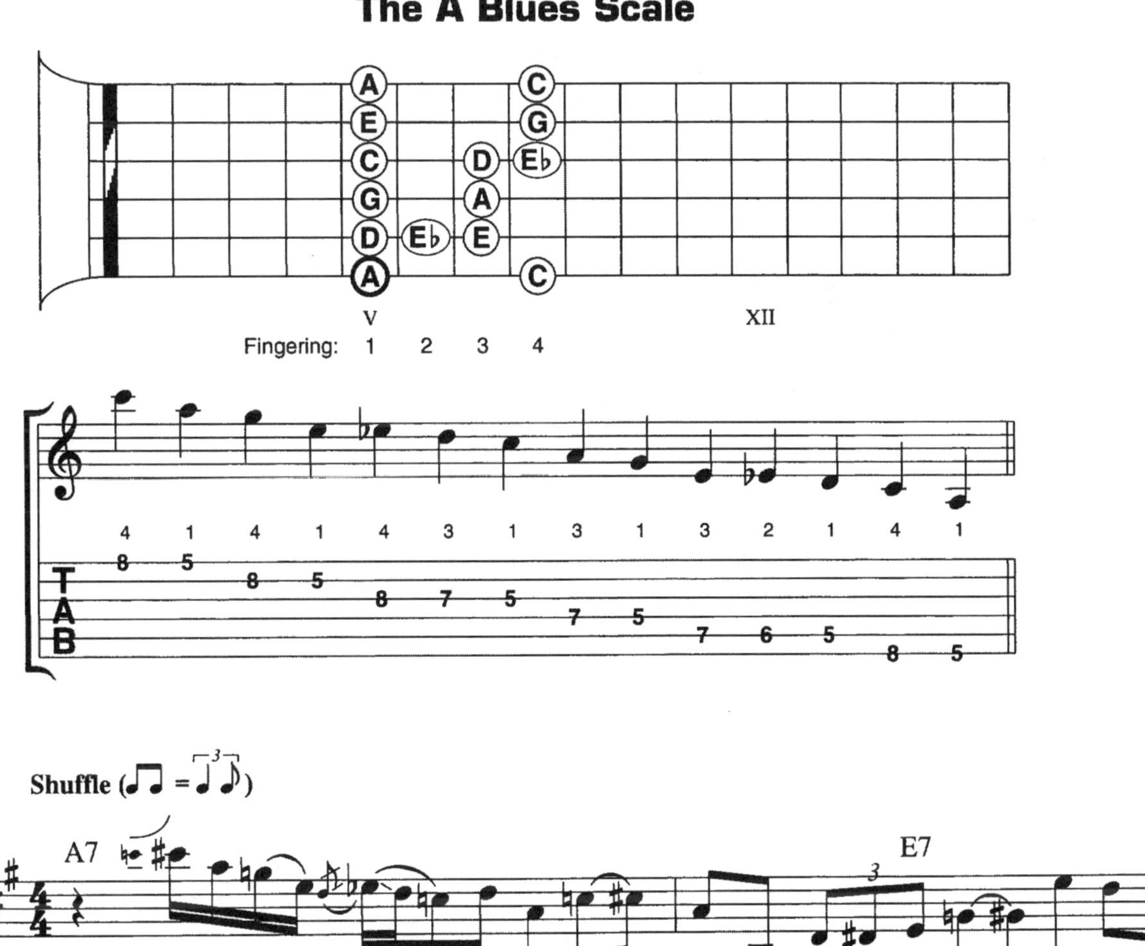

Shuffle

A7

E7

A7
D/F♯
A7
3
T
A
B
D/F♯
A7
E7
D/F♯
A7

Example 99

This entire example can be played using only a flat pick. This progression would be a great exercise to experiment with different right-hand techniques.

The first three measures of the intro start with the I7 chord and shifts down chromatically (in 1/2 steps) until the chords resolve on the next inversion, down in the open position. Measures 4 and 5 are a turnaround in E.

It is important to hold the necessary chord shapes and maintain a strong shuffle groove throughout the progression.

E7
B7
3
¼

A7
E7
E♭7
D7
E7
rit.

FINGERSTYLE GUITAR

ARPEGGIOS

Arpeggios are a useful tool for accompanying yourself or a singer. They can add a pianistic quality to your accompaniment as opposed to the more typical sound of strumming chords. In addition, employing open strings allows the frethand to exploit the full range of the guitar. When playing the arpeggio examples, allow all the notes to ring until you change to the next chord.

As you progress through the opening examples, keep in mind that the lowest note of each chord is the **root,** which is the note from which the chord derives its name. Any A, B, and C chords (major or minor) that you encounter will have their roots on the 5th string. G and E chords will have roots on the 6th string. Finally, D and F chords will have roots on the 4th string. Once you have mastered Examples 1–5, try to apply what you have learned to new songs or perhaps to songs you currently strum.

Example 100

This picking pattern involves a D chord on the top four strings. The thumb (t) picks the 4th string, the index finger (i) picks the 3rd string, the middle finger (m) picks the 2nd string, and the ring finger (r) picks the 1st string. You should adhere to these finger assignments in order to achieve good technique and stamina.

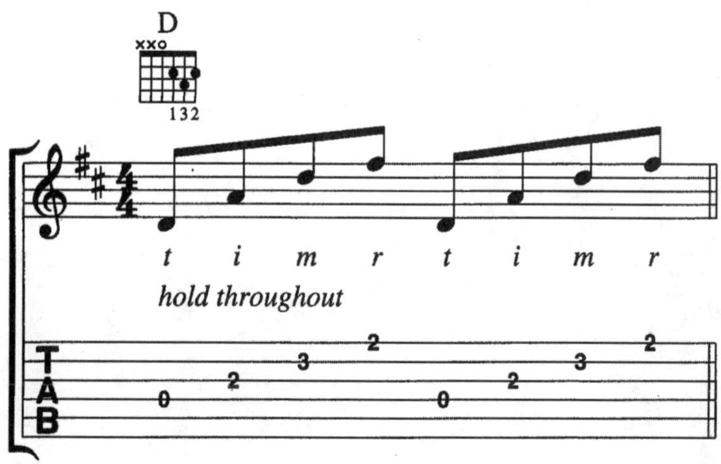

Example 101

This next picking pattern introduces the A and G chords. The finger assignments are similar, except these two chords have skipped (unplayed) strings.

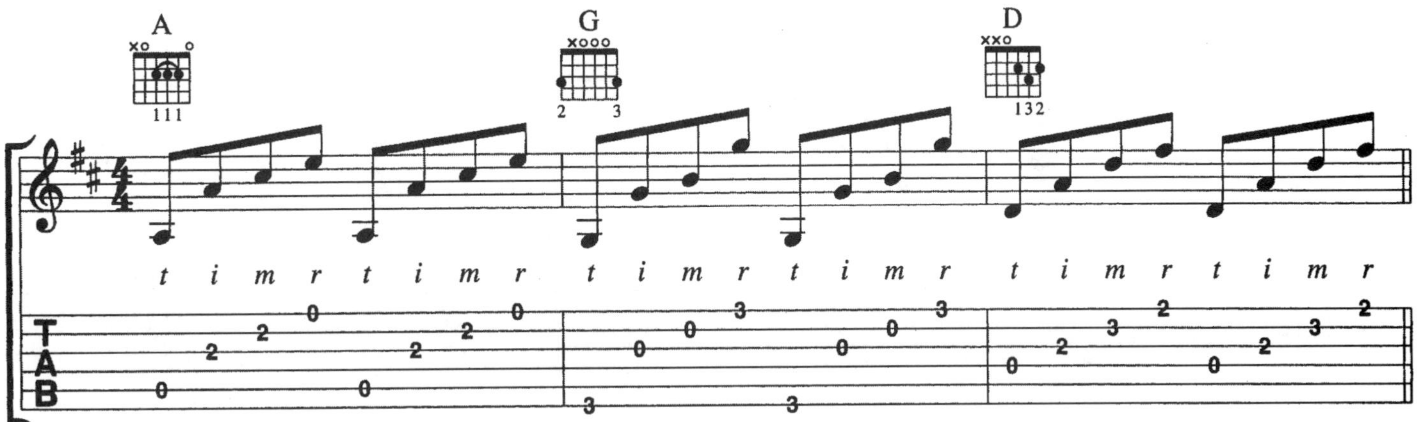

Example 102

Now we will connect all three chords together with continuous picking, beginning with the D. The arpeggio pattern is played two times for each chord. Remember, the root of each chord is on a different string, so make sure your thumb plays the correct strings. These chords all belong to the key of D.

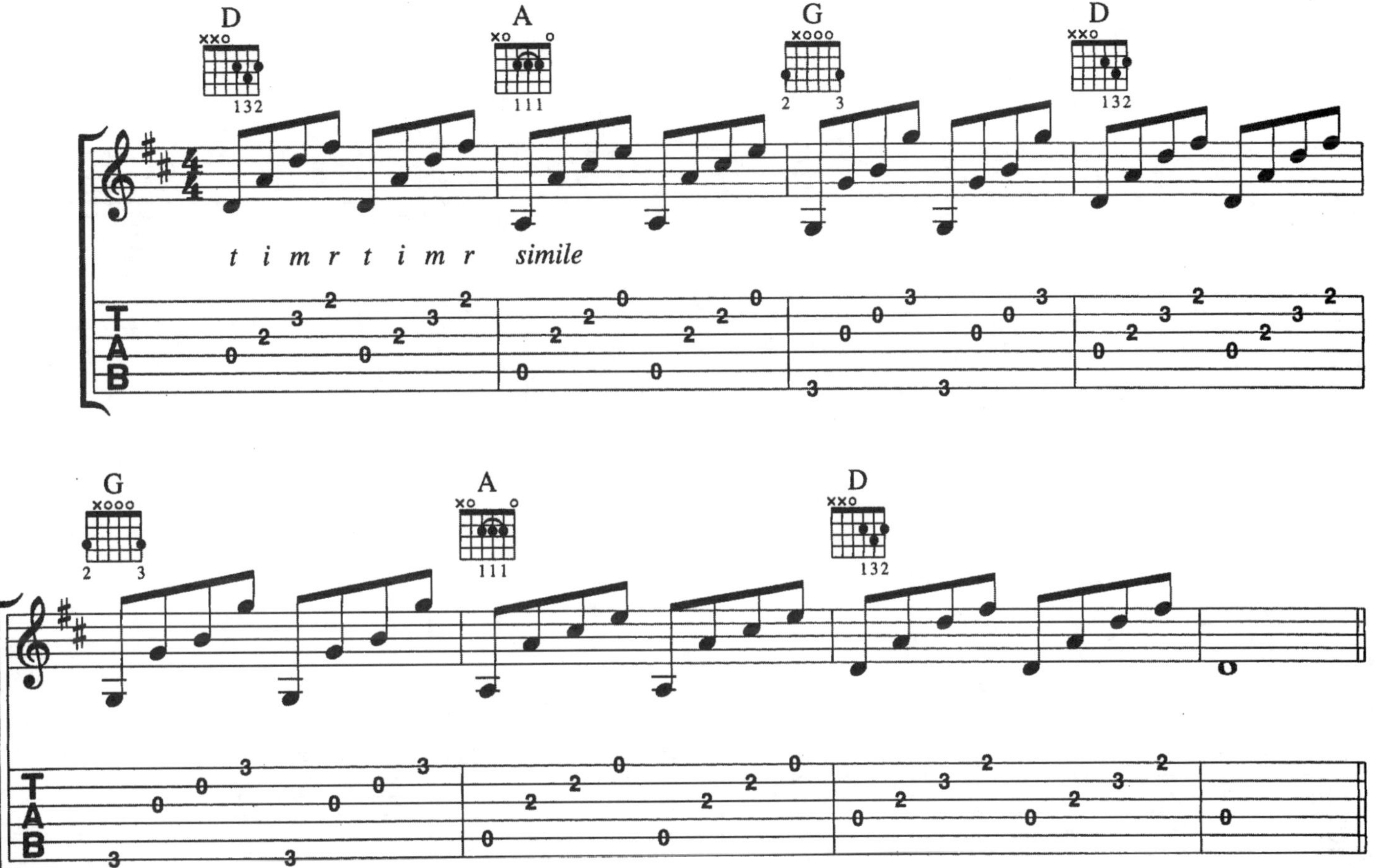

Example 103

This next example is in the key of C. We will apply the same picking patterns to the chords C, F (or Fmaj7), G7, Am, and Dm. Again, the thumb/bass-note shifts between the 6th, 5th, and 4th strings.

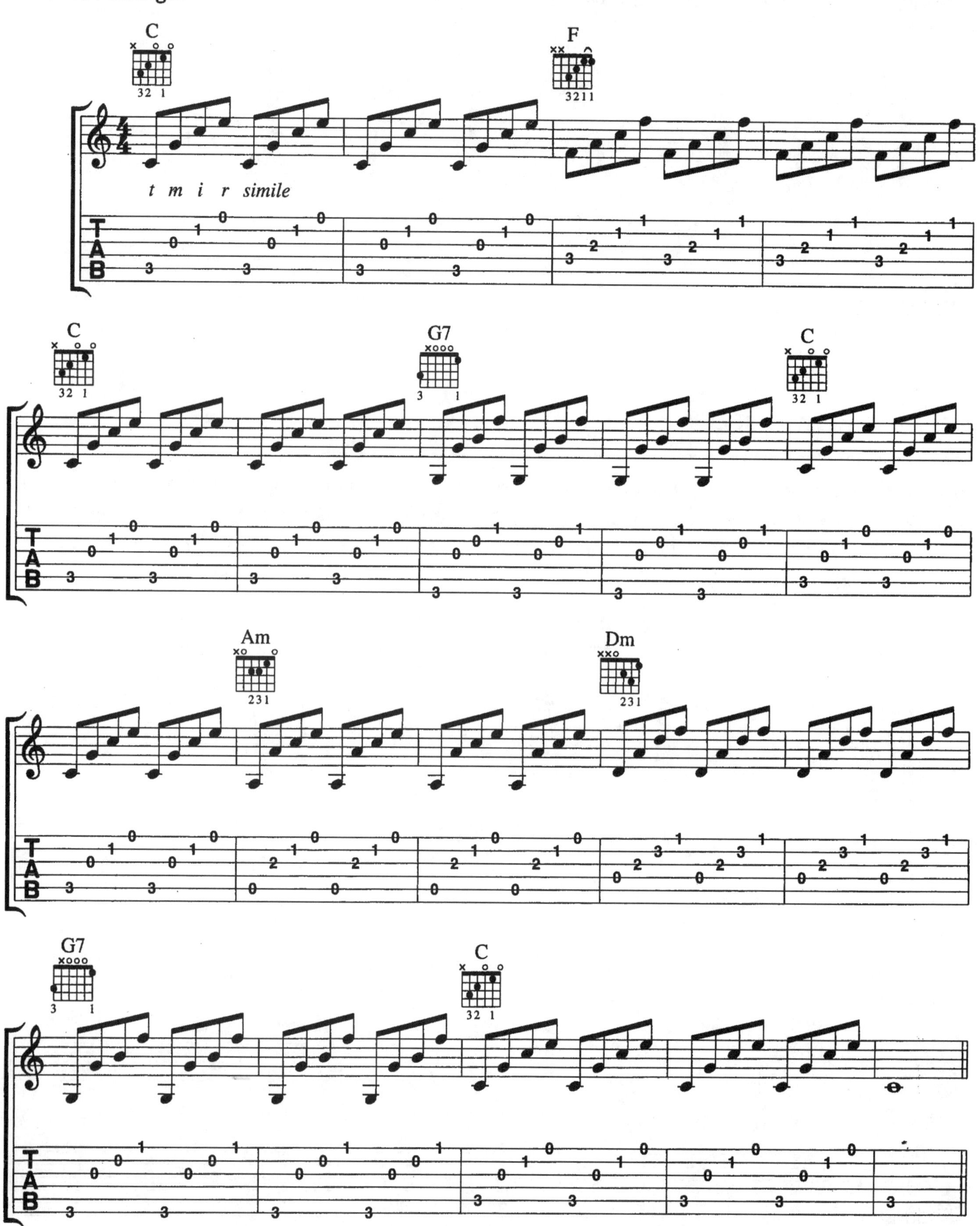

Example 104

Let's review two more chords: Em and B7. The Am chord we will borrow from the last example. Like the G and G7 chords, the Em skips both the 5th and 4th strings – with the thumb now playing an open E on the 6th string.

RIGHT-HAND POSITION

Follow these steps for good right-hand position:

1. Take your right hand and put your elbow on the guitar's side.
2. Aim your forearm at the ceiling.
3. Let your hand flop over and allow it to completely relax.
4. Straighten your wrist so that your hand is also pointing at the ceiling.
5. Maintain relaxation in your hand and fingers.
6. Bring your hand down to the strings with the crease of your elbow on the edge of the guitar, allowing it to support your arm.
7. Place your thumb on the 4th string and your index, middle, and ring fingers on the 3rd, 2nd, and 1st strings respectively.
8. The skin of your thumb and pick-hand fingers gives you richness of tone while the nails add definition and "bite."

CANYON CANON

This tune employs the thumb-index-middle-ring arpeggio throughout. The chords are mostly double-stops, which means that you usually are fingering only two notes at a time. These fretted notes are combined with open strings, providing lush chords without taxing your fretting hand

Example 105

This example introduces the E chord, combined with the A and D chords. This gives us a "I, IV, V" progression (the 1st, 4th, and 5th chords in the key).

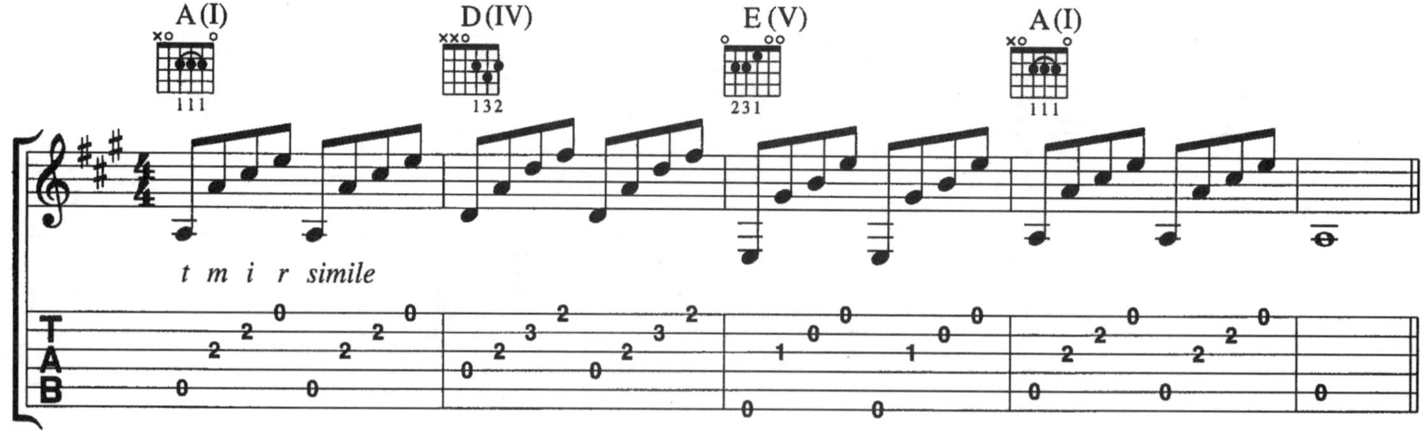

Example 106

All of the sections in this piece involve arpeggios on the four treble strings. Section 1 uses two fret-hand "shapes" combined with the top two strings played open.

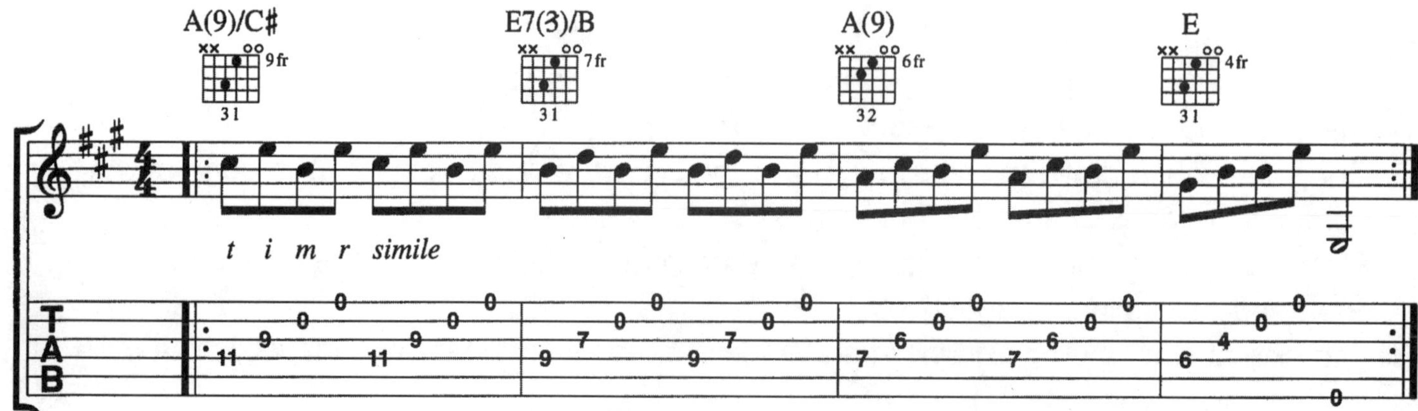

Example 107

Section 2 of the song begins with three chords using the open D (4th string) as a constant bass note played by the thumb, and the open E (1st string) as a *pedal tone* through the chord shapes. (A pedal tone is a note played through a series of chords.) For the final A(9) chord, the thumb still plays the open 5th string bass-note, while the index, middle, and ring fingers all shift down one string each toward the bass strings.

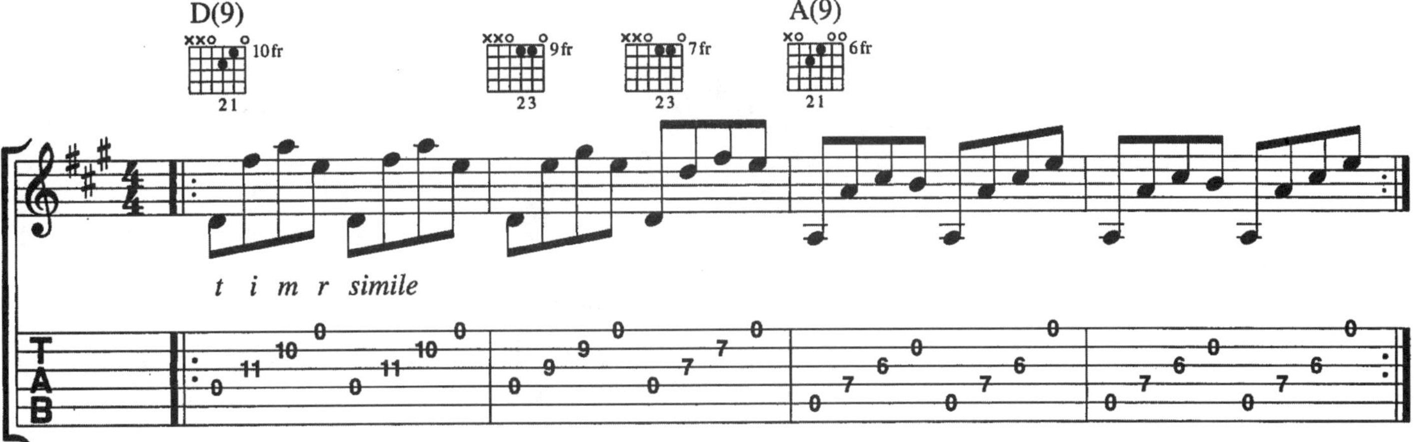

Example 108

For Section 3, your thumb has to pick the 6th string for the E chord, and the 5th string for the A chord.

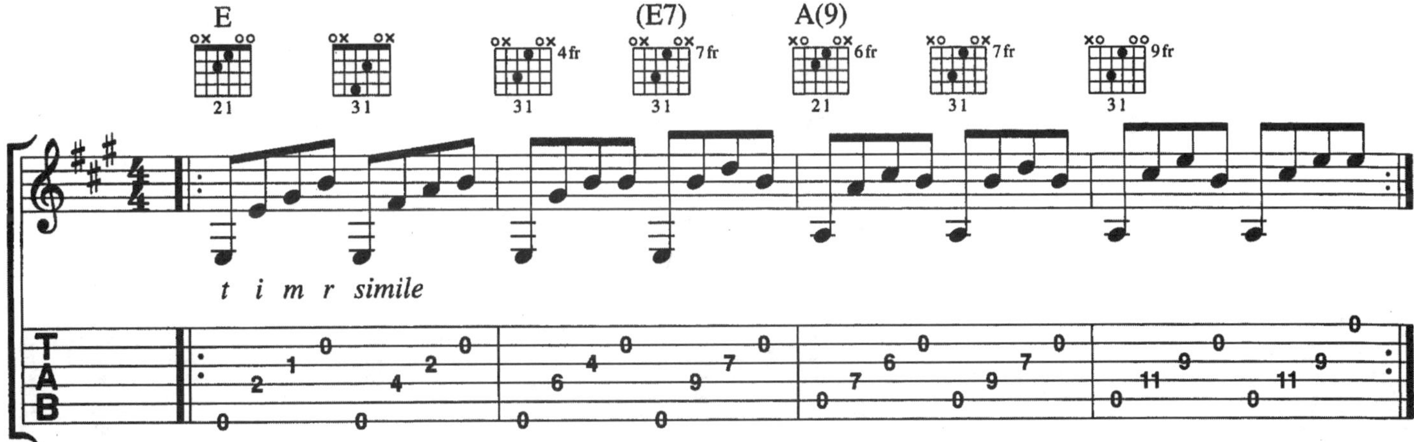

Example 109

The next section begins with a simple two-finger chord at the 10th fret [Dm(9)], slight alterations to the shape of that chord produce the Dm6 and the Dm7 chords that follow.

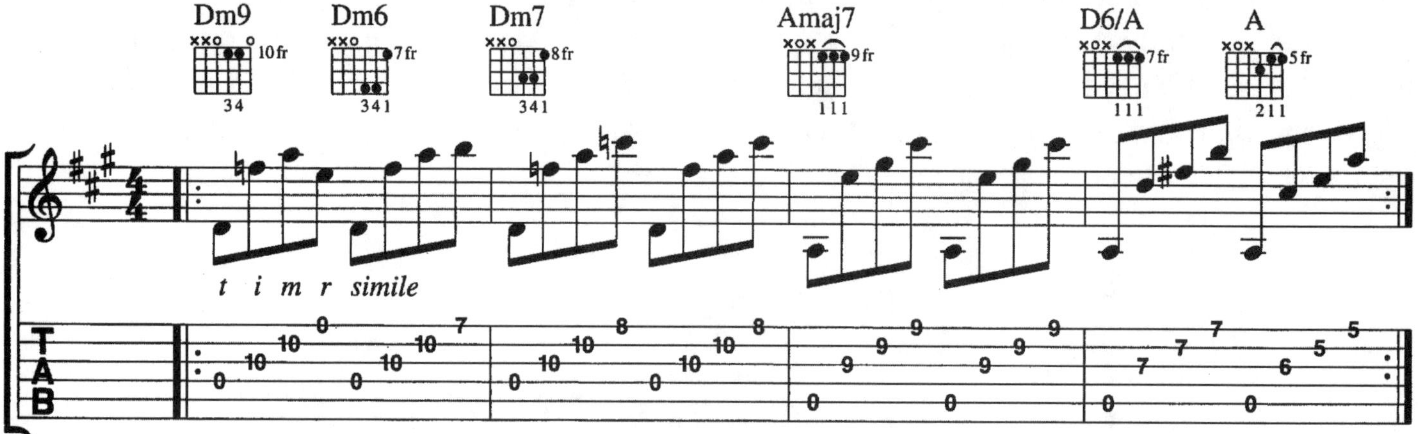

Example 110

The final section employs movable chord shapes that are related to simple, open-position chord fingerings. For instance, the first chord is like an open D shape, only it is moved up two frets. Playing the 6th string open E bass-note as the root makes it an E chord. Look for other familiar shapes in this section to identify with.

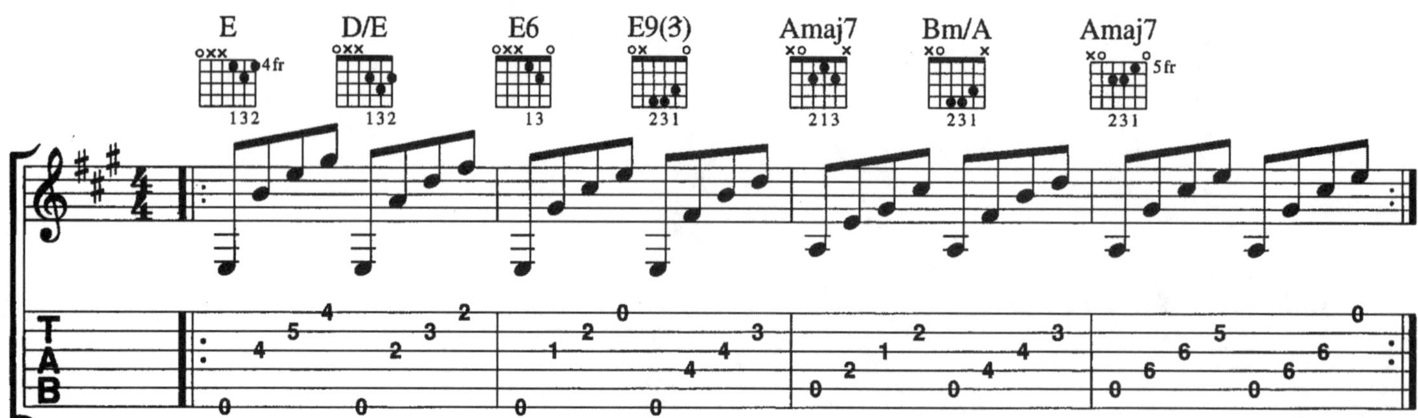

CANYON CANON

MARK HANSON

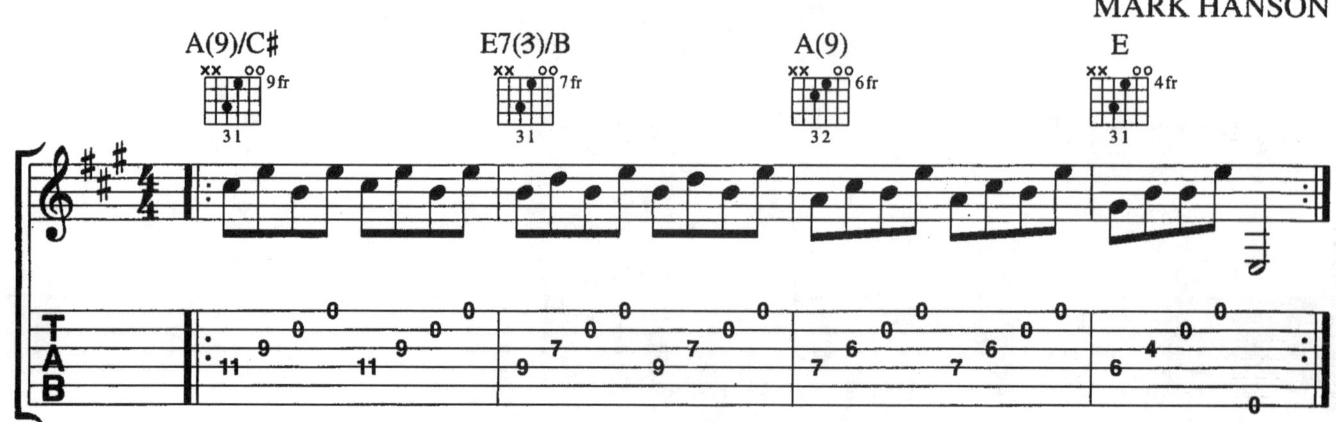

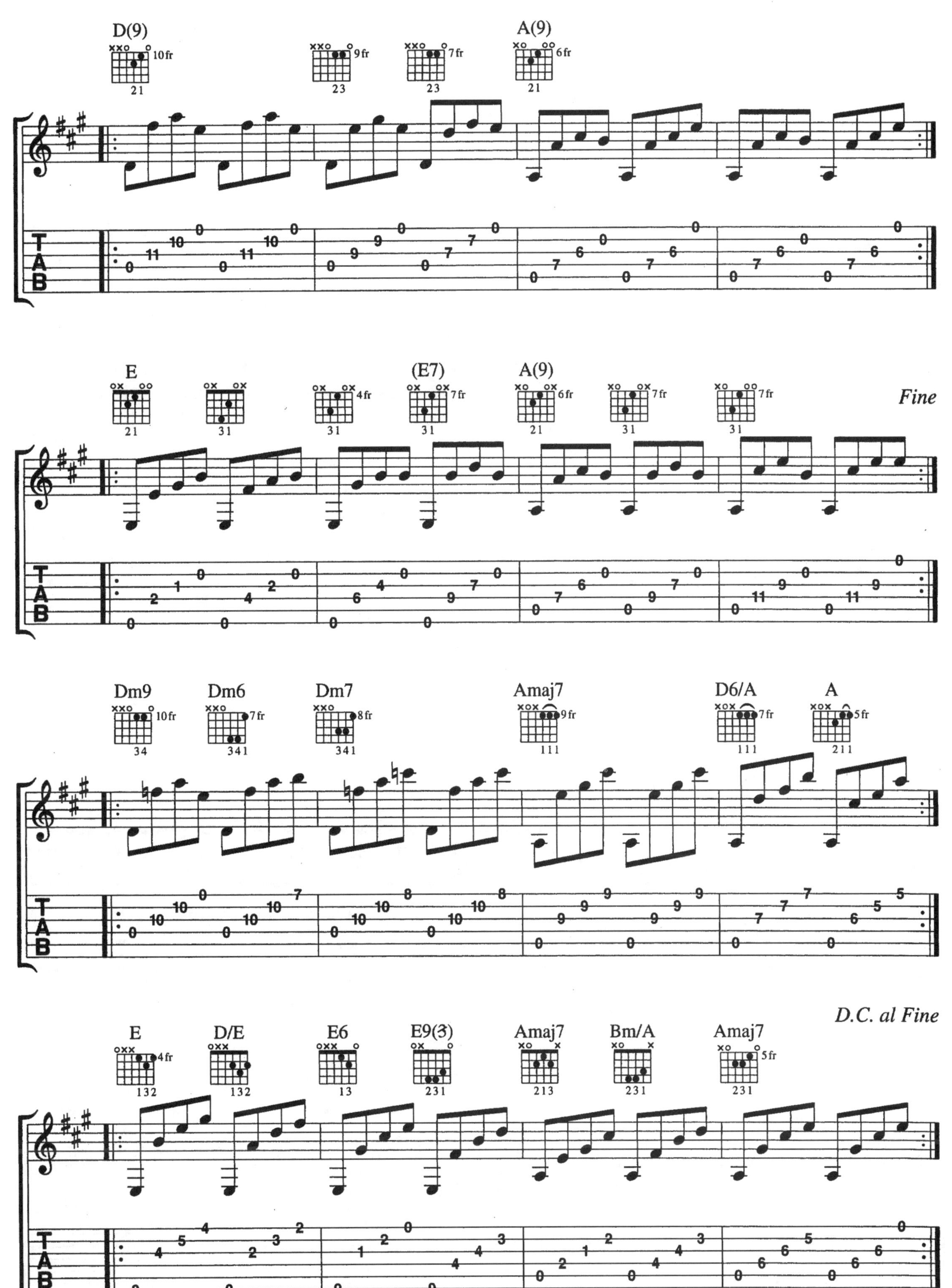

D(9)
A(9)
E
(E7)
A(9)
Fine
Dm9
Dm6
Dm7
Amaj7
D6/A
A
E
D/E
E6
E9(3)
Amaj7
Bm/A
Amaj7
D.C. al Fine

FINGERPICKING IN 3/4 TIME

So far we have been dealing exclusively with the 4/4 time signature which gives an "even" feeling of four beats per bar. Now it is time to learn how to fingerpick songs with three beats per bar.

Example 111

To produce 3/4 time we need to add two more notes to the basic pattern we have been working with. After playing the four notes of the pattern (t i m r), simply pick the middle- and index-finger notes again. These two notes add an extra beat to the measure, which produces 3/4 time. The pattern is now: t i m r m i. Applied to D, G, and A chords, it sounds like this:

Example 112

For experimental fun, let's apply this new "t i m r m i" pattern to Section 1 of *Canyon Canon.* You will immediately notice how this alters the "feel" of the piece. Try completing the entire song this way.

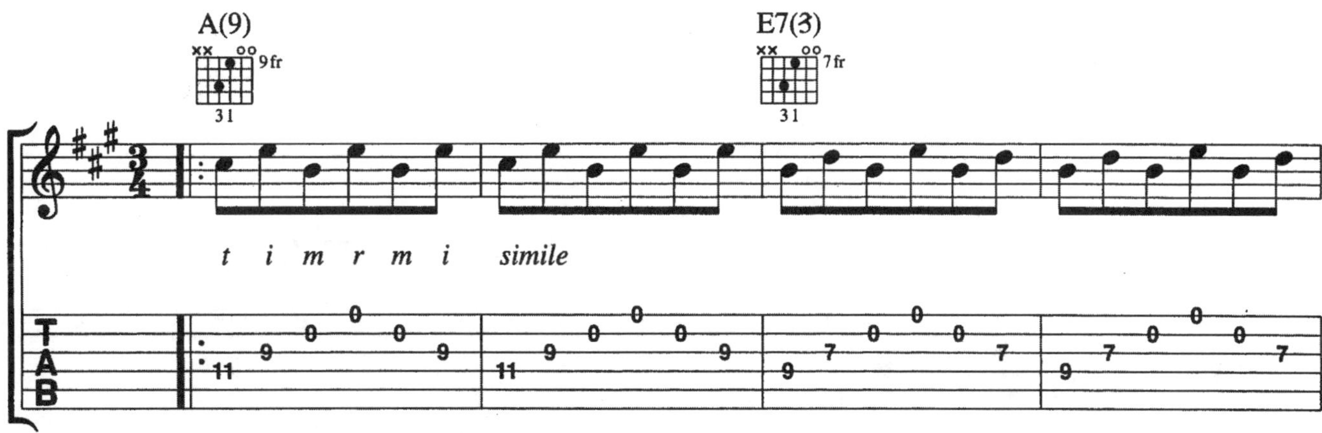

Example 113

For variety, we are going to learn another pattern for 3/4 time. It involves playing two strings simultaneously. Applied to D, G, and A chords, it works like this:

WINDOWS

Like ***Canyon Canon***, Windows was composed as an "etude," a piece that practices a particular technique. In this case, the technique is the 3/4 fingerpicking pattern from Example 113.

The title for this piece can be interpreted a number of ways. But the real reason it was chosen was that the recording session for this book took place in Seattle — home of computer software giant Microsoft.

Example 114

This section opens with a typical D chord at the 2nd fret. To understand the next chord, turn the D shape you are holding into a Dm by dropping the 1st string note (F♯) down one fret to F. Slide this shape up two frets and you will arrive at Em/D. Then slide the shape up two more frets to Dmaj7, after which you return to the D chord you began with.

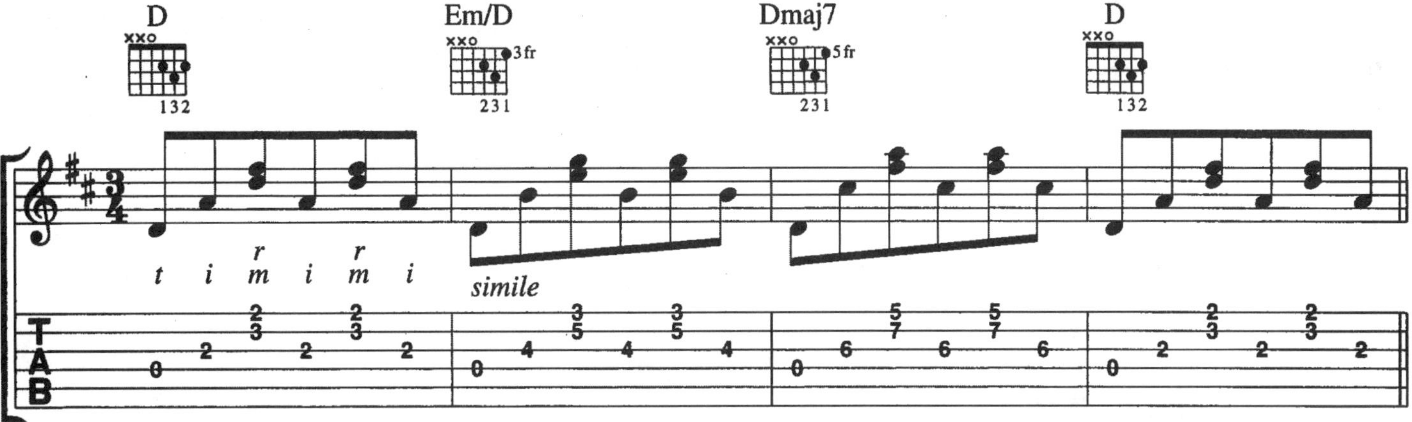

Example 115

The next chord is a G(9) (also known as a "Gadd9"). It has a 6th-string root played by the thumb. This chord leads to a D with the 3rd in the bass (D/F♯). It may be convenient to play the 6th-string F♯ with the thumb of your fret-hand. This section closes with Em and A7 and repeats to the top.

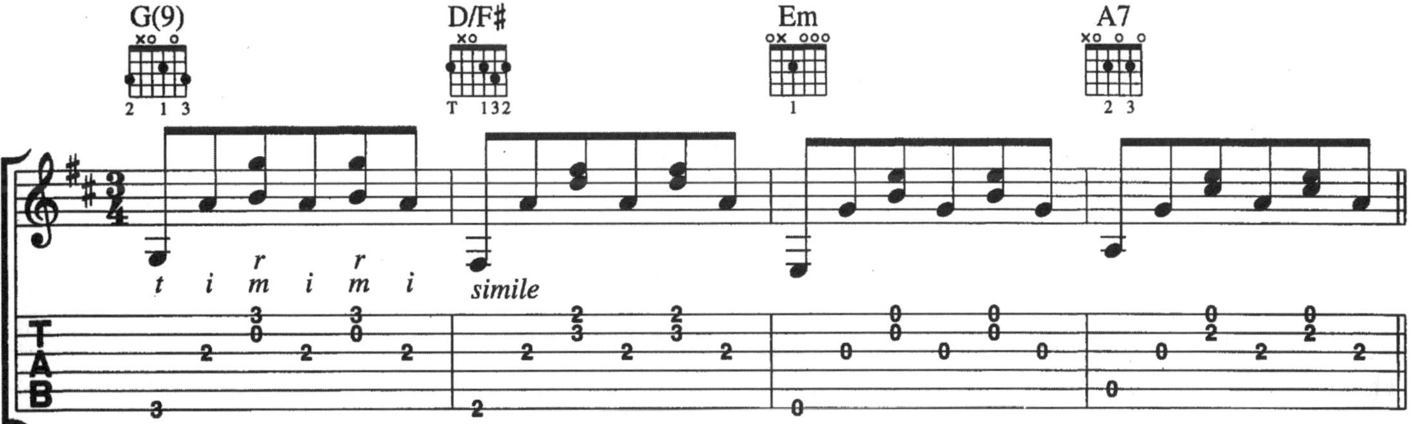

Example 116

Section 2 is in the key of C. It begins with a C(9) chord, which is like the usual C, except your little finger plays a D (the 9th) on the 2nd string, 3rd fret. The next chord is an inversion of G6, with the 3rd (B) in the bass. Last we have Am7 to D7, ending with a standard G chord.

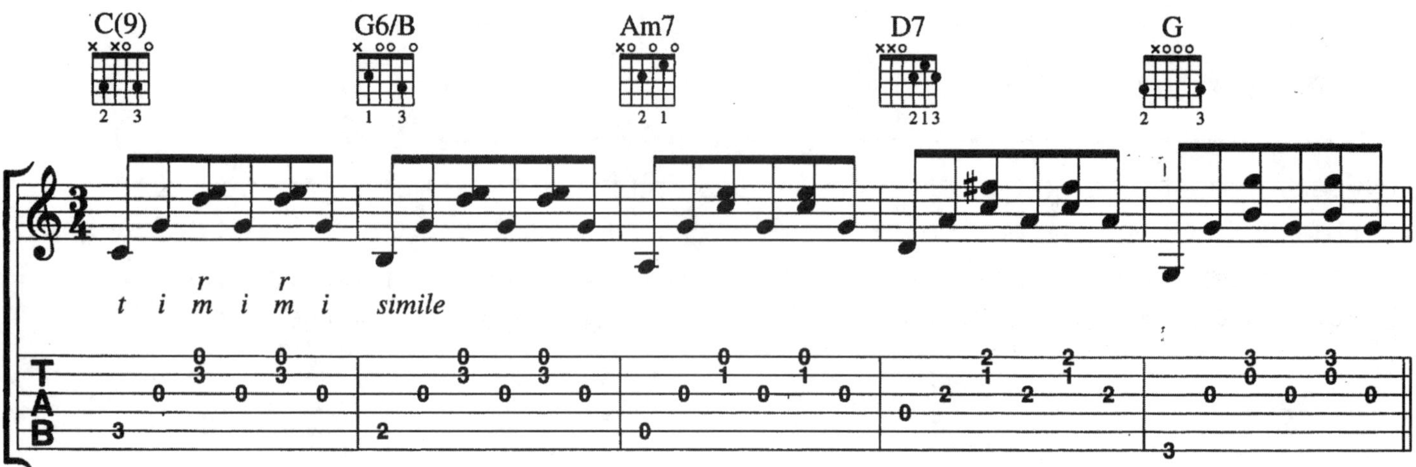

Example 117

The next chord change is from D to Em. This Em uses only the four treble strings. It is followed by Em/D (the open top-four strings). This chord is used in the 1st ending to connect back to the C(9) that began the section. The 2nd ending serves the purpose of connecting the music back to the top of the piece with the movement of A7sus to A7.

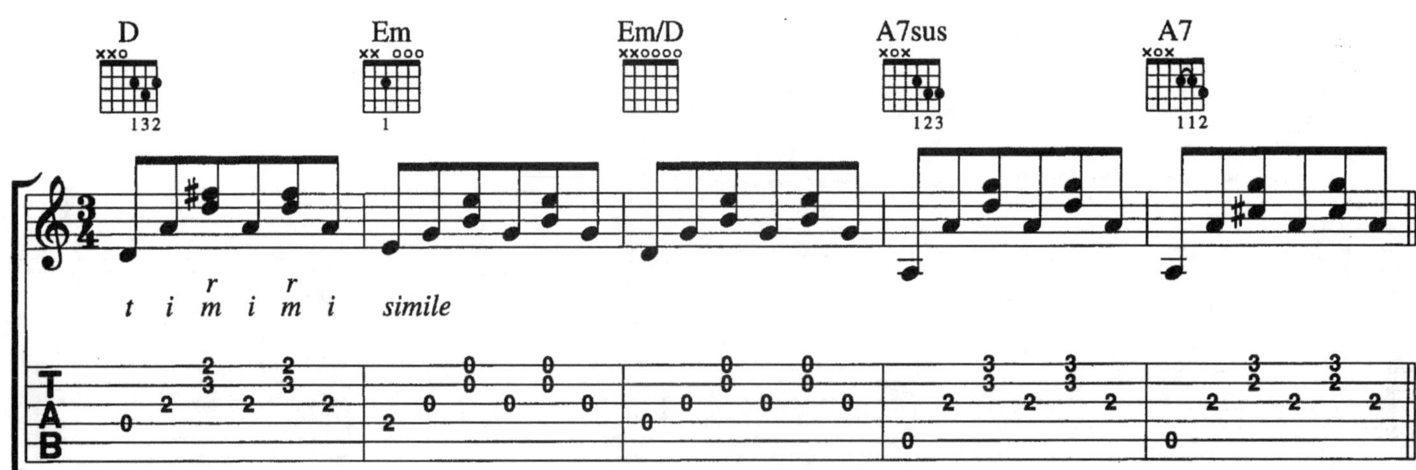

WINDOWS

D
Em/D
3fr
Dmaj7
5fr
D
G(9)
3/4
TAB
D/F♯
To Coda
Em
A7
C(9)
G6/B
Am7
D7
G
1.
D
Em
Em/D
2.
Em
A7sus
A7
D.C. al Coda
Coda
D

THE TRAVIS PICKING PATTERN
(Alternating Bass)

The Travis picking pattern is extremely popular and useful since it's applicable to virtually any musical style, including folk, rock, pop, blues, country, and ragtime. Travis picking (or alternating bass) can be used for everything from a basic accompaniment pattern to virtuoso guitar showcasing. When Travis picking, the thumb, imitating the left hand of a pianist, constantly alternates between the lowest bass-note of a chord (usually the root) and another chord tone (usually the 5th), creating the "oom-pa" feel. Once you've got your thumb going, your fingers are then free to play both "on the beat" with your thumb or off the beat — in between thumb strokes.

Example 118

Now let's apply a simple Travis picking pattern to a C chord. Notice that your thumb plays on each beat and your fingers play in-between the beats. (Once you become comfortable with this basic pattern you'll find there are hundreds of possible variations.)

Example 119

Now let's apply the same principle to the D and G chords. Depending on which chord you are playing, the fingers play different strings, but the Travis pattern just keeps rolling on.

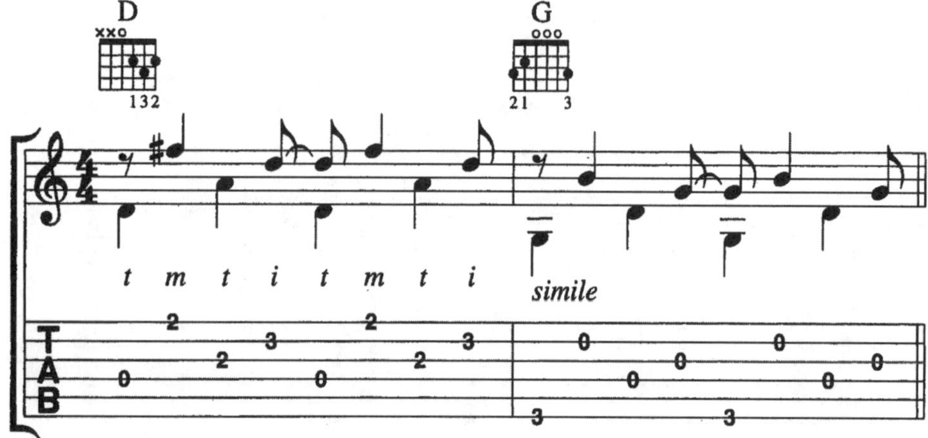

Example 120

In this exercise the Travis pattern is applied to three additional chords — Am, D7, and Em, at a faster tempo.

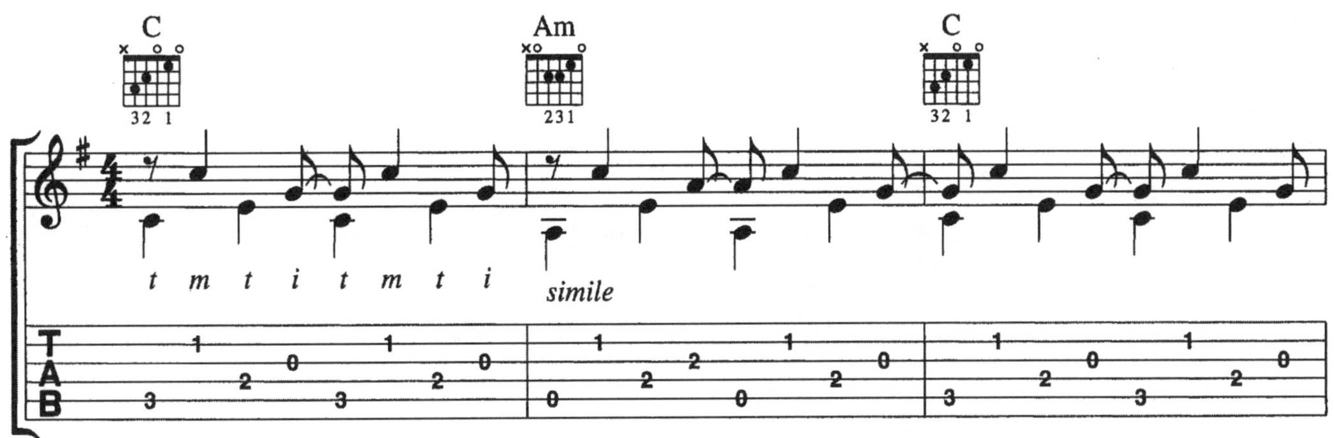

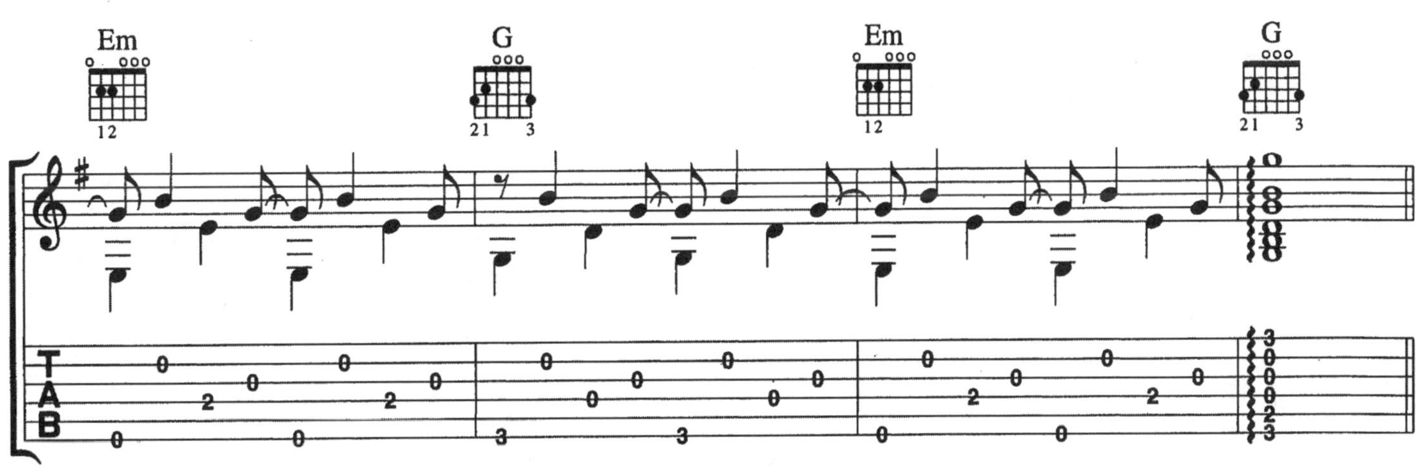

WHEELS

Wheels is a tune that uses a pair of chords per phrase with the Travis pattern applied throughout. You'll notice that the chords in this song are all "extended," containing interesting sounding notes like 9ths and major 7ths. Even though these chords are more "complex" sounding than your basic 1st position chords, they are all very easy to play. Let's take one pair of chords at a time and check out the changes in fingerings for the picking hand. Try to make the notes of the pattern flow with a steady, continuous rhythm, like a steadily turning wheel.

Example 121

The first two chords are Em9 and Am9. In Em9, the thumb/bass part alternates between the root and the 9th of the chord (E to F♯), an unusual but effective juxtaposition of bass notes. The Am9 alternates between the root and the 7th (A to G).

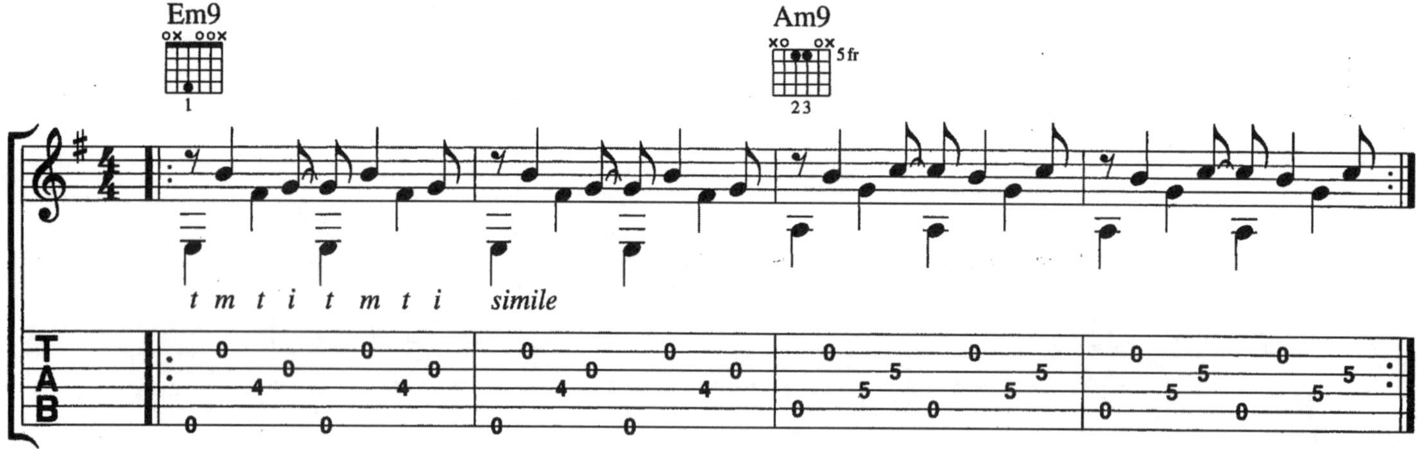

Example 122

The most important thing about the next pair of chords [D(9) and Am] is that they share the same "shape," only on different strings.

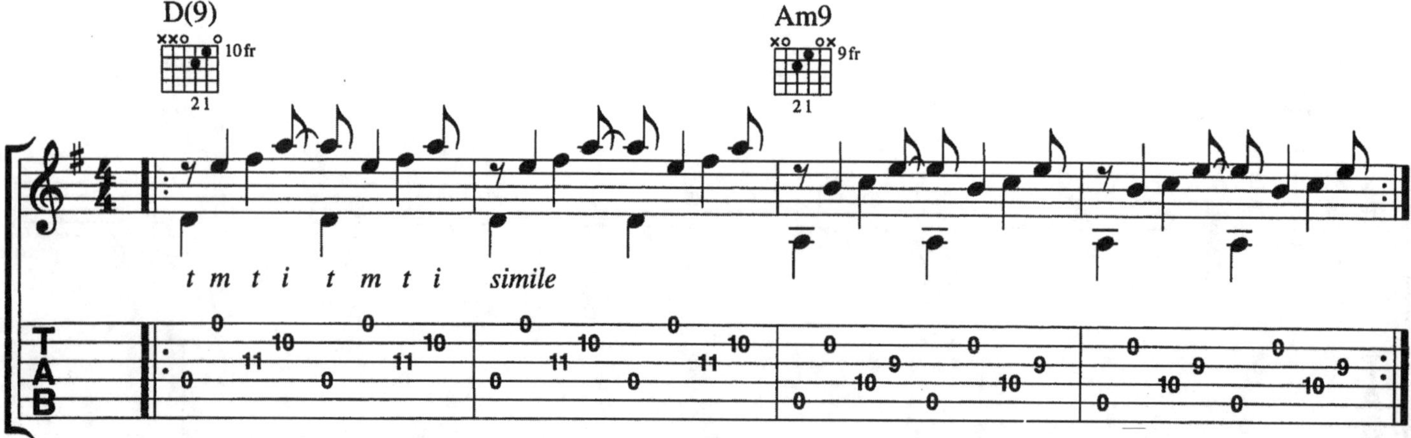

Example 123

You may remember G(9) from an earlier example. This is a 6th-string-root chord moving to a 4th-string-root Dm9 chord. The Dm9 feels like a regular first position D moved up to the 5th fret with your 2nd finger lifted off the 1st string.

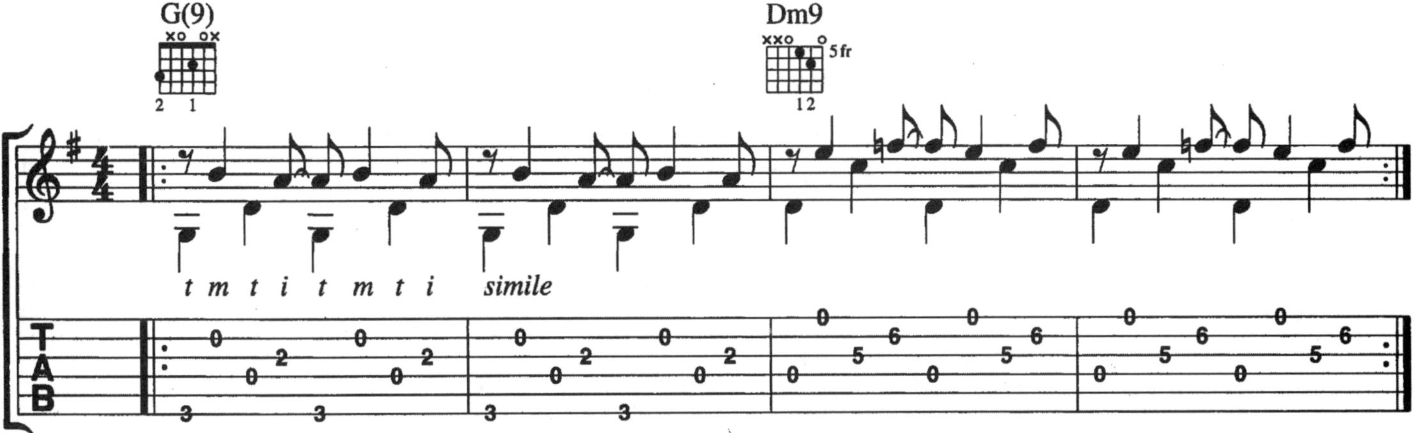

Example 124

The last segment to learn involves Cmaj7, Bm7, and a "turnaround chord" of B7. The B7 is the last chord of the piece; it leads back to Em9 at the top.

WHEELS

Em9
Am9
5 fr
To Coda
D(9)
10 fr
Am9
9 fr
G(9)
Dm9
5 fr
Cmaj7
Bm7
1.
2.
D.C. al Coda
B7
Coda
G(9)
T
A
B

OTHER ALTERNATING BASS PATTERNS

Now we'll look at the other Travis type patterns that involve two bass-notes in your fret hand (i.e. C and G for a C chord), as well as new alternating bass-note possibilities for chords you already know. Plus, we'll look at simultaneously picked bass-notes and chords, referred to as "pinched" throughout.

Example 125

First, check out the common C chord with the thumb alternating between the 5th and 4th strings.

Example 126

For the D chord, the thumb bass-notes alternate between the 4th and 3rd strings.

Example 127

With the G chord, the thumb skips the 5th string, alternating between the 6th and 4th strings.

Example 128

Now it is time to add the pick-hand fingers. While alternating bass-notes will always fall on the beats, the finger notes can fall on or off the beats. For now, let's practice picking different notes of the C chord on the beat with the alternating-bass pattern we established already. First we'll add the 2nd string C note with the middle finger. Next will be the 3rd string G with the index finger. Last, add the 1st string E note, picked by the ring finger.

Example 129

Here we will add another pair of simultaneously picked notes. The index finger picks the 3rd string G note along with the C bass-note. The middle finger picks the 2nd string C along with the E bass.

Example 130

Another possiblility is to use the middle and ring fingers picking the 2nd and 1st strings (C and E) along with the C and E thumb notes.

Example 131

This example will use the last three pinching combinations together in a pattern that goes i m r m. Each note picked is accompanied by a thumb note, C or E.

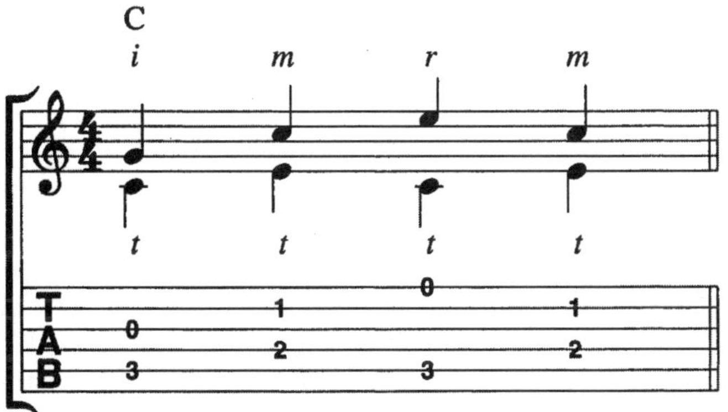

Example 132

Now a variation on the last pattern, picked as follows: r m i m.

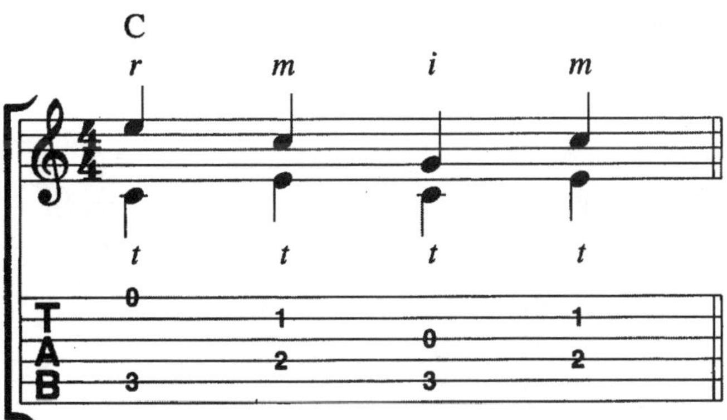

FOUR PER BAR

Four Per Bar consists only of pinches and stand-alone bass notes. The melodic phrases have identical rhythms, and nearly identical picking patterns. Once you have learned to pick the first melodic phrase, the others will be easy since your fingers will pick the same strings in almost the exact same order.

Example 133

The D7 needed for *Four Per Bar* has the 3rd of the chord (F#) picked by the thumb in the bass. You will need to alternate the bass notes between the 6th string (F#) and the 4th string (D). The pinching sequence is i m r m m i, ending on a G chord.

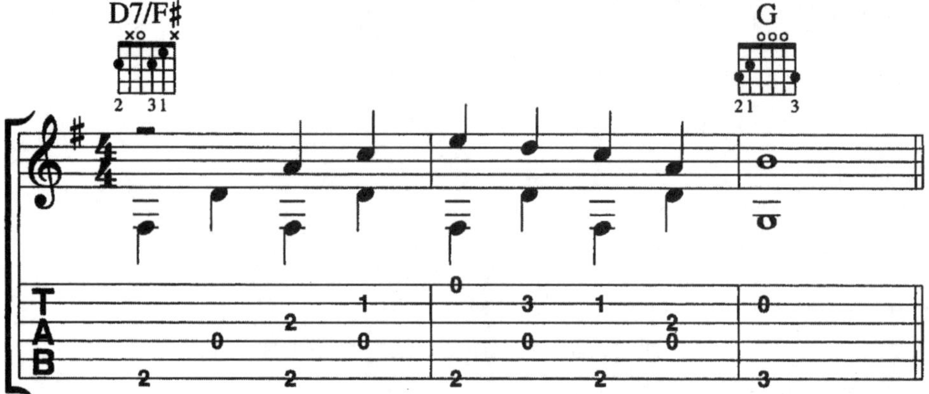

Example 134

The next exercise focuses on an E minor chord. The thumb notes are alternating between the 6th and 4th strings.

Example 135

This exercise teaches you how to connect the D7/F# and Em with other chords in the piece.

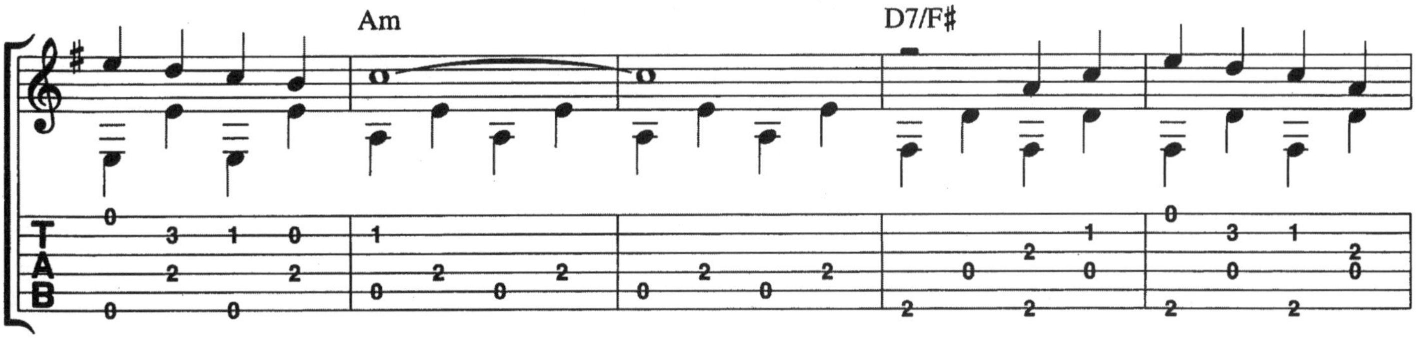

Am D7/F#

G Em Am

D7/F# G

Example 136

The first point of interest is the bass-line for the C chord. The third beat substitutes a 6th string G for a 5th string C each time. Now your thumb alternates among three strings to achieve a bass-line. Next point is the passing chord of G/F#, which creates a smooth bass-line, walking down to the Em chord. The passing Am/G chord sets up the D7/F# that follows. Last, a chord we have not yet played: C/G.

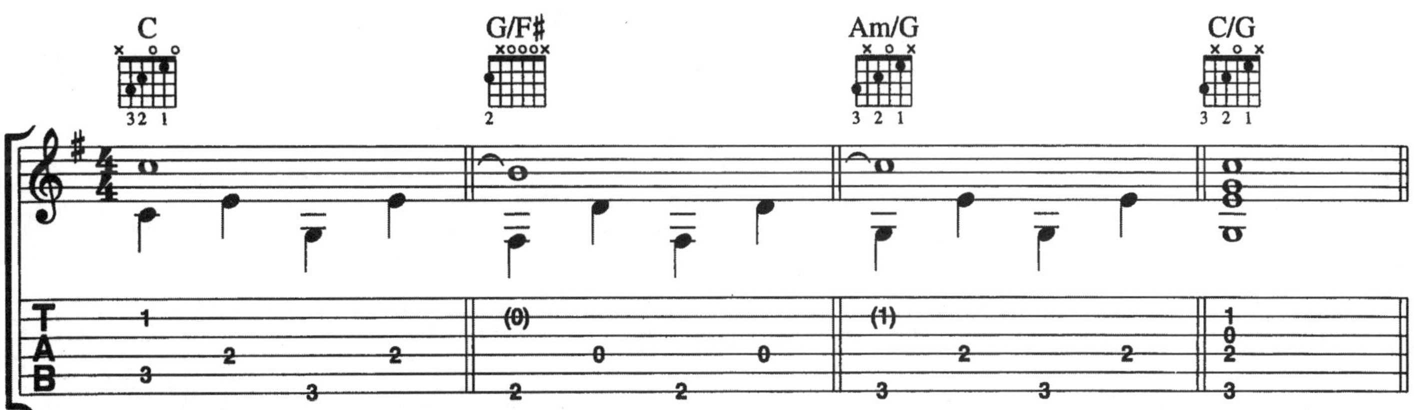

FOUR PER BAR

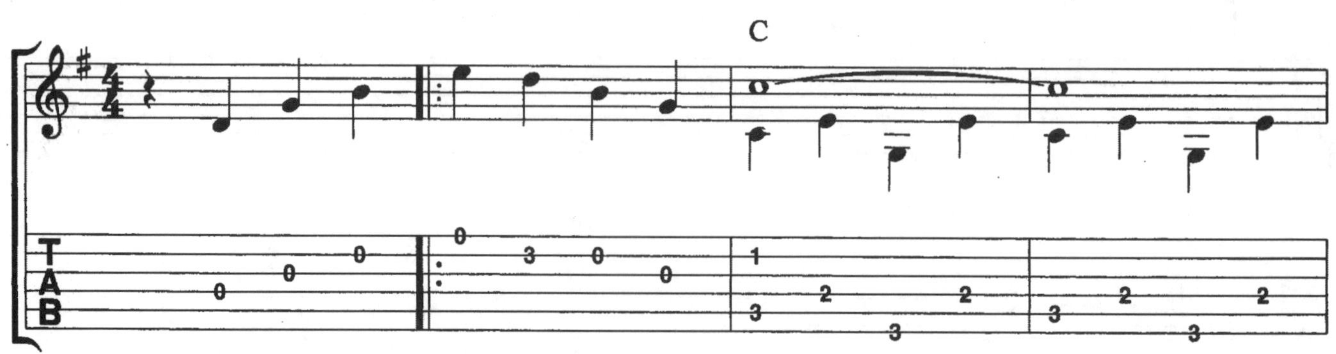

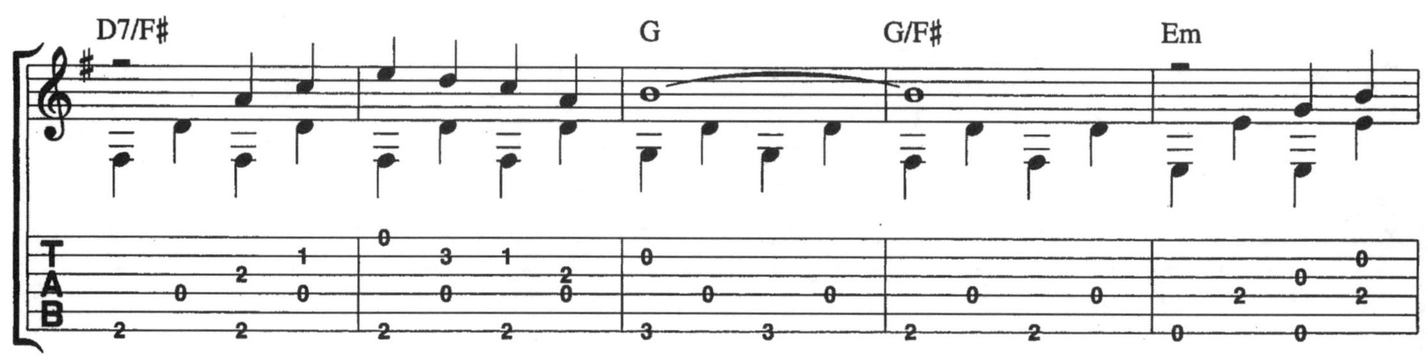

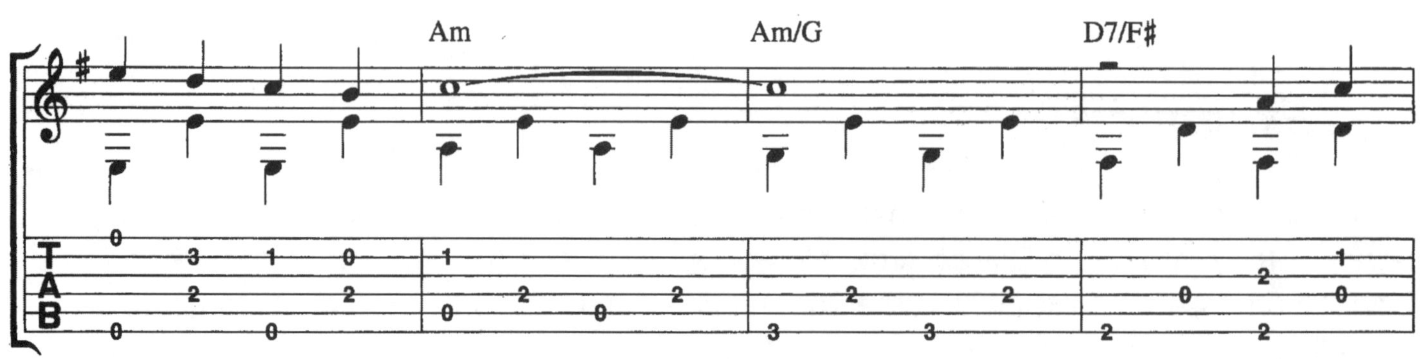

OTHER ACCOMPANIMENT PATTERNS USING THE TRAVIS STYLE

Example 137

This variation establishes a pattern in which a specific finger picks a string after each bass-note played by the thumb.

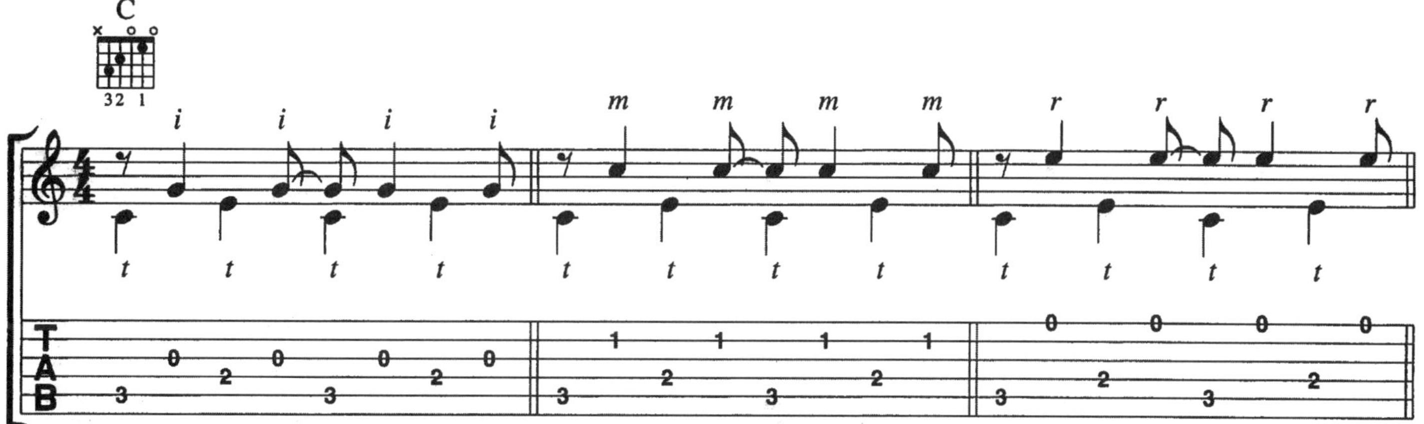

Example 138

Taking it one step further, we will now alternate between two pick-hand fingers while the bass-line continues its thumb alternation. The fingering of this pattern is: t m t i. Now apply it to the C, D, and G chords.

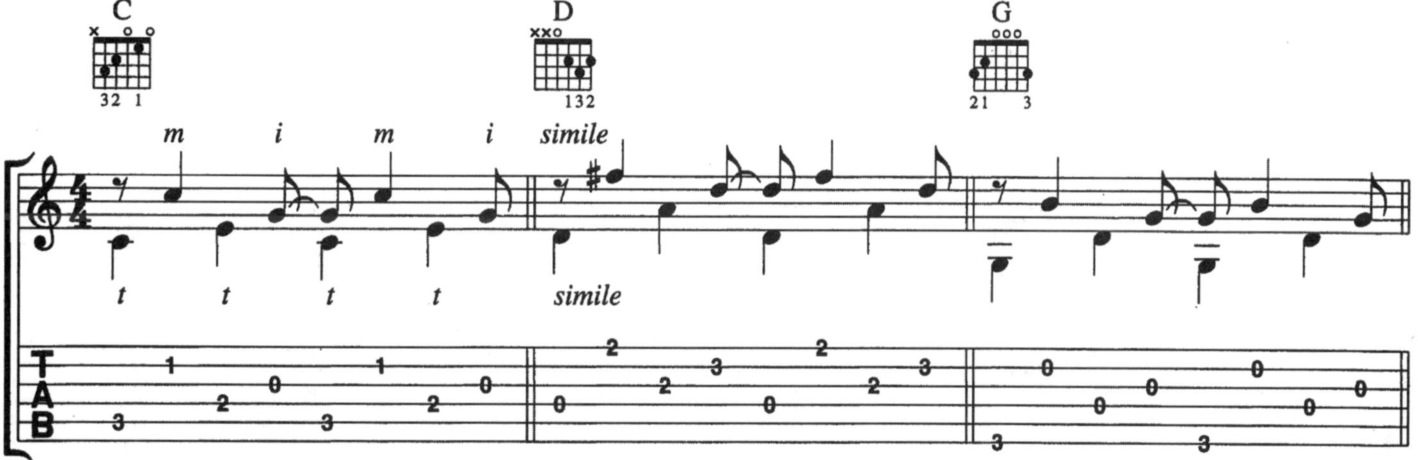

Example 139

The next pattern uses the pinch technique again — combining fingers both on and off the beat with the alternating bass. It is a four-beat pattern, divided into two parts. The first part has the pinch on the first beat, using the thumb and middle fingers. The second part has no pinch — it simply alternates the middle and index fingers between the thumb-notes. Again, apply to C, D, and G.

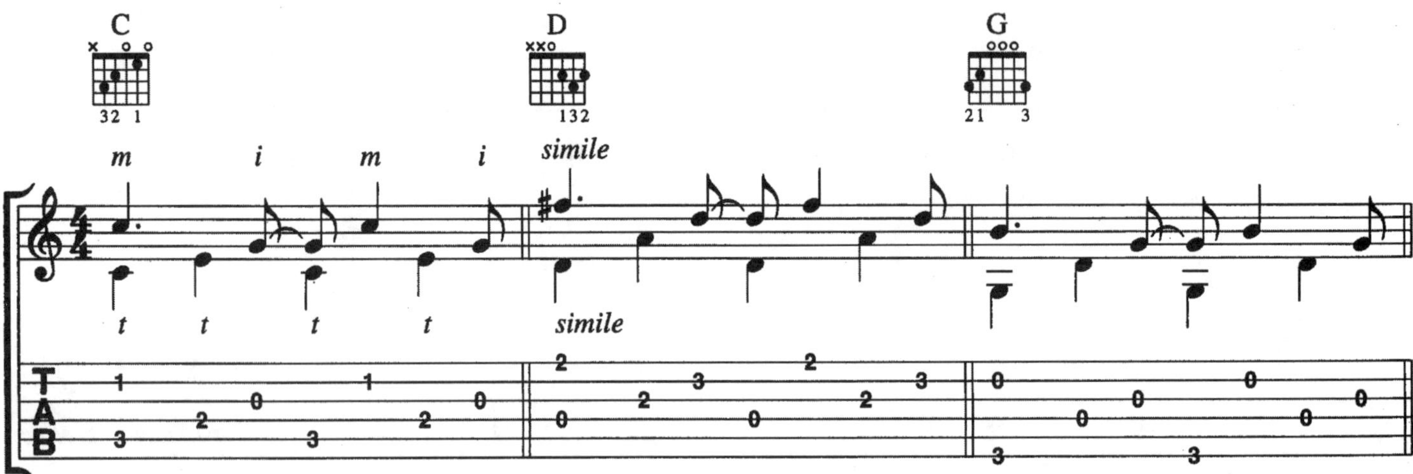

Example 140

Adding melodic interest to these basic chords is as simple as substituting a nearby note for a chord tone. C is altered to become C(9) and Am becomes Asus. This example contains other slight alterations for the G and C chords.

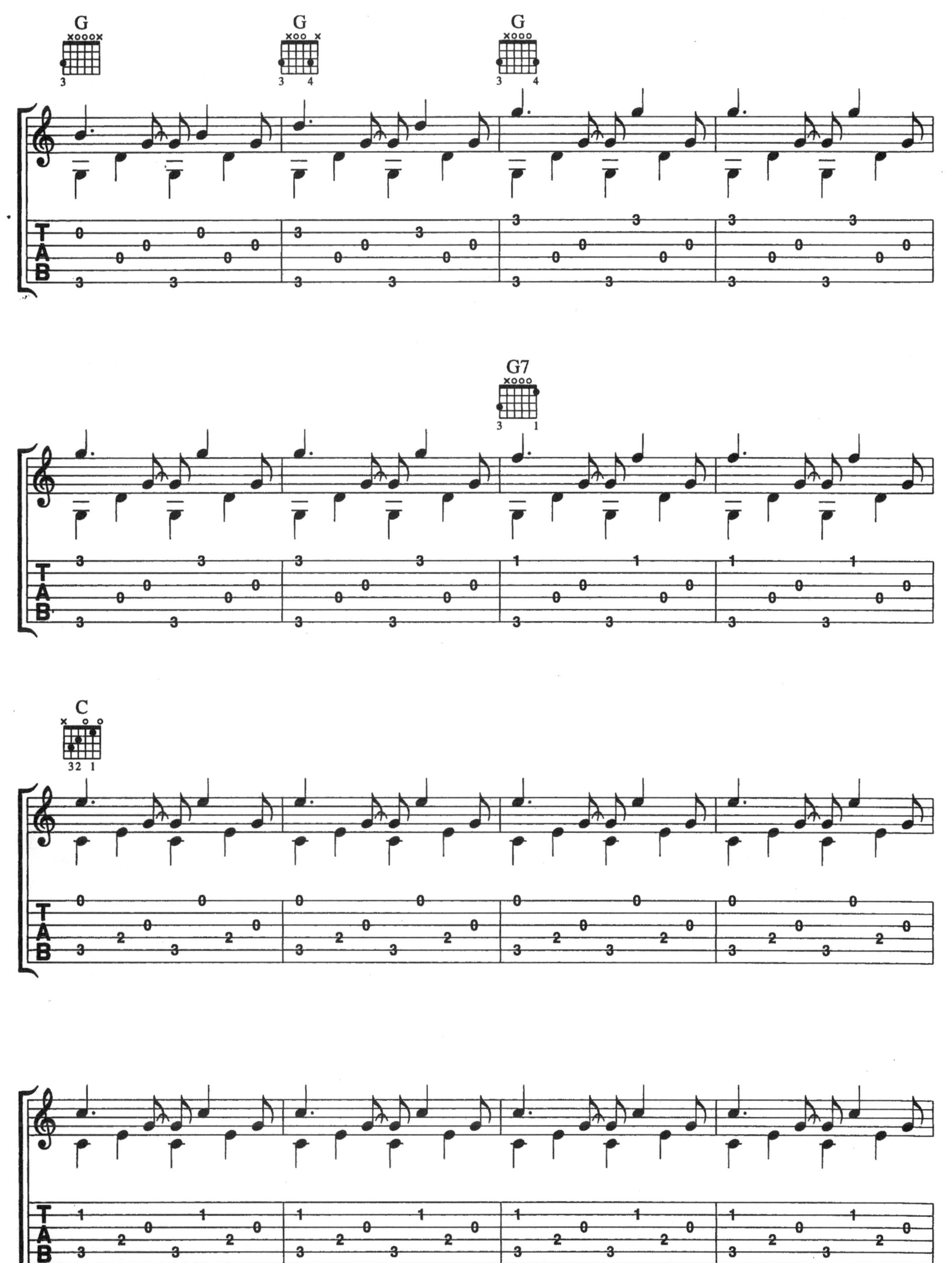
G
3
G
3 4
G
3 4
G7
3 1
C
32 1

Example 141

Pinching two fingers simultaneously with the thumb will enrich the sound of chords. Let's play two treble strings along with a thumb-note on the first beat of each bar, using G to G7 to C.

KEY TO THE KINGDOM

Key to the Kingdom highlights a number of picking techniques used by well-known virtuoso fingerpickers, notably Leo Kottke. It is an alternating-bass piece with a number of neat twists.

The first two beats of measure 1 contain a pinch on the second beat. This pattern, which repeats in the first measure of each section (measures 1, 5, and 9), is really part of the arpeggio that we studied in Example 114, combined with the alternating bass. In measure 9, notice that you add your ring finger to the pinch on the second beat.

Measure 2 has a "descending arpeggio" Travis picking pattern. It starts with a pinch, but immediately incorporates an index-finger pluck before the alternate bass note. This pattern of notes produces a descending arpeggio.

On the fourth beat of measure 10, an alternate thumb note is incorporated into the treble pattern. This is another useful technique in the alternating bass style. After some practice, you will find that it is easy to play consecutive notes on the same string with the thumb and index finger. The sequence of notes that you hear in this passage won't sound like what you normally hear in a Travis picking pattern, but the pattern of thumb-finger-thumb that characterizes Travis picking continues unabated.

Please notice that measures 3 and 4 and measures 6 and 7 are exact repeats of measures 1 and 2. Also, please notice that there is much repetition in measures 9–14.

Example 142

The first of three sections in *Key to the Kingdom* is based on a chord movement of Am to G, in the space of two bars. The first bar (Am) makes use of two different picking patterns that we have already learned. The G-chord bar is a hybrid based on a few of the patterns we have covered. This bar adds a jaggedness to the rhythm of the piece.

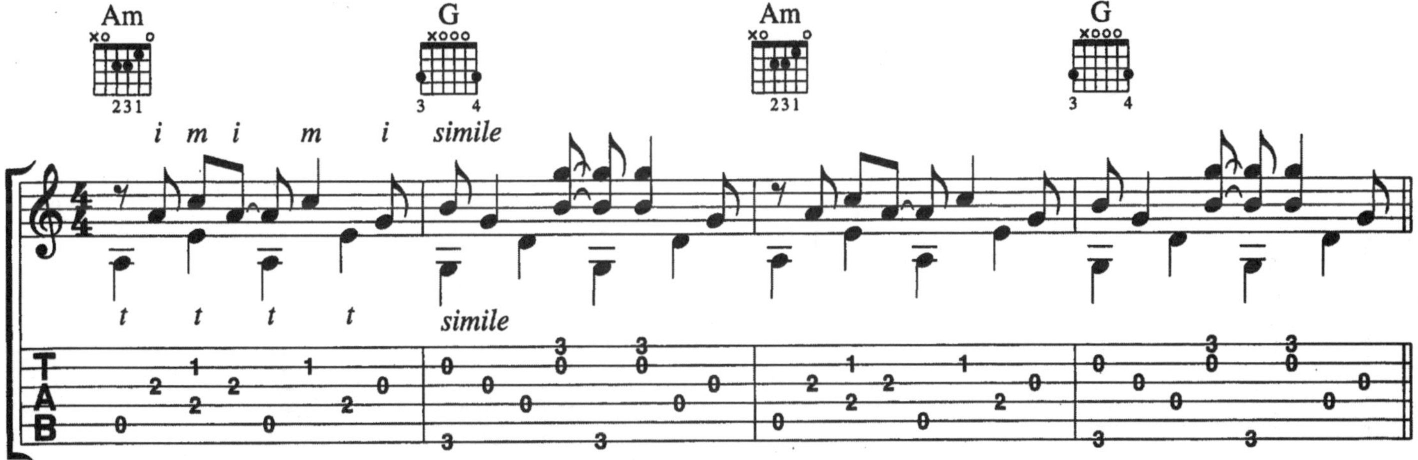

Example 143

Section two involves a pronounced high melody, found at the top of chords using the technique of three notes played together. The high melody connects an Am9 with a G chord and then is followed by "the vamp" — which is the Am to G of the last example.

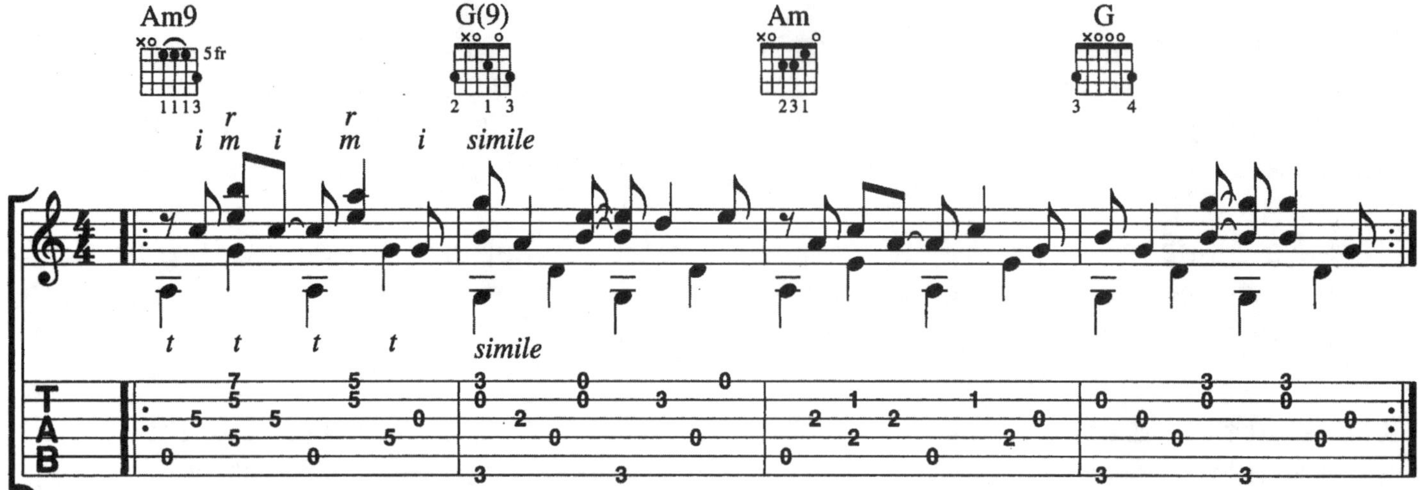

Example 144

The last section is six bars in length. It uses an Fmaj9 chord which is fingered like a simple 1st position C chord placed at the 6th, 7th, and 8th frets. You will play a three-note alternating bass pattern (F, A, and C) on the 4th, 5th, and 6th string. Be sure to keep your alternating bass-notes ringing beneath the falling melodic line on the G/B chord.

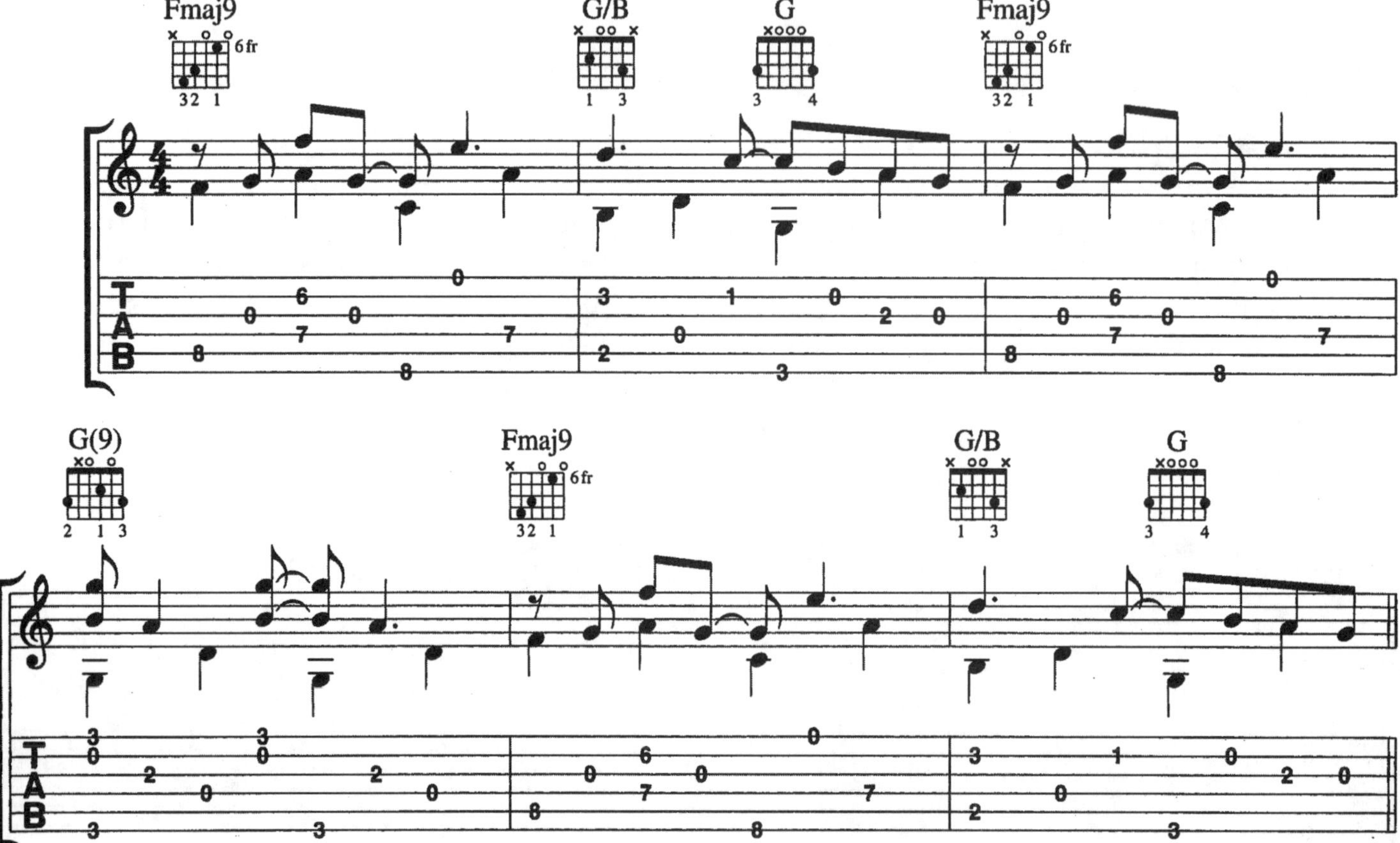

KEY TO THE KINGDOM

TAYLOR'S FERRY

This is a challenging piece in the ragtime style that brings together many of the techniques we have been working with, while adding a few new twists. It is named after a modern-day roadway in the Portland, Oregon, area. This roadway in turn took its name from one of the many ferries that crossed the Willamette River in the days of the Oregon Trail in the mid-1800s.

An interesting addendum to this story is Boone's Ferry Road, another main thoroughfare in the Portland area. It was named after a descendant of Daniel Boone, who also set up a ferry business across the Willamette in the burgeoning Oregon Trail days. The title of this tune may also have been affected by the fact that it was recorded using a Taylor guitar!

Example 145

The first section calls for you to position up at the eighth fret where it is more difficult to play cleanly, due to barre chord forms. With alternating bass-notes beneath, a melody is played on the top two strings. This melody creates chord forms with slight fingering changes heard as C, C6, G, and G6. In this example, use your left hand thumb "over the neck" to play the sixth string bass notes. This frees up your other fingers for the melody. This can be awkward at first, but once you get used to it, using the left hand thumb to play bass notes can become very natural.

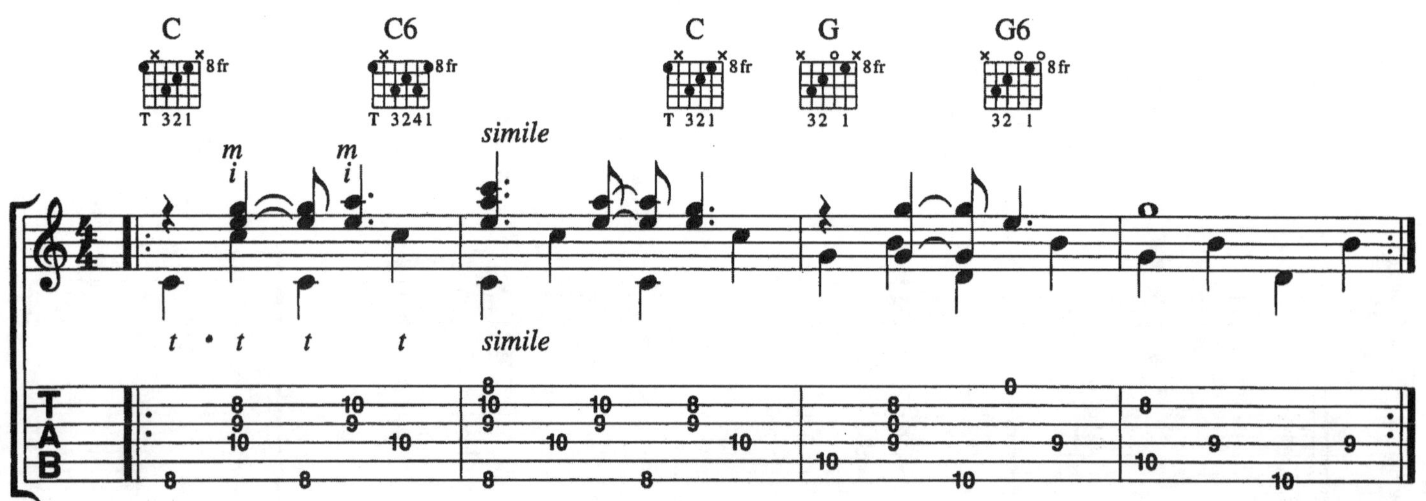

Example 146

The next four bars present interesting variations on the alternating-bass technique. The G, F(9), C/E, and G/D chords all involve sixteenth-note arpeggios where you assign the thumb, index, middle, and ring fingers to strings 5 through 2, respectively. These two bars do not use the 6th and 1st strings. The second two bars of the line continue the alternating bass with an added run within a C chord.

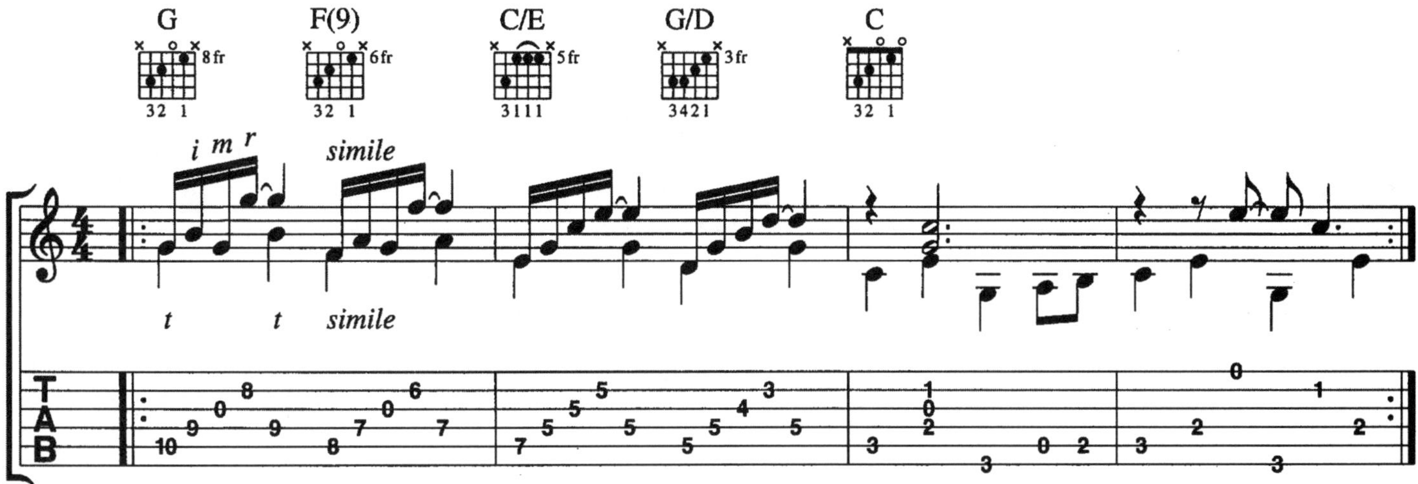

Example 147

The following 12-bar section uses lush voicings of Am9 and Em, interjected with harmonies that sometimes break the alternating-bass pattern. Try your best to make the harmonics sing out. Likely you'll need to pick them harder than the fretted and open notes.

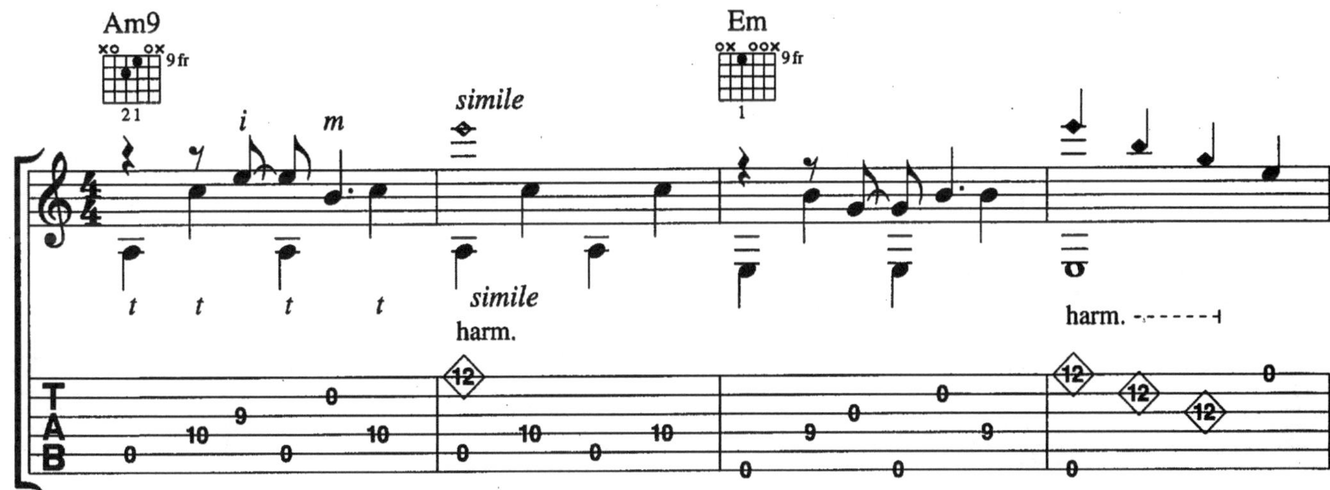

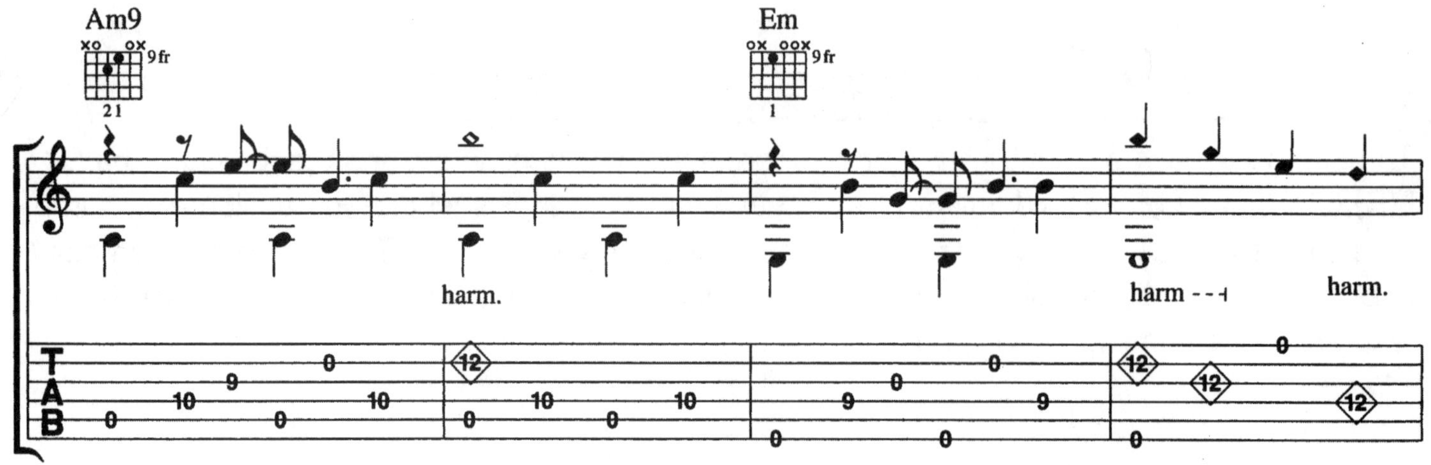

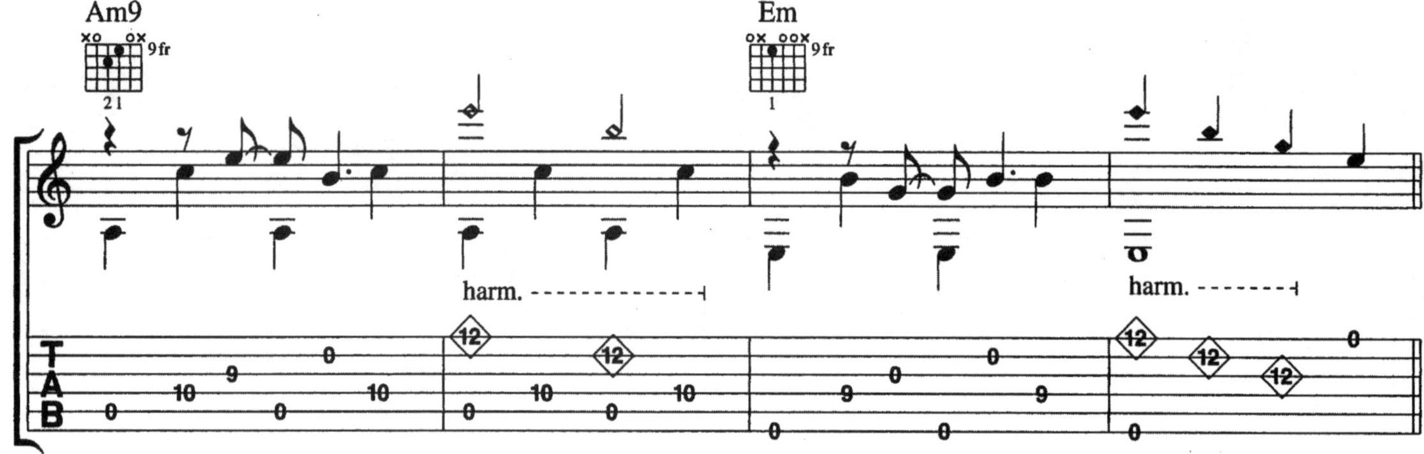

Example 148

These four bars serve as a transition back to the top of the piece. Another Travis picking variation is at work here, with harmonized half notes in the melody and alternating bass below.

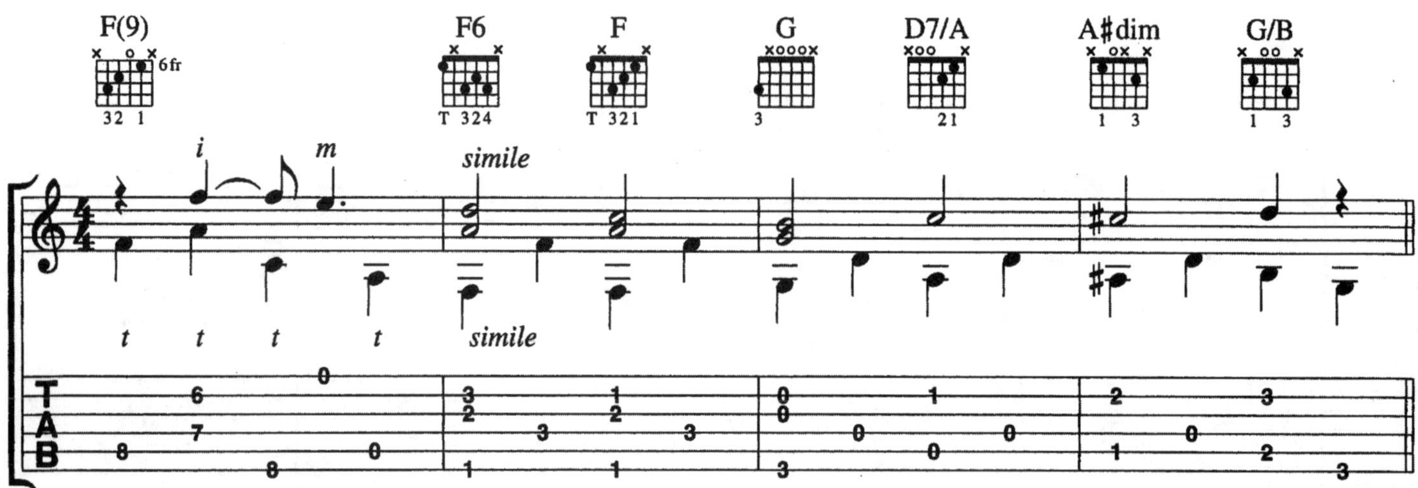

TAYLOR'S FERRY

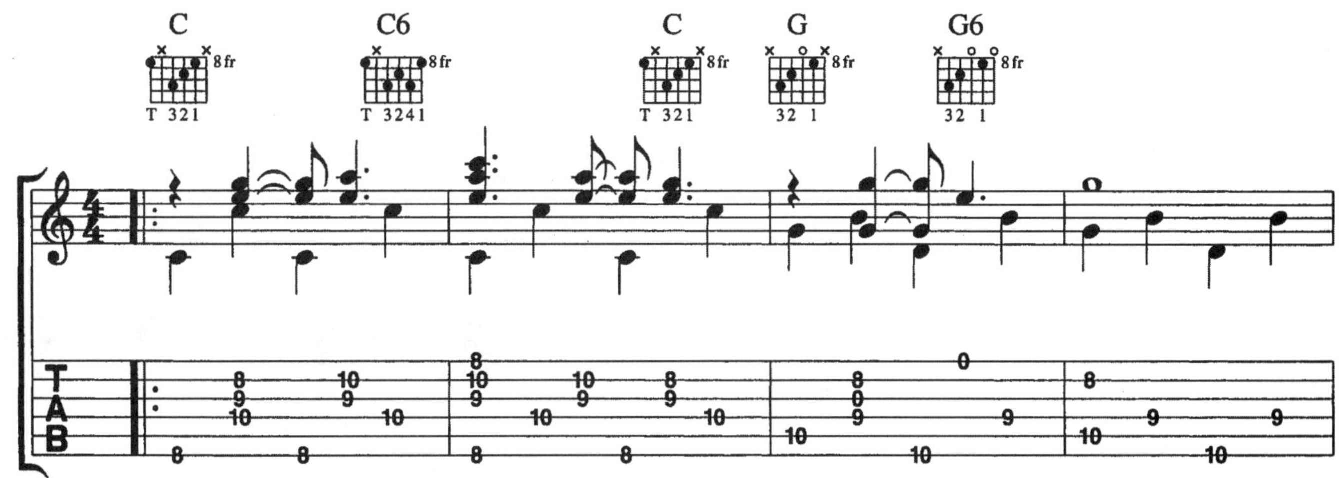

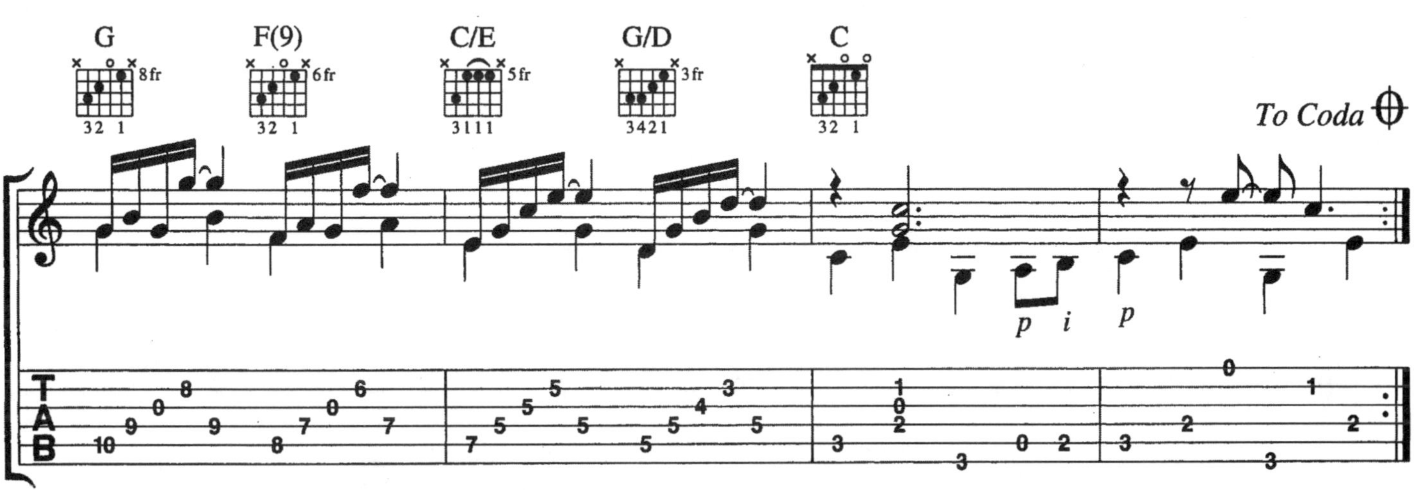

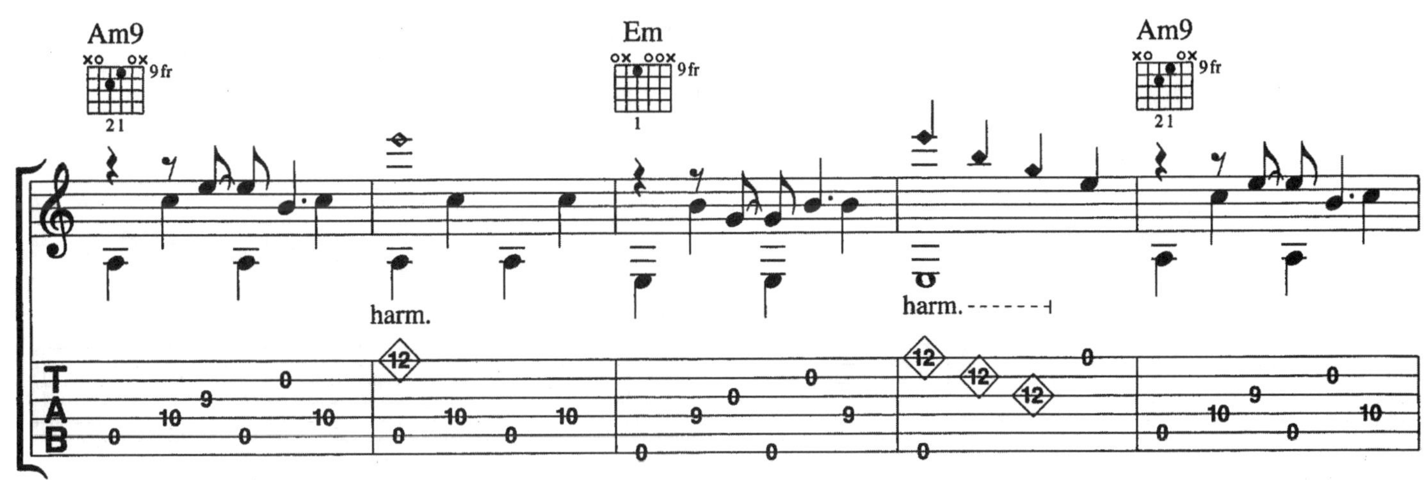

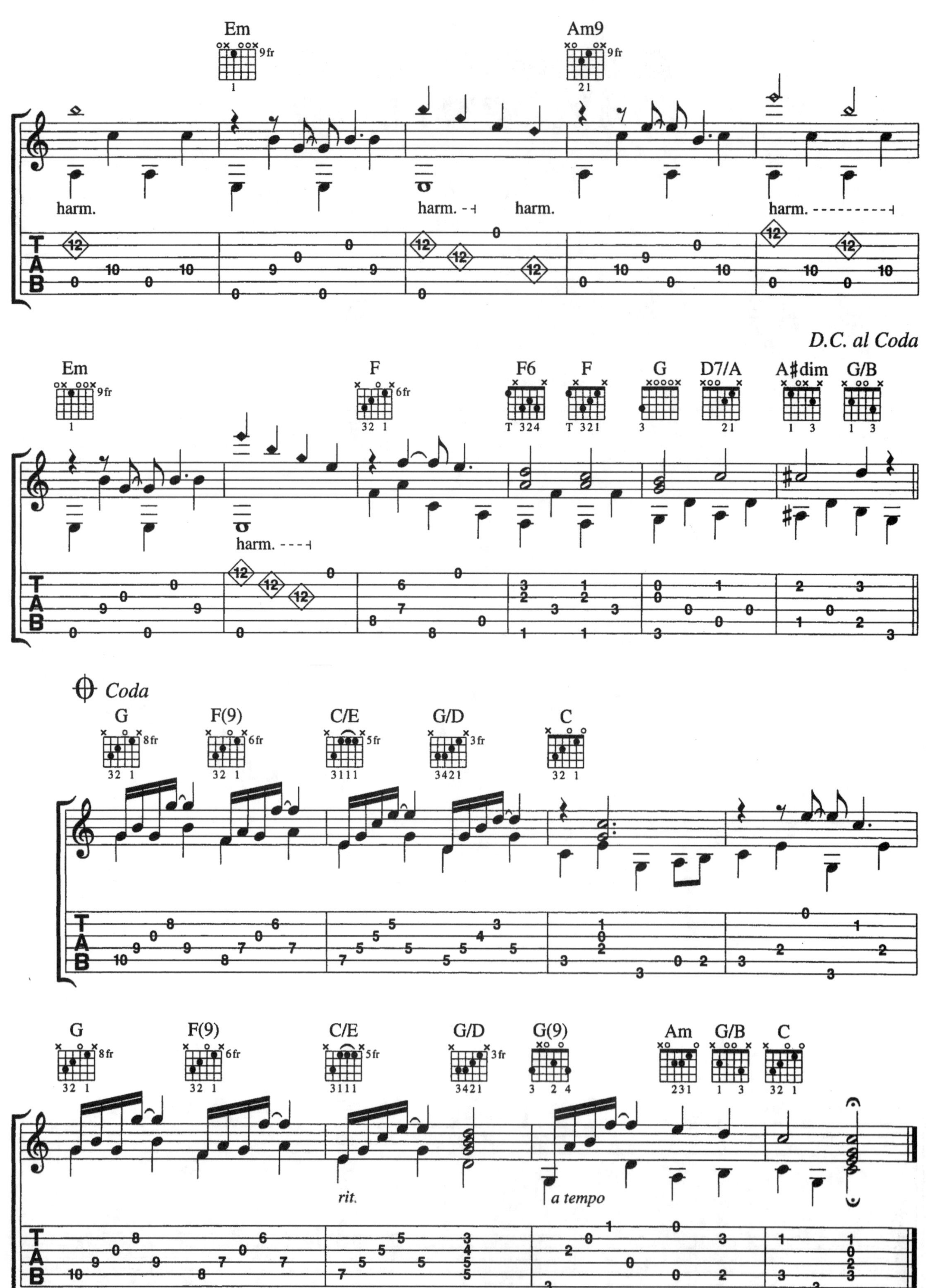

Em
Am9
harm.
harm.
harm.
harm.
D.C. al Coda
Em
F
F6
F
G
D7/A
A♯dim
G/B
harm.
Coda
G
F(9)
C/E
G/D
C
G
F(9)
C/E
G/D
G(9)
Am
G/B
C
rit.
a tempo

BRAHMS' LULLABY

This famous classical piece lends itself well to guitar interpretation. You will need to place a capo at the 2nd fret in order to match the pitch of the "Baby Taylor" guitar. The "Baby Taylor" is tuned a whole step higher than standard tuning, which makes it sound in the key of A, despite the chords appearing in the key of G on the fretboard. With a 2nd-fret capo on your guitar, you will also sound in the key of A.

Example 149 (Version I)

The first 16-bar section features a slow-moving bass-line, with chord pinches on all downbeats — while the melody is assigned to the top three strings. The next 16-bar section keeps the melody the same, as the bass accompaniment expands to broken chord movement. Be sure to play the broken chord accompaniment quietly so as not to distract the listener from the melody.

BRAHMS' LULLABY

(Version I)

Arranged by
MARK HANSON

G
C
G/B
G
D9/F♯
G
D9/F♯
D7
G
C
G/B
D9/F♯
G
C
G/B
D9/F♯
G

Example 150 (Version II)

The first half of Version II is almost identical to bars 17–24 of Version I. The last eight bars of Version II are where the new hot spots for harmonization are found. Here you will encounter some new chords which move with almost every melody note. These faster chord movements create a more "modern" color to the expected, traditional harmony.

BRAHMS' LULLABY

(Version II)

Arranged by
MARK HANSON